plot

dedication

For my husband again, who keeps the brambles away so that I might flower, and for the girls, who have tirelessly supported me throughout.

First published in 2005 by Murdoch Books Pty Limited

Murdoch Books Pty Limited Australia
Pier 8/9, 23 Hickson Rd
Sydney NSW 2000
Phone: 61 (02) 8220 2000
Fax: 61 (02) 8220 2558

Murdoch Books UK Limited
Erico House, 6th Floor North
93/99 Upper Richmond Road
Putney, London SW15 2TG
Phone: + 44 (0) 20 8785 5995
Fax: + 44 (0) 20 8785 5985

Chief Executive: Juliet Rogers
Publisher: Kay Scarlett

Concept: Marylouise Brammer and Alex Frampton
Design: Alex Frampton
Design Manager: Vivien Valk
Project Manager: Sarah Baker
Editors: Sarah Baker and Christine Eslick
UK and US Consultant: Ariana Klepac
Photo research: Amanda McKittrick
Production: Megan Alsop

Cover photographs: Joe Filshie (front cover, of Kennerton Green, Mittagong, NSW, Australia) and Mark Winwood (back cover)
Photographs by Andrea Jones (listed on page 435) appear by kind permission of the photographer.

Printed in China by Midas Printing (Asia) Ltd in 2005.

National Library of Australia Cataloguing-in-Publication Data:
Kirton, Meredith, 1969– . Plot: designing your garden. Includes index. ISBN 1 74045 395 6.
Gardens – Australia – Design. 2. Gardening – Australia. I. Title. 635.90994

Text © Meredith Kirton 2005. Design and illustrations © Murdoch Books Pty Limited 2005.

plot
designing your garden

Meredith Kirton

MURDOCH BOOKS

Contents

Possibilities

Fundamentals

Contents

Preface

At first the idea of writing a book on garden design was quite terrifying. What would my colleagues think about a horticulturalist and 'backyard' designer trespassing on their space? More importantly, what would a reader of this book think? I thought about it some more. Many gardeners are frightened of taking that one extra step and designing their own outdoor space. However, once armed with some information and ideas, this prospect may seem challenging rather than formidable. After all, the rewards of making your own stamp on your garden are great.

Each chapter of *Plot* begins with a gate, arbour or door, and I hope that this book opens up the world of garden design for you. The first part of the book covers the background to garden design. The first chapter, 'Past', is an historical overview of gardening and garden design. 'Possibilities' offers advice on working out the potential of your site, whether you are designing your garden from scratch or working with an existing garden. 'Fundamentals' includes useful guidelines and principles on garden design, encouraging you to approach designing your garden 'rooms' as you would decorating the interior of your house.

Each of the remaining four chapters, or 'palettes', covers five distinct garden styles. The first of these, 'Wild palette', examines five carefree and easy to manage types of garden — meadows, woodlands, rockeries, seaside gardens and water gardens. 'Exotic palette' covers five 'garden postcards', garden styles based on specific locations and cultures, such as the Mediterranean garden, while 'Colour palette' presents colour-themed gardens, from black and white gardens to pastel and hot gardens. The last chapter, 'Sculpted palette', covers five highly contrived garden styles, from classical to minimalist. Each of the twenty garden sections includes a mood board — with samples of plants, hard landscaping materials, fabric and accessories — that encapsulates the feel of that particular style.

I hope that the design ideas and planting suggestions in *Plot* will inspire you, and that you'll find a garden style that both appeals to you and suits your situation. Perhaps this book will sow the seeds for gardening adventures that will last you a lifetime. Gardening is one of the oldest pastimes known to humankind. It should bring only pleasure. *Bon voyage*.

Past

Inheritance. Inspiration from the classics. Tradition. Gleaning knowledge. History's lessons. Patina. Maturity. Long-term view.

Opposite: Looking through the gilded gate to Hatfield House in Hertfordshire, England, built by Robert Cecil, 1st Earl of Salisbury, in 1611. The gardens were originally designed by John Tradescant the Elder, who was chief gardener to Charles I.

Ancient times

Gardening goes right back to the beginning of known time when, as hunters and gatherers, we used wild plants for culinary and medicinal purposes.

Gardens in the Bible

The Bible mentions gardens frequently, and indeed talks about them not only in terms of food but also in relation to pleasure — from the Garden of Eden in the very first book, Genesis, through to Ecclesiastes, in which the author (who may have been King Herod) talks about his beautiful gardens. The Book of Daniel refers to King Nebuchadnezzar II, the ruler of Babylon, who is thought to have created the Hanging Gardens of Babylon, one of the Wonders of the Ancient World.

Egypt

Murals in pharaohs' tombs depict how ancient Egypt cultivated food staples such as dates and olives, wheat and figs. The Egyptians also developed aqueduct irrigation systems and designed conservatories within their homes. Gardens had religious significance: the sacred blue lotus blossom (*Nymphaea caerulea*) was regarded as a symbol of rebirth, and the sun god Aten was worshipped as a life-giving force.

In 1440 BC, Thutmosis III created 'garden' side chambers in the Karnak Temple to commemorate a military campaign against Syria. Here the wall carvings, known as the 'Botanical Garden' reliefs, depict 'all plants that grow, all flowers that are in God's land' — about 300 types of exotic plants, animals and birds in all. The open ceilings of these chambers suggest that living plants were also grown. These chambers were accessed internally only, and were thought to be special places for making offerings to the god Amon.

Less than twenty years before, Queen Hatshepsut's Funerary Temple (1458 BC) was being built. The carvings on the loggia walls show that what is now arid land was once planted with fragrant trees and avenues. Archaeological evidence has revealed plantings of sycamore, fig, palms and tamarisks.

Right: The striking bloom of the pink lotus (*Nelumbo nucifera*), introduced to Egypt from Persia. The sacred blue lotus (*Nymphaea caerulea*), which represented Upper Egypt, was the lotus depicted in hieroglyphs.

Below: Pomegranates, not apples, may have been the forbidden fruit sampled by Eve and Adam in the Garden of Eden.

Did you know? According to Greek mythology, the Hesperides were nymphs who lived in a beautiful garden, possibly near Mount Atlas. They are sometimes called the daughters of Atlas. The garden was guarded by Ladon, a dragon with 100 heads, and contained a tree that grew golden apples. This garden is said to be the first known earthly image of Paradise, and was possibly in Morocco.

Persia

It's clear from archaeological evidence and written accounts that the gardens of the ancient Near East were spectacular places, designed for enjoying an earthly paradise and all the trimmings of a decadent lifestyle. Filled with music, vibrant colours, the arts, lush plantings and dazzling water features, these garden oases offered relief from the dry, hot desert environment around them.

The garden ruins of Pasargadae Palace in ancient Persia (present-day Iran), date back to the mid-sixth century BC. Here, a monumental palace was built for Cyrus the Great. Made of stone, it featured a significant garden with avenues of cypresses, pomegranates and sour cherries. Elaborate water features were supplied by *qanats*, underground canals that carried water from an aquifer deep below ground. Loggias surrounded the garden, which contained two pavilions.

In 515 BC, Darius the Great built on the Persian tradition of wondrous gardens that were intended to be representations of the Garden of Eden. There is evidence of blooming watery paradise gardens, known as *pairi-daeza*, at the palace of Apadana, in Persepolis. Here, terraced gardens surrounded by engraved walls, vast colonnades and throne rooms looked out onto reflecting pools, trees, rows of pines and the vastness beyond. The bas-reliefs in this garden show that Darius borrowed styles and techniques from the many nations Persia had conquered, including India, Egypt and Greece.

Rome

It was probably the ancient Romans who first developed the now accepted concept of the garden room. Some villa ruins at Pompeii in Italy feature a courtyard planted out as an extension of the main house. The Romans grew flowers for victory wreaths and

garlands, and as they conquered Europe and Britain, they introduced many medicinal and culinary herbs that became the basis of physic gardens in medieval times.

In a villa near Pompeii (c. AD 79), a mosaic framed with fruit garlands depicts Plato teaching by the columns of a portico, under the shade of a tree, at The Academy.

Monastery gardens

During the Dark Ages in Europe, about AD 476 to 1000, the constant threat of attack by invading tribes resulted in the construction of fortresses and walled cities. Gardening went 'behind closed doors' for these 500 years or so, becoming the preserve

Above: A still channel of water, edged with clipped hedges of myrtle, reflects the sky in the Alhambra garden in Granada, Spain. This is the Patio de Los Arrayanes, or Court of the Myrtles. The hedges marked the path foreign dignitaries would take to meet the Granadine ruler. According to Islamic tradition, Adam and Eve brought a myrtle flower with them from the Garden of Eden.

Above: The kitchen garden at Hatfield House is a descendant of the physic garden. Flowers, vegetables and herbs are grown in rectangular beds, shaded by fruit trees.

Above right: The Patio de la Acequia, or Court of the Long Pool, in the Alhambra is a famous example of a Moorish garden that is found in Granada, Spain. The jets of water help to cool the two porticos at either end of the pool. Legend has it that Prince Ahmed al Kamel, also known as 'The Pilgrim of Love', learnt to communicate with birds while confined here.

Did you know? The word 'garden' is *alumina* in Arabic and *bagh* in ancient Persian.

of monasteries and nunneries. Monks grew medicinal herbs within simple box hedges in carefully designed 'physic' gardens, where herbs such as rue were prescribed for bad eyesight and feverfew was used for headaches. Not only medicinal herbs were important enough to be kept behind the walls: flowers such as lilies and roses were also grown for the altar, as were flowers for chaplets — strings of flowers, like rosary beads, for counting prayers.

These walled gardens were known as 'cloisters': an inner courtyard, comprising simple rectangular beds or quadrangles was often surrounded by a covered walk or a colonnade made of trellis, called a gallery. Through these grew wild roses and sweet honeysuckle (known then as woodbyne). Also featured were chamomile or turf seats, ponds for fish (known as stew ponds), beehives, poultry houses, dove cotes and bathing waters.

Beyond these cloisters were other walled gardens, only here the security was not as tight and the gardens were fenced with woven willow or drystone walls to keep intruders out. They featured fruit trees such as pomegranates, oranges, lemons, apples, quince, apricots, pears, peaches and almonds, planted in an offset grid pattern that allowed enough light to filter through to the ground. This meant that flowers could be sown through the turf to form meads or contrived 'wild' meadow gardens. These gardens doubled as burial grounds, and were considered the closest thing to paradise, or heaven, on earth.

The Moorish influence

At the beginning of the eighth century AD, the Moors invaded Spain, bringing their Muslim traditions with them. By now, the *chahar-bagh* style — an enclosed garden, divided into four sections by water channels — was entrenched in Islamic design. The Moorish garden, developed by the Arabs, closely follows Islamic teaching: the gardens as a whole are not symmetrical (as Allah would regard a symmetrical garden as arrogant), although the layout within courtyards is often very rigid, containing crossed paths and rectangular ponds. Islam also forbids the depiction of

man, so highly stylized images of plants and animals often feature strongly. Patterned stonework, simple pools and narrow channels of water are common — according to the Koran, water is an image of Paradise.

During the twelfth century, as Europe was emerging from the grip of the Dark Ages, the East was creating astounding gardens. For example, the Bagh-e Takht in Iran was built as a holiday retreat for the governor of Shiraz. The fortified site, in ruins today, contains a palace, seven terraces stepping down a rocky hillside, an artificial boating lake and intricate pathways linking all the terraces, with octagonal, star- and cusp-shaped designs. Elaborate water jets fed by a natural spring as well as stone-lined bowls and pools are also featured.

The Orient

A traditional oriental garden also follows strict rules. Today, this is often based on the Zen philosophy, which involves the enjoyment of beauty and the relaxation of the spirit. The elements are simple and symbolic, mirroring the rocky mountains, falling water, green valleys and lakes of the natural landscape.

Did you know? 'Chinoiserie' refers to the influence of Chinese style and motifs, particularly in the eighteenth century, on European art and decorative arts.

Above: This moongate in a Chinese garden reveals a glimpse of the garden beyond.

The **knot garden**

Above: One of the parterres at Villandry in France. The hedges are filled in with lavender.

Knot gardens were a sixteenth century expression of the medieval practice of embroidering knots and interwoven patterns. In turn, these were apparently based on ancient mythology: the knot garden was a symbol of the union between Mars and Venus.

The first printed record of a knot garden is in Venice in 1499. For the next two centuries, knot gardens were popular first in Italy, then in France and England.

A knot garden is basically a square comprised of geometric designs, formed by plants clipped into patterns. Typically, these plants were hyssop, germander, thyme and winter savory. Later, in the seventeenth century, box became the plant of choice.

The French parterre started off as exactly the same thing (*parterre* means 'on the ground', while *potager* means kitchen garden). These eventually evolved into a more flamboyant, curvilinear style.

The popularity of knot gardens dwindled, mainly due to the expense of their upkeep, but by the nineteenth century they enjoyed a revival. Many householders commissioned designs laid out in box, with gravel, sand, brick dust and other coloured materials highlighting the compartments.

Two fine examples of knot gardens can be found at Hampton Court and Barnsley House, both in England.

Did you know? An *allée* is a straight walk or ride bordered by clipped hedges or trees, called a *palissade*. Sometimes *allées* were finished at the boundary with a *saut de loup*, or deep trench, which prevented trespassing.

Some typical features of an oriental garden are winding paths, which reveal different views, glimpses through keyholes to borrowed landscapes and reflection pools at which to stop and contemplate or meditate. In both Japanese and Chinese garden design, 'borrowing' landscapes was commonplace. This was done by playing with the foreground, middle ground and background to create various layers. Stroll gardens were a popular form of garden design in the thirteenth century. Basically, a circuit was created so that different views and vantage points were gradually revealed as you strolled around the garden, crossing over bridges, stopping at tea-houses and contemplating artificial islands.

The Middle Ages

After Europe emerged from the Dark Ages in about AD 1000, wealthy people focused on peaceful pursuits such as gardening. Peace and prosperity resulted in the construction of the great gardens of Europe. English knot gardens of the Tudor and Elizabethan periods still retained the concept of a garden square, but became vast, and more intricate. Knot gardens — both 'open knots', which were filled with gravels, charcoal, sand and the like, and 'closed knots', which featured a mass of flowering ground covers such as violets, strawberries, wallflowers, primrose and thyme — were designed to be viewed from above, from windows in a building, raised platforms or from hills especially built for this purpose.

During this period, the Roman tradition of topiary was revived, and arbours, trellises and pleached trees, features of the monastic garden, remained popular. The orchard maintained its stature as a garden prized for both its fruit and beauty. Plants from around the world also started to arrive in Britain and Europe, and lilies, Jerusalem artichokes and hibiscus found homes in the Elizabethan garden.

Mughal gardens

Mughal gardens are a cross between the style of traditional Indian Hindu gardens and Persian gardens. This Indo-Persian garden style spans the sixteenth to the nineteenth centuries in India and was first brought from Kabul as a result of Emperor Babur's conquest of northern India in 1526. Enclosed symmetrical and axial parterre layouts, combined with stone terracing, geometric star patterns, hexagrams and foliate-shaped basins and fountains, water chutes and channels, and open-air pavilions typify the style.

The Renaissance

The French parterres and Italianate gardens of the Renaissance then became the fashion, with vast areas of countryside being redeveloped. Gardens such as Louis XIV's Château de Versailles and Vaux-le-Vicomte, both designed by the Sun King's gardener-in-chief André le Nôtre, are signature gardens of this grand formal style, as are the Boboli in Florence, built for the Medici family, and Villa d'Este in Tivoli, outside Rome, which was designed for Cardinal Ippolito Il d'Este.

Italian gardens comprised these elements: strong architectural lines, symmetry, clipped hedging and a formal water feature. Urns, stonework, balustrades, statuary and topiary were also key ingredients, as was the *grotto*, an artificial cave, an escape from the intense summer heat. Colours were mainly limited to the greens of foliage, with just touches of white jasmine and orange citrus, for example.

Above right: Climbing plants trained over archways in the cottage garden at Chatsworth in England.

Right: In the grounds of Hatfield House is an *allée* or path bordered by pleached trees, forming a *palissade*, which can be any sort of clipped hedge.

Opposite top: This bronze statue of Bacchus from Greek mythology at Versailles is typical of the Baroque style. In the background is an enormous shallow pond with a *jet d'eau*.

Opposite bottom: A striking example of a *jet d'eau* is the Emperor Fountain (1840s) by Joseph Paxton at Chatsworth. The garden was originally designed by Henry Wise and George London in the Baroque style, but was later redesigned by Lancelot 'Capability' Brown as a landscape garden. Some of the Baroque features remain.

Grand avenues were also an integral part of practically every large garden designed in the seventeenth century. These often included water parterres and *jets d'eau*. They were built on such an immense scale that sometimes villages were destroyed to open up vistas, rivers were redirected to fuel fountains and avenues of trees stretching for miles were planted. These gardens were outward looking, not inward or walled as before, and were the venues for extraordinary entertainments — theatre, circus performances and fireworks.

The landscape garden

Eventually, the labour-intensive scale and formality of Baroque gardens made them unfashionable. In the early eighteenth century, this led to the development of the romantic countryside or landscape garden, such as those created by Lancelot 'Capability' Brown in England and Robinson in Ireland, and painted by Constable. Gardens such as these were created in huge parklands, designed to mimic nature. The designers of these gardens often had to sweep aside great parterres to clear tracts for replanting forest and pasture. Sometimes a folly, usually an expensive but useless ruin in the Gothic or classical Greek style, was included for a touch of drama.

The cottage garden

The cottage garden style came into being in the second half of the eighteenth century, and was based on a desire to grow everything you needed, both ornamental and productive, within a small plot. Fruit, vegetables, herbs, flowers and shrubs were crowded into a small space, along with rose-covered roofs and clematis-smothered arbours. Also known as a romantic garden, the cottage garden has remained popular ever since.

Along the **avenue**

In ancient Egypt, avenues of sphinxes marked vistas. Avenues were popular throughout the Middle Ages. However, the most impressive were the grand axes defined by trees that were popular in the seventeenth century. At first these avenues would have been just cleared tracks through forests, but by the eighteenth century, elms and limes were regularly being planted. They served many purposes – from the aesthetic (creating avenues and highlighting distant features) and practical (acting as windbreaks) to the economic (providing future stocks of valuable timber).

Winston Churchill's birthplace, Blenheim Palace, in Oxfordshire, England, featured a 3 km (2 mile) quadruple avenue of elms, planted from 1705 onwards by Henry Wise, the royal gardener. This avenue eventually succumbed to Dutch elm disease, but was replanted by the present day Duke of Marlborough in the 1970s with limes (*Tilia cordata* and *T. platyphyllos*).

A modern day interpretation of one of these avenues would be a simple repetition of one species along a drive, or a pleached avenue to screen out the neighbours or unwanted views, or perhaps to frame a sculpture.

Left: A glimpse of an avenue through the gate at Het Loo, The Netherlands, a grand garden in the French style that was inspired by Versailles.

Did you know? *Jets d'eau* are columns of water, and were popular in the grand gardens of the French style in the seventeenth and eighteenth centuries. These water parterres were incorporated into le Nôtre's great gardens, notably Versailles. In the era of the landscape garden, they were replaced by more natural water features, but they enjoyed a revival in the 1800s.

Below: Densely planted beds of
annuals, perennials and bulbs in
a cottage garden at Abbey House
in England.

Opposite: Fiora's Temple, a folly
in the grounds of Chatsworth.

The Victorian era

During the Victorian age plants themselves became an obsession. Plantsmen travelled the world, and ships transported the first mobile glasshouses. It was an exciting period, when plants were swapped and detailed catalogues and seed lists were available. The garden became a repository of 'collections' rather than a designed space. William Robinson vehemently attacked this style of gardening, labelling it 'broken brick' gardening.

Twentieth century styles

By the end of the nineteenth century, gardens contained aloes, agaves, plumbago, citrus, olives, nasturtium, oleander and agapanthus; South African plants, Australian natives and American perennials were all popular. Building suburbs of single-storey homes was all the rage in the Western world, and people had room for a garden that combined pleasure and purpose. The suburban sprawl, common to so many cities, had begun. Architectural styles such as Australian Federation, Edwardian, Georgian revival, Arts and Crafts (promoted by designers like William Morris, John Ruskin, Gertrude Jekyll and Edwin Lutyens), Californian bungalow, Spanish Mission, Old English Tudor, P&O Streamline and Art Deco were in vogue during this period.

Did you know? Popular in the seventeenth and eighteenth centuries, Baroque is a style that used lavish ornamentation as well as asymmetry. Garden ornaments were in the form of richly carved and gilded statuary, while water features were theatrical. The term 'rococo' refers to the style of decoration popular in the 1700s when decoration and motifs were as important to garden design as form and structure.

Heated **glasshouses**

From as far back as Roman times, gardeners have been trying to grow plants either out of season or away from their natural habitat in a heated, controlled environment. In the ruins of Pompeii a heated brick structure with a thin mica roof has been found. The mica roof would have admitted the sun's rays and warmth.

This technology was lost during the Dark Ages, but reinvented during the Renaissance period when purpose-built greenhouses or orangeries were incorporated into the homes of the wealthy. A typical orangery was simply heated with a charcoal fire and had large windows that faced the sun, while its solid roof effectively excluded the cold and kept frost-tender species warm enough to survive over winter.

By the eighteenth century, plants were arriving in Europe from the Cape of Good Hope, the Caribbean and the Indies. Special pineapple houses or 'stove buildings' were built in gardens, allowing exotics such as banana, passion fruit, datura, hibiscus, aloes, guava and papaya to be grown successfully and, indeed, bear fruit.

These buildings evolved into what we now call glasshouses by the mid-eighteenth century. This was partly due to the advances in cast-iron manufacturing, which allowed the construction of curved structures that could support glass roofs. The famous Palm House at Kew in England, opened in 1841, and other glass palaces of the day epitomize a style that satisfied the hunger for plant exotica.

The twenty-first century has seen domestic garden design embrace the glasshouse yet again, whether it be the phenomenal Eden Project in Cornwall in the United Kingdom, a research centre that houses two enormous collections of plants in two conservatories, or the simple domestic conservatory. This is really just a glass-roofed addition to the family home, yet it provides those who live in colder climates with an opportunity to enjoy not only plants from other climes, but also some sunshine and warmth indoors.

Above: Designed by Joseph Paxton, the conservatory at Chatsworth was opened in 1840.

Above: An oak tree has been underplanted with hostas in this woodland garden in the Chanticleer Garden in Philadelphia, United States.

From the 1920s, garden design was greatly influenced by designers such as Jekyll, Vita Sackville-West and Lutyens, who were advocates of colour-themed gardens. This style is strongly plant based, with much of the effect achieved by perennials and flowering plants in borders with carefully chosen colour schemes.

The woodland garden is synonymous with the traditional English garden — peaceful, with trees, shrubs and herbaceous plants in appropriate garden beds, generally edged and curving. One of the finest examples of this sort of garden is Hidcote in the Cotswolds in England, designed by Lawrence Johnston.

Australia also had its stars of the gardening world. Edna Walling and Professor Wilkensen teamed up to create great homes and gardens, and Paul Sorensen designed many sites in the Blue Mountains. Everglades is one of his best known gardens.

These traditional 'English' styles remained popular until the Modernist movement of post war society. Modernism was characterized by mass-produced materials such as concrete and by geometric shapes such as the simple cube house.

After World War II, the Bauhaus school of design, established in Weimar, Germany, in 1918 by Walter Gropius, started to rekindle the ideas that Hitler had stamped out, and the 1940s to 1960s saw a new garden era. The aim of the Bauhaus school was to combine all the practical and applied arts,

removing the distinction between design and production. The Bauhaus workshops produced prototypes for mass production — from a single lamp to a complete dwelling. The Bauhaus philosophy led to the popularization of indoor and outdoor garden rooms, ultimately resulting in modern landscape theory.

The twentieth century saw other influences from around the world too. For instance, in Barcelona, Spain, Antonio Gaudi designed many extraordinary buildings that look rather like dripping wax candles. In the same city he designed the spectacular Parc Guell, once intended as a residential garden city. And Roberto Burle Marx, a Brazilian landscape architect and artist who designed over 1500 public and private gardens, is sometimes touted as 'the inventor of the modern garden'. Both designers tended towards biomorphic, organic shapes and borders in their work. (See pages 374 and 377.)

This exuberant, outlandish and flamboyant style of garden design and plant use is also evident in the fabulous Lotusland in Santa Barbara, California, designed by Ganna Walska, a retired singer, during the mid-twentieth century. Named in honour of the lotus flower that grew in one of the ponds on the 15 hectare (37 acre) property, Lotusland is a botanical garden full of rare plants, collected by Madame Walska over a 30-year period (see page 374).

Above: A lime tree shades an eating area at the end of a path scented with lavenders in Luberon, France.

Opposite: Designed by Andy Sturgeon for the 2001 Chelsea Flower Show, this 'Circ Contemporary Man's Garden' won a silver gilt medal. The innovative water feature and the use of bold colour, geometric forms and architectural plantings provide a glimpse of what gardens may be like in the future.

Some modern trends in garden design

As the world becomes more and more cosmopolitan, so too do our gardening tastes. Drawing inspiration from our travels has become *de rigueur*, and themed gardens such as the Santa Fe, Mediterranean, Oriental, Balinese, Middle Eastern and French provincial have become popular, their chief objective being to capture the mood of another place.

The latest major influence on garden design has been the environment itself. The importance of the impact of human activity — water consumption, and the use of pesticides and fertilizers, for example — has seen the development of gardens that emulate nature and capture some of the natural beauty of their surrounds.

Meadow gardens or the 'prairie' look, combining soft grasses with self-seeding annuals and bulbs, became popular in the 1980s. Paths are usually beaten earth or simple mown tracks through the 'meadow'.

Similarly, the new perennial garden, a more contemporary style, combines the softness of ornamental grasses with mass plantings of perennials. It follows a free, flowing form, with pea gravel paths and soft edges.

The popularity of the grass garden has been fostered by renowned contemporary designers such as Piet Oudolf (his plants look wild but his gardens do not) and James van Sweden, an American designer who creates bold but romantic gardens.

The native plant movement has been influential in the Middle East, South Africa and the United States as well as Australia. Nineteenth century horticulture tended to feature exotic plants, whereas late twentieth century gardening reversed that trend, emphasizing plants that occur in the wild in any given area.

For example, the Australian native bush garden has been Australians' concession to the environment. Rainforest and dry forest plants are used to replicate a bush-like feel. Surfaces are usually natural — leaf litter, pea gravel or sandstone — and edges, if any, are either of bush rock or timber. Unfortunately, misconceptions about the care and maintenance needs of Australian native gardens have led to their decline and lack of popularity in recent years.

The future

The challenge of the decreasing size of urban gardens, the cost of land, labour, water and plants, and the ever-diminishing amount of spare time in which one is able to garden will all be factors that determine the gardens of tomorrow.

Possibilities

The blank canvas. Framework. Perimeters.
Limitations and opportunities. Measure. Plan
and design. Intention. Build and grow. Evolve.

Opposite: A flight of steps leads to an arbour, and beyond lies a
place full of promise and possibilities. Your dream. Your garden.

Identifying your space

Making a garden and an outdoor living space is an exciting endeavour. Whether you have just moved in or want to make major improvements, hold off from any radical changes and survey your site first, assessing its possibilities and your commitment to the project ahead.

The actual process of designing a garden is a three-step procedure. The first step involves working out exactly what you have, the second is working out what you want, and the third step is the marriage between possibility and practicality — working out what is best.

Like all marriages, this process inevitably involves compromise. A grand plan may be impossible with a small budget, and space and accessibility issues will also play a role in the eventual design. But the great thing about good design is that it is a blend of form and function, so solutions that meet the needs of a particular site and personality are possible.

A garden is rarely a completely blank canvas. You usually inherit components from previous owners — existing trees and shrubs, the garden shed, a clothesline, concrete drive and perhaps some bulbs or other herbaceous plants that may pop up and surprise you. In a newly developed area you may be unlucky enough to unearth a rubbish tip of broken bricks and builders' rubble.

While some of these items may not be welcome, you should always consider everything. Clearing the backyard as if a team from a makeover TV show is about to move in for a day isn't necessarily the right strategy. In fact, it is often the accumulated effect of past owners' endeavours and the growth of plants over time that gives a garden its character and depth.

So, before you bring in the chainsaw, bobcat, bulldozer or television crew ready to work on a slash and burn exercise, stop and map out what's there already; the process may lead you to discover your garden's potential.

Sketching a plan on paper will help you to assess how much space you have for your garden. From this you will be able to work out a number of things, such as the number of plants you will need to buy and which parts of the garden are in the sun or shade — factors that will help you choose the right plants for your garden. A plan will also help you to work out how to meet their needs in order for them to flourish.

To then move on from this point and design your own garden is a real adventure: the reward can be truly wonderful spaces, filled with your own character, personality and style, coupled with the inherent style of the building and its environment.

Below: A small shaded niche is the perfect spot for this wall fountain, surrounded by Chinese star jasmine.

Opposite top: Making the space for outdoor entertaining is often a priority in gardens today.

When to enlist **professional help**

If you lack confidence or expertise in any area, and you can afford it, consult a professional landscape designer or horticulturalist. Gardening and landscaping are really different things, and even if you are expert at one, you may be a novice at the other.

If your site is tricky — for example, it is difficult to access, has drainage problems or is simply not giving you any inspiration — seek help. But have a clear idea of what you want as well as what you are capable of doing yourself or are able to outsource to others.

You may not want to venture beyond making up a scrapbook of ideas before handing over to the professionals, or you may draw up your own plan and implement the entire design yourself. Another option is to project manage your design and organize the various trades until the planting stage, which you may choose to do yourself.

Above: Whether you consult a professional or design your garden from scratch on your own, you'll need a plan.

A site survey

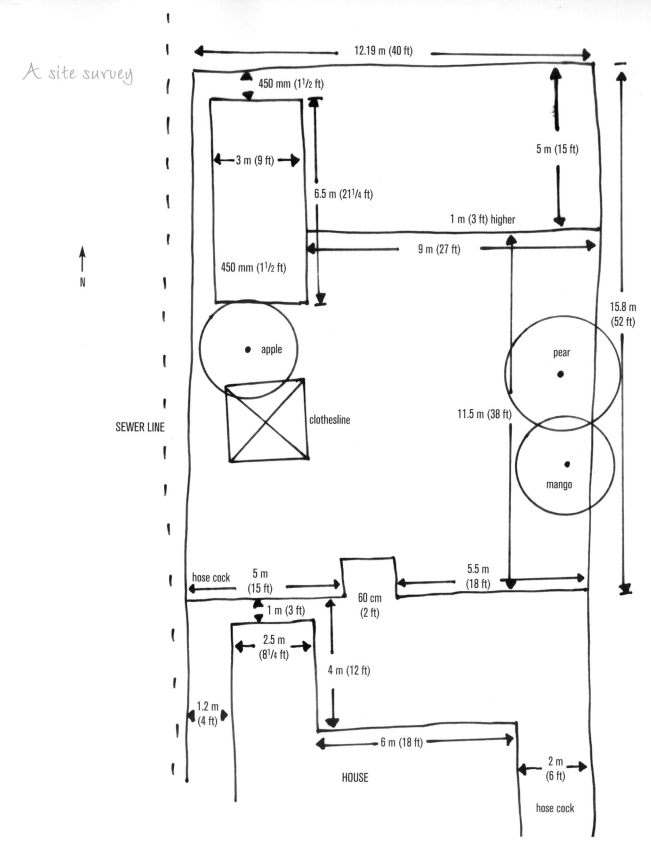

12.19 m (40 ft)

450 mm (1½ ft)

3 m (9 ft)

6.5 m (21¼ ft)

5 m (15 ft)

1 m (3 ft) higher

450 mm (1½ ft)

9 m (27 ft)

N

apple

pear

15.8 m
(52 ft)

SEWER LINE

clothesline

11.5 m (38 ft)

mango

hose cock   5 m
(15 ft)

5.5 m
(18 ft)

60 cm
(2 ft)

1 m (3 ft)

2.5 m
(8¼ ft)

4 m (12 ft)

1.2 m
(4 ft)

6 m (18 ft)

2 m
(6 ft)

HOUSE

hose cock

Site survey

Whatever your level of commitment, the following will help you to understand plans and gauge the knowledge and expertise of various tradespeople. It will also arm you with enough information to ask the right questions and make informed choices.

What do you have?

Before undertaking any design work, make a thorough analysis of your site. This means looking at the size and shape of your block, its undulations, levels, services and existing planting, the climate zone and microclimate of your garden, its aspect and exposure, the soil and drainage.

Size and shape of the block

Drawing a plan of your block is a useful first step. Draw a rough sketch of the site, just a 'mud map', like a simple drawing in the sand. Indicate all the features, services and the like. Start off by 'guesstimating' rather than measuring. Pace out the lengths of boundaries, buildings, walls and tree plantings. Make sure you have an even stride, and that you know the length of your pace. Mark these features on your rough plan. Then check to make sure you counted correctly. Try and do this roughly to scale, and indicate north. This is called a site survey. It should include all these aspects, as well as existing plantings.

Next, get out the tape measure and measure these features exactly (for step by step instructions, see the project on page 32). On this rough sketch, transfer accurate figures such as the length of boundaries, the distance from the house to the boundaries and the exact location of trees. Also, topography or level changes need to be shown on this plan. The fall of an area can obviously be measured with equipment such as a dumpy level, but clear plastic tubing with water in it will also

find its own level, and allow you to measure the various drops or increases in ground level. If accuracy isn't your strong point, don't despair. Design is a combination of art and science, and your strength might lie in the former rather than the latter.

So if the mere thought of technical drawing puts you off, remember that this step is just a very useful tool for exploring different concepts. It is much easier to rub out a pencil mark than rebuild a wall, so it's worth a try.

To make the process as painless as possible, photocopy the cut-outs on pages 439–40 to scale, and simply stick them onto your outline where appropriate. You can use the plan to work out correct quantities and costs, so your work will pay dividends. Your design will work better too.

If you are lucky enough to have a surveyor's plan of your property, simply use the reducing function on a photocopier and print out a 1:100 scale plan. A useful tip here is to make sure that the scale is drawn on the plan (rather than represented by a ratio) before you reduce or enlarge your copy. This way, when you photocopy your plan, the scale will automatically change at the same rate.

Soil type, water and drainage

As everything that goes on above ground level is affected by the soil (virtually half of each plant is in fact unseen), you also need to note soil type, pH, drainage patterns and wet spots. You can then manipulate these as desired by raising beds, creating wet or dry gardens, and adding compost and gypsum, for example, as required.

Remember that plants do not tolerate soil levels being changed dramatically around them, and that you can easily kill beautiful, significant trees by changing levels or manipulating drainage patterns if you don't carefully consider the consequences first.

how to...
Use a water level

To measure the fall of an area with a water level, pour water into a length of hose, then adjust the height at both ends until the water is just starting to spill out of both at the same time. This means that both ends are level. Next, measure the height above ground level at both ends and subtract the lower figure from the higher one to give you the fall.

project

Drawing a site survey

To make an accurate site survey, plot your site onto grid paper, then mark in all the relevant information. You'll need a scale rule, grid paper, a long measuring tape, a pencil and your rough survey. Let each square on the grid paper represent one square metre (yard) on the ground. This scale is called 1:100. Use a scale of 1:100 for medium-sized and larger gardens to show trees and shrubs. If your garden is small and more detailed plantings are needed, use a scale of 1:50. Finally, a scale of 1:20 is useful for showing details such as pot plants.

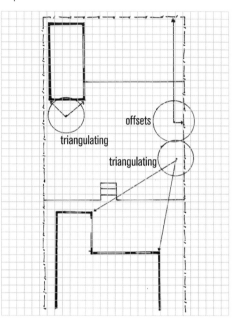

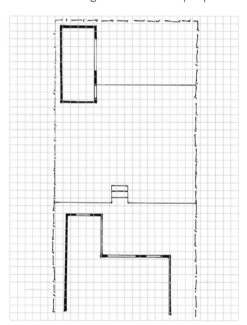

1 Use the measurements from your rough survey and plot them yourself. Use a piece of grid paper that is large enough for you to leave space around the plan, as this will be a useful space for details later on. Count the squares and plot these property lines out on the paper. Draw the outline of your home onto the grid paper. Draw the shape of the back and sides, and mark the positions of windows, doors, bays and recesses.

2 Next, plot the position of trees and garden beds from fixed objects, such as the house or boundary fence. For example, measure the position of a tree from two fixed points. This is called triangulating. Take measurements for both the canopy and the trunk of each tree so you can plot its spread accurately. To make the plan easy to understand, draw a circle to represent the spread of each tree. Another way of plotting trees and beds is by offsets. Lay a length of tape flat across the garden, and place pegs opposite the features you wish to mark out. Then measure the distance from the start of the tape to each peg, then from each peg to the relevant feature. Double check this offset by triangulating. For defining curves, sketch the general shape of the beds, and then measure 90-degree offsets at regular intervals. Mark each measurement, and join the dots freehand.

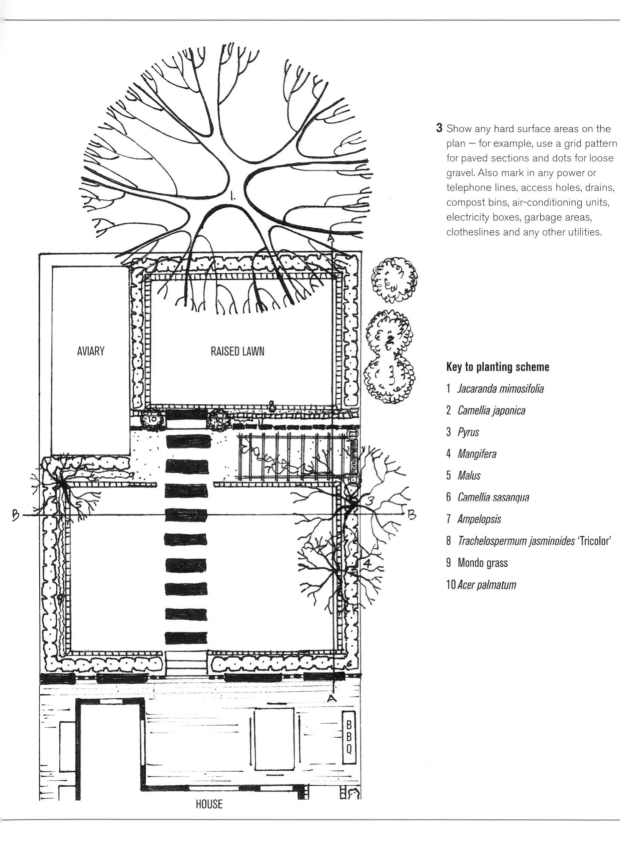

3 Show any hard surface areas on the plan — for example, use a grid pattern for paved sections and dots for loose gravel. Also mark in any power or telephone lines, access holes, drains, compost bins, air-conditioning units, electricity boxes, garbage areas, clotheslines and any other utilities.

AVIARY

RAISED LAWN

B

B

A

A

HOUSE

BBQ

Key to planting scheme

1 *Jacaranda mimosifolia*

2 *Camellia japonica*

3 *Pyrus*

4 *Mangifera*

5 *Malus*

6 *Camellia sasanqua*

7 *Ampelopsis*

8 *Trachelospermum jasminoides* 'Tricolor'

9 Mondo grass

10 *Acer palmatum*

Centre: A raised planter box makes it easy for you to adjust the soil pH to suit the plants you want to grow.

Your soil is a mixture of various components and is affected by many things, such as the parent material or bedrock from which it was derived, the subsoil and the most fertile, plant-friendly layer, the topsoil, which includes humus or decayed organic matter that feeds and nurtures plants. The parent material and level of organic matter will greatly affect the pH and structure of your soil, whereas the texture of your soil is a result of the mineral components — for example, the amounts of silt, clay and sand in each soil.

Is your soil acid or alkaline?

If soils contain lime or chalk, they are known as 'sweet' or alkaline soils. This means that if you test the soil's pH it will show up in the range of 7–14. Conversely, a peat-based soil lacking in lime will show up as a 'sour' or acid soil, which will have a reading of less

Testing the soil pH

It's easy to test the soil to find out exactly what you're dealing with. It's just a simple matter of buying a pH test kit, taking a soil sample, adding water, shaking the solution around with a few drops of indicator fluid and then allowing it to settle. Once the dust has settled, so to speak, you can match up the coloured liquid to the chart that comes in the pack. You'll need a pH testing kit, a small amount of water and a soil sample that is moist but not wet.

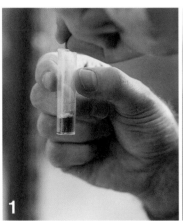
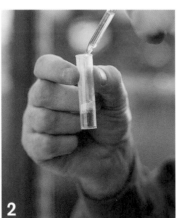

1 Place the test chemical and the soil sample in the test tube.

2 Add some distilled water up to the level indicated on the test tube, replace the cap and give it a vigorous shake for about a minute.

3 Once the solution has settled and cleared, check its colour against the colour chart. This will indicate the lime content of your soil.

than 7. A neutral soil has a reading of 7. The scale is a sliding one, with a pH of 6 being 10 times more acid than a pH of 5, which in turn is 100 times more acid than that of 7.

Soils can be manipulated, however. If your soil is too acid, it can be sweetened by the addition of lime, blood and bone or many poultry manures and mushroom composts. If a radical adjustment is necessary, you may need to add calcium hydroxide (hydrated lime). To increase the pH by 0.05, add hydrated lime according to the manufacturer's instructions. A heavy clay soil will need twice as much lime as a light, sandy soil. Winter and autumn are the best times for adding lime, but you shouldn't fertilize the soil for a month before or after as this will affect the pH too. Sulfate of ammonia-based soils will lower the pH, as will the addition of peat and many animal manures. See the plant lists for particular soils on page 53.

Soil **texture** tests

You can use a few methods to test your soil texture. The first test, known as 'the worm test', is done by hand (above left). Simply squeeze a small sample of moist earth in your hand. Pure clay feels smooth, sticks to your hand and can be rolled into long, thin worms. Silt is also smooth, but tends not to keep its shape as well and the worms break up after they reach about 3 cm (1 in) in length, as this sample is starting to do. Sand will just crumble, whereas mixtures, or loams, may form some worms, then break, but still stain your hand.

The other test is just as straightforward (above right). Place a sample of soil in a clear jar with some water and shake it vigorously. Allow it to settle. After some time, the components will fall to the bottom of the jar, the heaviest first, with the lightest, organic matter floating on top. From this strata effect you'll be able to identify the sand at the bottom, then silt and finally the clay particles on the top layer. This will clearly show you the proportions of sand, clay, organic matter and silt in your soil.

Right: The footprint test: if you walk on the grass and it fails to spring back in a few minutes, then it needs water.

How much to water

Water is a precious resource. Using it judiciously will not only benefit your garden, it will also help the environment.

The sprinkler test: Before watering your garden, place a bucket or similar container on your lawn or garden bed, then turn on your sprinkler or irrigation system. When the bucket is 15 mm (1/2 in) deep, your plants should have had enough water. You can test that the water has penetrated to the roots by digging a hole and checking the colour of the earth. Obviously where the earth is darkest, water is soaking in properly.

However, if water has not penetrated at all, you may need to change your mulch or treat your soil with a water surfactant, which will break down any waxy coatings or the repelling factors of some soils and allow water penetration. By only watering in this way, you'll minimize water runoff and encourage roots to grow deeply to where they are best protected from weather extremes.

The footprint test: To check if your lawn needs watering, try the simple footprint test. Walk on your grass and see how long it takes to spring back. If you can still see your footprints from your stroll after two minutes,

Weeds

Another consideration at this point is the weed factor. If your garden has suffered bad infestations of weeds, then attend to these before you embark on new plantings. Seed source can remain viable in the soil for many years, so correcting the weed problem may involve using weedicides or, in worst case scenarios, replacing the plant-growing media. In hot climates, solar sterilization of the soil may be an option. Drape plastic sheeting over the soil and pin it down. In hot weather, the sun's rays heat up the soil until any seeds are 'cooked'.

the grass needs water; on the other hand, if it springs back quickly, it has enough.

The question of drainage

Wherever you have altered the natural course of water or added hard surfaces, drainage is crucial. Paved areas should have a gentle fall so that water can run off into either subsurface drainage and pipes or a grassed or planted area. Walls too should be protected from water pressure by drainage. Make sure your walls have weep holes, swale drains (a ditch parallel to a wall that directs water away at either end), or agricultural pipes diverting water away from the wall so that it won't collapse during downpours.

Soil porosity test: Depending on your garden style and design, wet spots in the garden can be either drained or planted with appropriate water-loving species. A simple test, known as the soil porosity test, will determine how well your site drains. Simply dig a couple of holes, each about 60 cm (2 ft) deep, and fill them up with water. If the water stays in each hole for more than a few hours, it needs either extra drainage or planting with plants that like wet feet, known as bog plants. A herringbone pattern of agricultural pipe is the most common sort of artificial, subsurface drainage for gardens. See page 53 for a list of bog plants.

Below: These stone retaining walls have weep holes at regular intervals to allow water to run off.

Laying agricultural drains

There are three types of drains that are easy to lay — agricultural pipes, soakaways and swale drains.

The best solution for drainage problems is to install underground agricultural pipes, which are made from perforated polythene. They are usually laid in a herringbone (reticulated) pattern from the wettest area you are trying to drain — for example, a paved section — to the lowest point, where you'll need to connect the main drain line with the stormwater or sump, or you may need to install a soakaway (see opposite).

Perforated agricultural pipes, or 'ag pipes' as they are called, are really an updated version of terracotta or unperforated poly pipes. They are laid end to end, with gaps at the joins to allow water to enter and be redirected. Whether you use perforated or unperforated pipes, line your trenches with geotextile material (landscaping material) and backfill with crushed gravel before replacing the topsoil. This will help stop your pipes becoming clogged with silt. Also, make sure the grade you use is sufficient for the pipes to be self-cleaning — water doesn't run uphill! A 1:60 fall along the pipe's length is about right.

1 Dig a trench about the same width as a spade. Lay enough geotextile material in the trench so that it will wrap around the top of the pipe and fill you use. Spread the fill along the bottom of the trench, then lay the agricultural pipe on top.

2 Backfill over the top of the pipe to about 5 cm (2 in) from ground level. Wrap the geotextile material over the top.

3 Replace the topsoil and turf, if appropriate.

Soakaways and swale drains

A soakaway is a really simple way of dealing with isolated spots of dampness. Basically, it's just a hole about 1 m (3 ft) wide and 1.2 m (4 ft) deep, located at the damp spot. It helps water to drain into the subsoil. The hole should be filled with stones and rocks, then coarse gravel or rubble, the geotextile material, subsoil, and finally the topsoil and planting. Make sure soakaways are located away from buildings and structures that have footings, so that they don't weaken them. If you have agricultural pipes directed into your soakaway, make sure they enter the crushed gravel layer.

Digging a shallow trench, or swale, is a good way of redirecting runoff that would normally run sheet-like down a hill. Swales are often built at the top of road embankments and the like to divert water away from thoroughfares where it may cause hazards. Pitch the swale in the direction you want the water to run, and mound up the soil from the ditch on either side, compacting the soil around the downhill side. On very steep ground you may need to place geotextile material over the soil to prevent erosion, but in most cases just replacing the turf or planting with ground covers is enough to prevent erosion.

Above: Piet Oudolf is regarded as one of the world's most inspiring garden designers. His work is often closely married to nature, with the site itself and the wildflowers of the region often directing the design. The plants he chooses are always the best cultivars available, and his treatment of them nothing short of masterly. This wetlands garden, Pensthorpe Waterfowl Park, in Norfolk, England, is typical of his style.

Did you know? Chicory, valerian and cow parsnip grow happily in chalky soils. A 'calcifuge' is a plant that won't grow in alkaline soil.

Climatic conditions

Climate affects plant growth enormously, and determines what selection of plant life is available to the gardener. Choosing plants that are either indigenous, or grow in a similar climate elsewhere, is fundamental to the success of your garden. Without this initial sensible decision process, you are doomed to always fight a losing battle.

Climatic zones are determined by proximity to the equator, distance and height from the sea, and usual direction of the wind. The elements of climate that affect plant growth are temperature, sunlight, rainfall, wind, humidity, frost and snow. There is no point in trying to grow alpine plants in the hot tropics, but a similar style of rock garden planted with succulents may provide you with the sort of garden look that you want. Not only does climate affect the success of your chosen planting scheme, but it also relates to the comfort of your outdoor living areas.

Luckily for gardeners, microclimate, or the peculiarities of a particular spot — such as aspect, protection and shelter, hours of sun and watering practices — extend the possibilities of what you can grow successfully. By mapping areas in the sun (and shade), wind channels, drainage

Below: *Iris laevigata*, or rabbit ear iris, backed by the giant leaves of *Gunnera* sp. Both plants love growing in a moist environment, so no drainage is necessary in this garden.

patterns and frost pockets, you can manipulate these areas and extend your plant selection by providing protection in the form of glasshouses, covered areas, windbreaks and shade trees. Extending the functionality of outdoor spaces by including outdoor fireplaces, braziers and pergolas may also be a sensible option.

Right: Over winter, protect cold-sensitive plants in a glasshouse.

Below right: Succulents are the perfect plant choice for this drystone wall as they don't need special care and can cope with the lack of water.

Above: A well designed garden should seem like a continuation of the house.

Right: A veranda or porch is an intermediate area that links the house with the garden. Style it as you would a room in your house.

Climate change

The greatest challenge for gardeners in the future will be climate change. Reliably wet areas may experience periods of drought and extreme highs in temperature, while formerly dry places may be hit with flooding rains and cyclonic storms. Be prepared for the worst. Check the hardiness of all plants before introducing them into your garden, and landscape with storms and the like in mind, making sure that your drainage system can cope with flash floods. Carefully choose trees for their strength, with brittle-barked ones planted away from any structures in case they fall and cause damage. As the carbon dioxide levels increase with the greenhouse effect, it is likely that plants will grow much faster, but consist of weaker woody matter and therefore break easily.

Left: In this low maintenance garden, *Restio tetraphyllus* and *Dianella* sp. both form grassy tufts that tolerate a wide range of conditions.

Site appraisal and analysis

This step is all about working out the potential of your property and addressing any problems. When appraising and analyzing your space, try to look at it afresh. You can become so familiar with a place that you fail to see the problems or advantages that a stranger might notice straightaway. Try asking a friend to tell you what they see, as another person will always see things differently.

The site analysis plan

Once you have drawn up your site survey, photocopy it a few times and then start work on the next plan, called the site analysis plan. To make the plan more professional, try using the different tree symbols that are in the back of this book on pages 439–40. Photocopy them to the right scale and place them on your grid paper in the appropriate positions.

Walk around the site to get an idea of its potential. Are there any views? Is there any opportunity for borrowing landscapes (see page 44)? Are there any plants or landscapes in surrounding gardens that you could incorporate into your garden? What needs screening? What is the 'feel' of the place? Do you need summer shade or more sun? Are there any shaded, dark spots? Where are the nicest places to sit? Is your garden near a busy road or noisy thoroughfare? What are the existing materials? What plants do you want to keep? Where is the connection from the house to the outdoors? Can this be improved by the addition of French doors, picture windows or concertina doors?

Now mark down these attributes, possibilities and problems onto your site analysis plan. Think about your neighbours too. Planting a large tree might block their view or the sun, so work out if there are any potential contentious issues now, at the planning stage, to save yourself problems in the future.

The **borrowed** landscape

Above: A hedge of *Camellia sasanqua* 'Showa-No-Sakae' successfully masks the boundary, making the neighbouring trees seem as if they are part of the garden.

No garden, unless it is totally surrounded by tall walls or buildings, operates without some glimpses outwards. The 'borrowed landscape' is a term used to describe how capturing or including that view can augment your own garden.

It may simply be a matter of planting or building to frame views, or removing boundaries to increase the number of glimpses of an attractive site. Another trick that is used less frequently is to repeat elements outside the boundary in your garden in order to link features together. This may mean repeating the same species of tree, or planting one with a similar form. It could be including a water feature to mimic a greater body of water that is seen at the same time. Often it is simply a matter of enjoying the shade cast by a neighbour's tree canopy, and screening out your fence so that you can imagine that the tree is in your garden.

The Japanese and Chinese were masters of this technique; in Japan it is called *shakkei*, while in China it is *chie ching*. Both cultures utilized the layered effect of background, middle ground and foreground, but successfully incorporated borrowed views as the background to each garden.

Use an arrow to mark in north, and the direction of any strong prevailing winds. Indicate any views that need either opening up or retaining, and use large squiggly lines to roughly mark out where planting and screening should be used to block out buildings, utilities and neighbours.

Now your plan shows you what you have, and the deficiencies of the site that need rectifying. The next step is to work out some broad concepts for your garden, but before doing this, it's worthwhile asking yourself what you really want the space to provide. This is called a design brief.

The design brief

The next step should be to give yourself a design brief. Actually articulate things that are important to you. Ask yourself some simple questions before you start digging, as this process will help you to formulate a design brief. You can then use this design brief to ensure that your garden will fulfil your needs and be the right space for your personality and lifestyle.

What are your needs?

Before you garden, make a priority list of what you want from the space and in order of need. How many 'rooms' does your garden need? Do you need an area for outdoor entertaining? Do you want a lawn for small children or animals? For each item on your list — for example, storage, utilities area, outdoor seating, outdoor cooking, transitional space from indoors to out, vegetable patch, paved section, compost area and flower garden — indicate any special considerations, such as sun requirements.

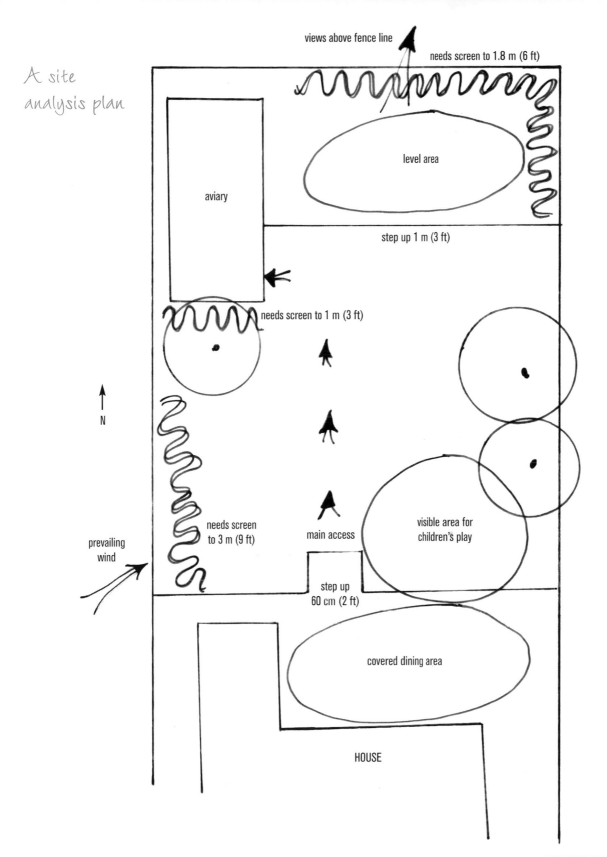

A site
analysis plan

views above fence line

needs screen to 1.8 m (6 ft)

level area

aviary

step up 1 m (3 ft)

needs screen to 1 m (3 ft)

N

needs screen
to 3 m (9 ft)

main access

visible area for
children's play

prevailing
wind

step up
60 cm (2 ft)

covered dining area

HOUSE

How much time and money do you have?

Ask yourself some questions about time constraints, special loves and lifestyle. For instance, how much time do you want to spend gardening each week?

Decide on a time frame for your garden. Are you planning on selling in a few months and want a 'makeover'? Are you renovating, or planning to extend in the future? Will your needs change dramatically (because you're planning to start a family or your children are starting to leave home)?

Work out what you can afford in terms of both maintenance and installation. Put together a budget. Allow about half the allotted amount for labour (unless you can do it all yourself), and the rest for materials and plants. Remember that you can save on costs by planting young specimens or tube stock rather than mature or advanced stock, while still sticking to your selections and quantities. Your costs should be measured both in financial terms and the time needed to implement and maintain them.

What is your style?

Your garden should be an extension of your own personality, likes and dislikes. Consider whether you prefer drama or fantasy, privacy or an 'open' garden, simplicity or complexity, neat and tidy or messy.

Collect pictures of things you like from magazines, and use them to make up a scrapbook or poster. When you stick these pictures down together on a couple of pages, does a theme or style emerge? How do you want your garden to feel?

Opposite: Making room for a children's play area, and even for a children's garden, should be a priority in all family gardens.

The **low maintenance** garden

Above: A natural garden needs less maintenance: leaves dropping to the ground only add to the ambience. A garden with hard surfaces, however, should be swept regularly.

Some gardens are hard to maintain because they contain features that are difficult to look after. Small ponds, lots of garden edging that necessitates cutting lawn edges by hand, plants that are water dependent or vast areas of mown grass are all examples of what to avoid if you are trying to cut down on the time you'll need to spend in the garden.

Low maintenance options include raised beds, curved lawn areas (they can be mown continuously without turning the mower around and are therefore easier to mow), and drought-tolerant or climate-specific plants. They will all aid in the creation of an easy-care garden. Limiting the number of plants that need regular trimming — such as formal hedging, flowering perennials and resource-dependent annuals — will also ease the load. Planting with informal shrubbery and ground-covering plants will significantly decrease the garden maintenance required.

Another tip is to choose your garden floor carefully. While decking or paved areas are easy enough to sweep, they still require attention. A leaf-litter floor with carpeting ground covers and stepping stones may be a better option for the parts of your garden where open areas with access rather than hard surfaces are required.

Did you know? Plants are a lot cheaper than hard materials, especially when you factor in the cost of skilled labour for construction. Planting is called 'soft landscaping', whereas construction work like paving and building walls and other outdoor structures is called 'hard landscaping'.

What's the feel of your suburb?

The style or atmosphere you want for your garden should be carefully balanced by the aesthetic needs of the house, the streetscape and a sense of place. Your local environment and the character and history of the neighbourhood should all help determine the direction your garden takes.

There should be lots of local clues to selecting elements you may wish to include. Any original buildings will be built from local products. Timber, stone, clay bricks and slate roof tiles are all sources of inspiration for compiling your palette of materials, but don't overlook other clues such as walls, fences and gates that may give you an idea of the existing character of your local area.

If these elements have all been destroyed, there may be photographs in the local library or historical society that may help, but even looking at the street names — for example, Orchard Lane, Quarry Road, Gardeners Street — will give you an idea or starting point.

Below: Corrugated iron is a roofing material that can seem sleek and modern when used in another context — for example, as a boundary wall in this minimalist courtyard.

Research

The next step also involves researching and collating all your ideas. Find out about original water features and lighting if they are part of your concept.

Set out a plant list, incorporating elements such as colour, texture and form. Look around at building materials and work out a selection of construction materials for your garden. From these, you can display elements on a board and get a sense of the mood they will create. Finally, you can start imagining what the garden will look like — its style and materials, and the actual composition and choice of plant material. Examples of these 'mood boards' can be found in the four chapters on garden design palettes. (For example, for a woodland garden mood board, see page 139 in 'Wild palette'.)

Concept plan

For those of us who love flowers, trees and the wonderful diversity of nature, it's very difficult to ignore plants. However, a garden space is not only a place for plants, it is also a valuable extension of your living area and extremely important to your psyche.

The problem for city gardeners is the limited amount of space, and many of us try to incorporate everything into one little plot. The result is all too often a grand-style garden on a small scale, which never looks quite right, and which doesn't fulfil its potential to improve your lifestyle.

The answer is garden design — an understanding of styles and the elements of design as well as being able to subjectively appraise your site and select plants according to set criteria. You need to be able to find the right spot for all those favourite flowers and special plants, not just in terms of their horticultural requirements, but also how they will work within the design framework.

This should show you how by planning your space, in both a visual and practical sense, you can have a garden that suits your way of life, the character of your home, and the surroundings in general.

Now you have decided what rooms you already have and the ones you want, your task is to design a garden that incorporates your needs. The next step is to complete your concept plan, playing with the areas you want and the spaces available until you have a suitable combination of the two — that is, what you want and what's attainable. Try to

devise quite a few concepts. Each one may incorporate components that you like, that can be used to work out your final design. Be willing to try ideas and throw them away. You may discard many pieces of tracing paper before settling on a final plan.

Making a concept plan

If you find it difficult to plan or think in two dimensions, try building a three-dimensional model. A simpler method is to play with shapes, rooms and space, so try this technique. At this stage of the planning

Below: A change in level has been utilized to create a private seating area in a tropical courtyard garden.

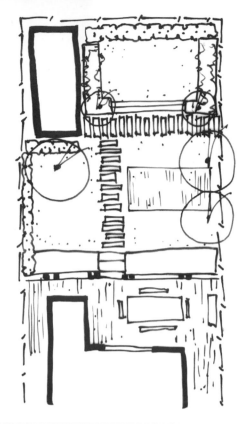

Right: A rough concept plan that will be developed into a final garden plan (see opposite).

Below: Paper in different colours and patterns can be used to play around with design ideas. These layouts show how different areas can be created in a small rectangular garden.

process you can have fun with loads of ideas. It is worth considering moving the garage or shed on a plan, or even changing the entrance to your house, when changing your mind is as simple as moving a piece of paper or rubbing out a line.

Step 1

First, either photocopy or copy a 1:100 plan of your garden onto white paper. Then, using coloured paper, cut out different shapes in various sizes to represent the house and outbuildings, lawn and paved areas — for example, use a colour code (light green paper to represent lawn, brown for any hard surfaces, blue for bodies of water and dark green for planting beds). Manipulate these different elements to form interesting links and help you visualize garden rooms.

Step 2

Once you've settled on, say, three good layouts, draw these up into draft concept plans. This will allow you to see how the design works as a whole, and to check measurements for practical purposes — for example, make sure that the paved area is large enough for a table, and that the sandpit will be large enough for the children. A scale representation of your key pieces, such as furniture, may be useful too, so that you can

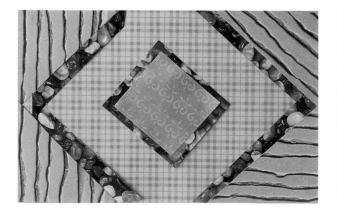

move them about on your concept and see where they fit best. See the back of the book for plan view drawings of plants (pages 439–40) that may be useful at this stage.

Step 3

The next step is to trace these cut-outs onto tracing paper. Now you have three complete concept plans. You can use one of them as your final garden plan.

Structural plan

Use a structural plan to show details such as paving patterns, walls, pergolas, a barbecue or outdoor kitchen layout in more detail. The scale is normally 1:50 or 1:20, which is in effect a close-up look at garden features. It may be worth drawing up some cross-sections so that you can also check on the vertical aspects of your concept. Indicate the heights of buildings, trees and shrubs as well as accent plants on this plan.

Planting plan and plant lists

The next stage is to play with your green areas. Again, design these by playing with shapes. This time, however, try and think in three dimensions and look at plants as forms or basic outlines. Use them as units to make up groups and associations, but make sure you include only plants that are suited to your garden's aspect and climate.

A useful tool at this stage of the process is to use cheat perspectives. Photograph some parts of your garden, then enlarge the images up to A3 or A4 size on a photocopier.

Right: If you are designing your own garden, it's probably easier to combine the structural plan and planting plan, as shown here. A landscape architect would draw up two separate plans — one for the builder and one for the 'soft' landscapers.

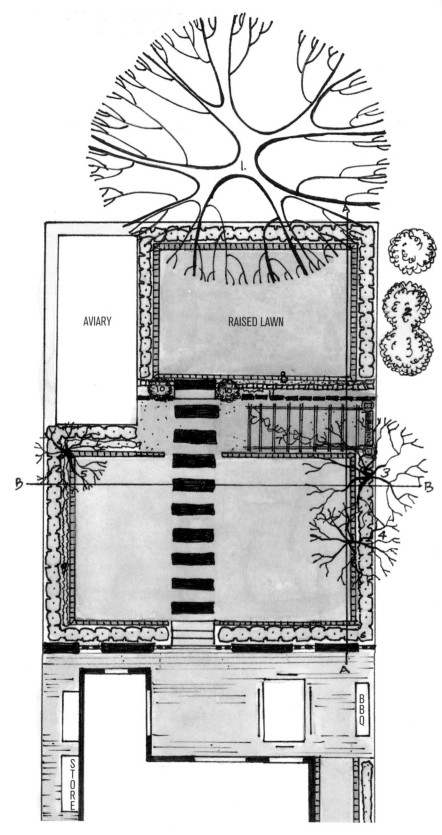

AVIARY

RAISED LAWN

STORE

BBQ

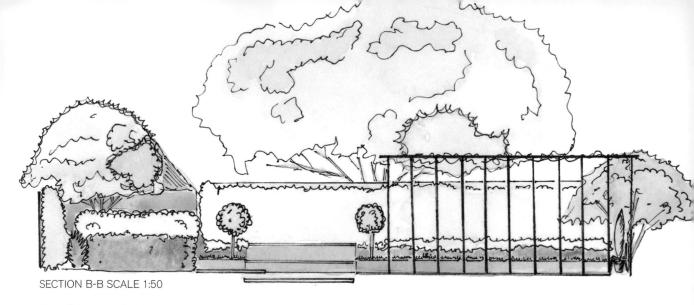

SECTION B-B SCALE 1:50

Above: This cross-section shows
what is known as the elevation
from one side boundary of a
garden to another.

Opposite, from top left to
bottom right: *Dietes grandiflora,*
Cistus sp., *Viburnum tinus,*
Escallonia bifida, Aspidistra
elatior, Yucca sp., *Ginkgo biloba,*
Gunnera manicata, Cercis
siliquastrum and *Nicotiana* sp.

Draw onto these photocopies your ideas
in silhouette form, or use the silhouette
shapes in the back of the book (see page
438). Practise organizing your plants
into different groupings to see which
combination works best.

When you are satisfied with your
combinations, find plants that fit the bill. The
lists of trees with different shapes and foliage
on page 59 will help. Then mark them on
tracing paper. This is known as a planting
plan, which is often like an overlay for your
main plan. Use colours to highlight various
flowering schemes or planting arrangements.
Another option is to again use a scale such as
1:50 that leaves enough space for adding lots
of information, such as plant varieties and
cultivar names.

Use keys or symbols to show various
types of trees and shrubs. Try and put
different symbols next to each other so that
any overlapping plants are still easily
distinguished on the plan. Use a broken
line to indicate a tree that needs removing.
(Refer to the plan view drawings on pages
439–40 and use these as a guide.)

Again, use cross-sections like the one
shown above to highlight key areas in your
garden, such as the position of seating,
steps and gateways, feature pots, focal
points and other prominent features. You
can also show the heights of various
planting schemes on the cross-sections.
This will help you to visualize your garden's
framework and pinpoint any design
problems, such as a lack of a top tier.

Right: Paper cut-outs
representing different plant forms
can be used in different
combinations to help achieve
various effects.

Plants for **tricky places**

Dry shade
Annuals: *Lamium* sp.
Fern: *Dryopteris* sp.
Perennials: *Clivia* sp., *Dietes* sp.,
Vinca sp.
Shrubs: *Elaeagnus* sp., *Hypericum* sp.
Trees: *Acer negundo*, *Cercis* sp.

Front line salt spray
Annuals: *Brachyscome* sp.,
Dorotheanthus bellidiformis,
Gazania sp.
Perennials: *Phormium* sp.
Shrubs: *Atriplex* sp., *Coprosma* sp.,
Cordyline sp., *Genista* sp., *Yucca* sp.
Trees: *Albizia* sp., *Arbutus unedo*

Shallow soil, sun-baked tops
Annuals: *Agrostemma githago*,
Argemone sp., *Calendula* sp.
Perennials: *Agapanthus* sp.,
Eryngium sp., *Sempervivum* sp.
Shrubs: *Ceratostigma* sp., *Cistus* sp.
Trees: *Acacia* sp., *Banksia* sp.,
Pinus sp.

Heavy frost and snow
Annuals (plant out when this has
lifted): *Brassica oleracea*,
Glaucium sp.
Perennials: *Delphinium* sp.,
Digitalis sp.
Shrubs: *Calluna* sp., *Euonymus
fortunei*
Trees: *Betula* sp., *Chamaecyparis* sp.

Winter shade, summer sun
Annuals: *Myosotis* sp., *Primula* sp.
Perennials: *Anemone* x *hybrida*
Shrubs: *Camellia sasanqua*,
Euonymus sp., *Mahonia* sp.,
Viburnum tinus
Trees: *Ilex* sp., *Podocarpus* sp. and
virtually any deciduous tree

Permanently boggy soils
Annuals: *Mimulus* sp.,
Ranunculus sp.
Ferns: *Blechnum* sp., *Pteris* sp.
Perennials: *Acanthus* sp.,
Gunnera sp., *Hemerocallis* sp.,
Pratia sp., *Rheum* sp.
Shrubs: *Bauera* sp.
Trees: *Cornus* sp.

Clay soils
Annuals: *Campanula medium*,
Cleome sp.
Perennials: *Dahlia* sp., *Lupinus* sp.,
Paeonia sp.
Shrubs: *Abelia* sp., *Cotoneaster* sp.,
Escallonia sp., *Hypericum* sp.
Trees: *Acer* sp., *Alnus* sp.

Chalky soils
Annuals: *Erysimum* sp., *Iberis* sp.
Perennials: *Alchemilla* sp.,
Campanula sp., *Oenothera* sp., *Phlox*
sp., *Thymus* sp.
Shrubs: *Berberis* sp., *Buddleja* sp.,
Buxus sp., *Mahonia* sp., *Weigela* sp.
Trees: *Cercis* sp., *Crataegus* sp.,
Pyrus sp.

Heavy root competition
Annuals: *Ageratum* sp., *Alyssum* sp.
Perennials: *Aspidistra* sp., *Clivia* sp.,
Eranthemum sp., *Erigeron* sp.,
Eupatorium sp., *Kohleria* sp.,
Liriope sp.
Shrubs: *Hypericum* sp.,
Sarcococca sp.
Trees: *Alnus* sp., *Ficus* sp., *Pinus* sp.

Acid soils
Annuals: *Nicotiana* sp., *Petunia* sp.,
Zinnia sp.
Perennials: *Aster* sp., *Dicentra* sp.,
Paeonia sp.
Shrubs: *Berberis* sp., *Cistus* sp., *Hakea*
sp., *Rhododendron* sp.
Trees: *Acer* sp., *Betula* sp., *Malus* sp.

Transplanting a shrub

It's best to move conifers and deciduous plants in late autumn and winter when they have stopped growing and are dormant. Conversely, palms and most other tropical plants, which don't really have a dormant period, are best moved in summer so they can recover during their new season. This cordyline had been planted in the wrong position and was getting burnt. Moving it to a more sheltered position in the garden will give it a boost.

1 Dig around the root ball with a sharp spade so that the roots are cut cleanly. If they happen to tear, trim them with secateurs.

2 Lift the plant into an easy-to-lift container such as a large bucket, or wrap it with hessian and transport it to its new position in a wheelbarrow.

3 Prepare the new planting hole. Dig in well rotted manure or compost if the soil needs improving, but never more than 20 cm (8 in) deep as the soil can turn anaerobic (that is, lack oxygen) at greater depths.

4 Replant, being careful to maintain the original soil level, neither building up over or exposing the roots. Mulch, then water well.

Transplanting

When reworking your garden, you may find that some plants don't fit into your new design, but you would still like to keep them elsewhere in the garden. It's easy to transplant shrubs, conifers and deciduous trees, providing you have timed it well, and you have patience and a sufficient number of strong and willing workers or suitable equipment (see the box at left).

The advantage of transplanting is that your specimens are usually larger than you might otherwise be able to afford. Also, they tend to be garden hardy, already adapted to your particular climate, soil and location. Besides, it is great to be able to reuse material in a garden, as most people with green thumbs are conservationists.

Plant associations

This simply means combining plants together so that they make interesting combinations. You can devise beautiful plant pictures by playing off individual specimens against each other rather than letting one dominate.

Successful plant associations aren't just about leaves and flowers, however: they also depend on berries and seed pods, shape, texture and form, and rely heavily on the season and timing. An easy mistake to make is to overlook flowering times when choosing plants; in your mind they look great, but in reality they flower weeks apart and don't create the effect you expected.

A good trick here is to actually buy the plants you want to combine at the same time. Place them together in your trolley and assess the effect. This is a similar technique to shopping for clothes. Unless you actually have the garment with you, how can you be sure of getting the right coloured shoes? Colours in your mind almost always end up different in reality, especially with tricky shades such as red and green, which seem simple but actually have a variety of nuances.

Another technique worth trying is to copy someone else's successful plantings. As the old saying goes, copying is the sincerest form of flattery. Visiting other people's gardens on open days is not only a nice day out, but also a great opportunity to learn about plant associations that work.

The laburnum arch at garden designer Rosemary Verey's house in England is probably one of the most copied. The golden chains of pea flowers are underplanted with mauve alliums; the colour contrast is superb.

Rather than slavishly copy this combination, you could adapt the successful elements of this union. Yellow and purple work well because they are on opposite sides of the colour wheel. The flower shapes also contrast — one being pendulous chains, the other round globes. A similar effect could be achieved with mauve spires of spring larkspurs planted with the yellow disc flowers of *Rudbeckia* sp. Other opposites, such as green and red, or blue and orange, are also exciting.

Year-round interest and seasonality

Gardens that look good year round don't happen by accident; they are usually planned. This can be a simple thing: for instance, you can visit your local garden centre every six weeks or so, and buy something that looks good each time. After a year, you should have just about every season covered! Alternatively, you could be a bit more proactive, and actually choose plants to create certain effects in different seasons, or plants that look good year round or for at least half the year. Pay particular attention to winter. It is a season that is often forgotten, but it can be an enchanting time in the garden if you plan it well.

Above: An arch shows off the long pendulous flowers of laburnum to perfection.

Left: The red flowers of *Astilbe* sp. make an attractive contrast with green foliage because red and green are opposites on the colour wheel.

Seasonal guide to planting

Finding the right plant for the right place is harder than you might think. Visit your garden centre and you'll soon see how easy it is to be seduced by the displays of flowers and shrubs that in reality have little chance of survival in your garden. A Louisiana iris may look superb in the shop, but if you plant it in a garden that is predominantly dry and sandy, it will die. A bearded iris (or the extremely hardy daylily) would be a better choice of plant and yet serve the same purpose. Your local horticulturalist could steer you towards more suitable selections. Write down a clear list of criteria first, then ask your local horticulturalist for advice in fulfilling it. Consider the flowering time, position, height, form and colour of each plant as well as the climate and soil of its new location.

For planting suggestions, see the four 'Palette' chapters and 'Plants for tricky places' on page 53.

Using annuals and perennials

Beds and borders are the most common locations for annuals and perennials. A bed is usually an island of soil — square, rectangular, oval, round or kidney-shaped and surrounded by paving or lawn. The most pleasing way to plant beds is to group tall plants in the middle, then circle them with intermediate-height plants and an outer ring of low-growing plants. This 'cookie cutter' style of planting was very popular early in the Victorian era.

Opposite: A metal arch planted with a rambling *Rosa* 'Black Boy' softens a high wall and draws attention to the doorway.

Below: When planning your garden, consider how it will look all year round. This garden looks wonderful in autumn because of the flowering *Camellia sasanqua* hedge and the flame-coloured Japanese maples, but it will look just as good in spring with fresh new growth punctuated by the living wall.

Above: Plants with a suckering habit, such as these forsythias, will help cover up placement errors in a new hedge by sending up suckers to fill any gaps.

Opposite, from top to bottom: *Acacia cardiophylla*, *Prunus* x *subhirtella* 'Pendula', *Cupressus sempervirens*, *Fagus sylvatica* 'Purpurea', *Gleditsia triacanthos* 'Sunburst', *Cedrus atlantica* 'Glauca' and *Corylus avellana* 'Contorta'.

A border is generally a strip of soil backed by a hedge, wall, fence or path. The planting may be formal (neatly geometrical) or informal (with a wavy edge). Tall plants should be placed at the rear, intermediate plants in front of them and low-growing plants as an edging. A line of shrubs, such as forsythias or hydrangeas, makes an excellent background for a border of shorter flowers.

Annuals only live for one season so don't use them as the basis of your design, otherwise you will need to constantly replant them. But do use annuals for adding splashes of colour, emphasizing a particular scheme or colour combination, trying out new schemes or keeping up with trends. Annuals work best in places where people will see them often, such as in strategically placed pots or in beds along a path or driveway.

Perennials, on the other hand, are a more permanent feature. Their flowering season may last some months, but often flowering is part of an attractive life cycle that may include pretty foliage, interesting seed capsules or dried tops, all useful for seasonal interest. Many perennials are herbaceous, which means they die down to a permanent rootstock for part of each year. Some examples are bulbs, hostas and some ferns. These need to be mixed in with more permanent plantings, or if enough space is available, devoted to a bed for that particular season.

Group perennials in odd numbers, but plant accent plants singly. For a more natural effect, plant in drifts. Planting in blocks will create a more modern feel, while rows will result in a formal effect.

Designing with trees

Playing with space as infinite as the sky is a wonderful experiment that only home owners with plenty of land can indulge in. This aside, the effect of contrasting trees against each other, playing with the various canopy shapes and experimenting with coloured foliage, wonderful blossoms and statuesque outlines is a task worth careful consideration: you can't change your mind as you can with shrubs, perennials and ground covers (see opposite).

Spacing plants

Working out how many trees and shrubs you need for your garden is not hard. Your plan will help, as the size circles that you draw will correspond to the actual plant sizes and make counting up the number of plants easy. However, it is a little trickier to work out hedges, ground covers and perennials, where plants will overlap each other. Also, as a plant's size will vary over time, it's worth plotting your garden design so that it reflects a reasonable time frame — say, five to ten years.

Did you know? The Leyland cypress (x *Cupressocyparis leylandii*) is a hybrid of two genera, *Chamaecyparis* and *Cupressus*, which is quite unusual. It's the plant kingdom's equivalent of crossing a horse and a donkey to end up with a mule.

After this time be prepared for some changes, as some plants may outgrow their position, need pruning to keep them compact, or be overshadowed by larger trees and no longer grow well. A garden design is not a static work; you should continually tinker with it during its life.

When you buy a plant, check the label for its ultimate size, then verify this figure in a reliable gardening reference book. Some labels indicate the size to which a plant will grow only within a certain time frame — say, ten years — which can be misleading, especially when it comes to trees. If you plant new cross-breeds, only time will tell how tall they'll grow. For example, the Leyland cypress (x *Cupressocyparis leylandii*) has surpassed all estimates and has now towered out of control in many gardens.

If you are planting a perennial border, the key is to plant lots of the smaller growing plants en masse so that they have greater impact. The closer you space them, the faster the border will be finished and the less room there'll be for weeds. On the other hand, the maintenance level will be higher as you'll need to keep the plants watered and divided. If your plants are immature you need to be disciplined about watering, and if you live in an area with water restrictions, when and how much you water can be a significant factor. For instance, watering 200 plants with a watering can takes an hour.

Estimating quantity

Gardening is not an exact science and plants tend to be forgiving, eventually growing over mistakes. However, planting a few extra shrubs that can be pulled into place is a prudent practice, especially if losses will spoil the design, such as with formal hedges. Consider the following points before buying plants for your garden.

Trees to suit

Fast growers
Acacia sp., *Agonis* sp., *Citharexylum* sp., *Eucalyptus* sp., *Fraxinus angustifolia* 'Raywood', *Grevillea* sp., *Lophostemon* sp., *Melia azedarach*, *Robinia* sp., *Virgilia* sp.

Pendulous habit
Acer palmatum 'Dissectum Atropurpureum', *Alnus jorullensis*, *Betula pendula*, *Fagus sylvatica* f. *pendula*, *Morus alba* 'Pendula', *Prunus* x *subhirtella*, *Pyrus salicifolia* 'Pendula', *Salix babylonica* 'Pendula'

Fastigiate habit (upright, narrowing towards the top)
Cupressus sempervirens, *Gleditsia* 'Pyramidalis', *Juniperus chinensis* 'Keteleeri' and 'Pyramidalis', *Prunus* 'Amanogawa', *Pyrus calleryana* 'Chanticleer'

Purple foliage
Acer platanoides 'Crimson King', *Cercis canadensis* 'Forest Pansy', *Dodonaea viscosa* 'Purpurea', *Fagus sylvatica* 'Purpurea', *Gleditsia tricanthos* 'Ruby Lace', *Malus* x *purpurea*, *Prunus cerasifera* 'Nigra', *Prunus* x *blireana*

Golden foliage
Acer negundo 'Auratum', *Catalpa bignonoides* 'Aurea', *Fagus sylvatica* 'Aurea Pendula', *Gleditsia triacanthos* 'Sunburst', *Robinia pseudoacacia* 'Frisia', *Ulmus* 'Van de Houte'

Silver foliage
Cedrus atlantica 'Glauca', *Cupressus cashmeriana*, *Eucalyptus gunnii* and *E. cinerea*, *Picea pungens* 'Glauca', *Populus alba*, *Pyrus nivalis*, *P. salicifolia* 'Pendula'

Weird and wonderful
Adansonia sp., *Corylus avellana* 'Contorta', *Cyathea* sp., *Dracaena draco*, *Ginkgo* sp., *Pandanus* sp., *Robinia pseudoacacia* 'Lace Lady', *Salix babylonica* var. *pekinensis* 'Tortuosa', *Sequoiadendron* sp.

Above: The layered effect of the planting along this wide walkway, with shrubs sweeping down to the path, hides the base of the tree and attracts the eye to the tree canopy above.

Did you know? Some trees have extensive root systems. You should never underestimate them. The weeping fig (*Ficus benjamina*), which is often sold as an indoor plant, has been known to grow a canopy nearly 1 km (½ mile) in circumference, sending down aerial roots from every branch to support itself.

• Most annuals are happy with 30 cm (1 ft) spacing. Determine how many plants you will need for a given area. Use coloured pens to shade in the beds and borders you have sketched on graph paper. Use different colours to represent different plant groups — for example, twelve yellow squares to show a planting of a dozen marigolds, or 24 red squares to show a planting of two dozen wax begonias.

• To create a visually interesting bed or border, remember to include low edging plants and tall background plants. If a perennial grows to, say, 50 cm (20 in) wide, then that is 0.5 x 0.5 m (20 x 20 in) or 0.25 square metres (33 square ft), which requires four plants per square metre/yard. Perennials may need as much as 90 cm (3 ft) if they are larger growers.

• Space hedges at approximately two-thirds their width — that is, if a plant grows naturally to 1 m (3 ft) wide, then space a line of them 60 cm (2 ft) apart so that they merge together fairly quickly.

• When spacing ground covers, overlap them by half their diameter. Normally these areas are vulnerable to weeds, and overplanting reduces the likelihood of an invasion.

• Copses of trees are best planted in random groups. Edna Walling, a famous Australian garden writer and designer, advocated throwing a bag's worth of potatoes onto the ground and planting a sapling where each potato landed. Whatever method you use, placing odd numbers of trees in a haphazard manner usually works best. This will give a natural effect, and your garden won't look rigid or contrived.

• Climbers are so vigorous that they can be spaced 3 m (9 ft) or more apart. Often you'll need only one plant.

Use your imagination

After you have drawn up your plans, try this simple exercise. Visualize your landscape. Close your eyes, clear your mind, then focus on your plan. Walk around your virtual garden. Try and feel the effect of sun or shade on your face, the surface you're walking on and the smells as you wander from one area to another. By doing this you can perhaps ensure, while there is still time, that you have in fact catered for everything needed for the sort of garden you imagined in the first place.

Practicalities

The next step is to plan how you'll get the job done. Very few of us have the luxury of a free weekend away at a luxury resort while the TV makeover team does it all.

Look at access to the site, ways of moving heavy plants, pots, materials on- and off-site, services that may need moving, access for machinery where necessary, delivery costs (both of materials onto the site and fill or excavated material off the site). Any one of

Above: A simple planting scheme complements modern architecture. Here, ground-hugging knawel (*Scleranthus* sp.) forms a carpet in a shallow bed, while the shrub helps to break up the angular wall.

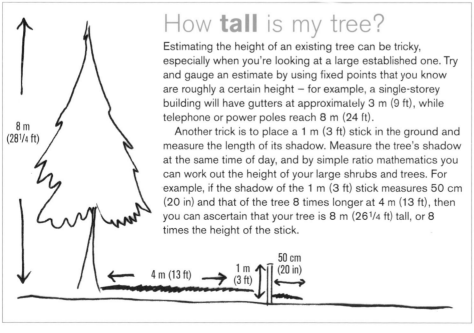

How **tall** is my tree?

Estimating the height of an existing tree can be tricky, especially when you're looking at a large established one. Try and gauge an estimate by using fixed points that you know are roughly a certain height – for example, a single-storey building will have gutters at approximately 3 m (9 ft), while telephone or power poles reach 8 m (24 ft).

Another trick is to place a 1 m (3 ft) stick in the ground and measure the length of its shadow. Measure the tree's shadow at the same time of day, and by simple ratio mathematics you can work out the height of your large shrubs and trees. For example, if the shadow of the 1 m (3 ft) stick measures 50 cm (20 in) and that of the tree 8 times longer at 4 m (13 ft), then you can ascertain that your tree is 8 m (26¼ ft) tall, or 8 times the height of the stick.

8 m (28¼ ft)

4 m (13 ft)   1 m (3 ft)   50 cm (20 in)

Above: Some bricks showing the bricklayer's trade marks.

these factors may have an impact on your design. It may be an impossible dream. So before you pick up a spade, consider whether you need to make any changes.

The large space set aside for your paving may look like a good spot to have a load of mulch delivered, but remember you'll have to remove it before you can level your sand for paving and that the garden beds might not be ready for mulching by then. Another often overlooked logistical element is rubbish. Think about where a skip bin might be placed, how long you can have it on council land and when you'll need the bulk of the material removed.

Estimating quantities

This is where your plan will be invaluable. Measure up the square metres or feet of paving needed and order about 10 per cent more to allow for wastage. Loose materials, such as mulch and gravel, are sold by volume rather than weight, as it is like comparing a bucket of feathers with a bucket of wet sand. If materials are sold by weight, ask your supplier to calculate the weight from the volume, as this is much easier for you to work out.

If you want to mulch to 10 cm (4 in) thick, simply work out the square metres or feet on your plan of mulched beds, and multiply it by 0.1 to get a cubic metre or feet measurement. For example, if your bed is 3 x 2.5 m (10 x 8 ft), then your square metre or feet measurement is 7.5 square metres (80 square feet). Times this by 0.1 and you know that you need 0.75 cubic metres (8 cubic feet) of mulch. Add 10 per cent more to allow for waste.

Stones are usually sold in square face metres or feet, as they are normally used for building walls. Some rocks may be sold by weight, flagging by the square metre or foot, while other materials such as rough stone and broken slates are ordered by the pallet. Special rocks — natural rocks or boulders or water-carved limestone suitable for Chinese gardens, for example — may be sold piece by piece.

The pros and cons of a makeover

The most common landscaping mistake is to underestimate the time it will take to complete a task. For example, you could lay a path in a day, but then you might not be able to walk on it for 24 hours, so your weekend job may become two.

A handy rule of thumb is that if you think a job will take a professional a day to do, it may take you a week. If you think it will take you a week, then double it. It's safer to over-perform than under-deliver, especially when you're trying to maintain domestic bliss!

Another option is the working bee, although the 'many hands make light work' approach really only works when one person knows what they are doing and has set out a list of jobs and the order in which they need to be achieved. If you don't expect the deck to be built in time for a barbecue that night, your workers will remain your friends. Also, supply your team with plenty of food and drink (not alcohol, if you want the job to last until the next gathering or working bee), and don't forget to return the favour.

Some garden clubs have a rotation system where members meet at each other's place every fortnight, working as a team on each garden — a great way to handle tough jobs.

Did you know? Carpet bedding was a nineteenth century practice of mass planting annuals to create patterns of colour (also known as *mosaiculture* in the slightly more sophisticated French and Italian style).

Far left: A temporary gravel path makes it easier to move around the garden while you're building the hard landscaping features and digging new garden beds.

Left: To give paving a professional finish, use an old piece of pipe to rub the joints smooth.

Ten steps to success

An action plan is a vital step in the realization of your dream. The order of tasks done will vary from job to job, but as a guide, this is the usual run of tasks.

1 Prepare and finalize your design, but be prepared for some small changes.

2 Decide on what parts of the design are going to be contracted out to landscapers, and which sections you are going to attempt yourself. Get quotes and settle on contractors, and make a booking to secure each of them.

3 Mark out your design with marking paint, string lines, agricultural lime, hoses and the like. Make sure that what you've marked out matches up with your vision, and try and pinpoint any problems that you may have missed. For example, have you misjudged any levels that will affect the design?

4 Excavate any necessary areas and prepare the subsurface for such things as drainage, footings, conduit for lighting and/or wiring and sublayers. It is often the stuff you can't see that will make or break your landscape down the track. Store topsoil for reuse.

5 Install or build any hard landscaping features such as paving, decks and walls.

6 Prepare soil for planting, restore the topsoil and add compost, water-storing crystals and slow-release fertilizers. Prepare areas with turf underlay — that is, the level bed of sand or loam onto which you'll lay the grass. Lay pipe for surface irrigation. Order plants.

7 Following your design, lay out plants, but again be prepared for change. Your drawings are a guide; sometimes tweaking your design at this stage will yield better results. Order mulch and turf, or buy seeds.

8 Mulch garden beds and lay turf, or sow grass seeds.

9 Dress your garden by adding the final touches and details.

10 Enjoy your garden as it evolves.

Safety tools

Wear protective goggles whenever you're cutting bricks, tile or stone. Even when you are just working outside, wear a hat and sunglasses, which not only protect you from the sun but also keep the dust out of your hair and eyes. Wear ear pads whenever you use drills, circular saws or other noisy power tools. Gloves and boots will protect your fingers and toes, and kneepads, although not essential for safety, can make kneeling for long periods easier. If necessary, use a barrier to keep children away, and always completely block off access to excavation sites where water may accumulate.

Above: Marking paint is an easy way to outline garden beds and key features. If you change your mind at this stage, all you need to do is mow off the paint.

Above right: Use a dibble to make planting holes for seeds and bulbs.

Opposite, bottom: A wheelbarrow should be in good working order.

Getting started

Careful preparation at this stage will save you a lot of time and effort in the long term.

Laying out beds and borders

To transfer your planting plan from a piece of graph paper to the garden, take a sharp stick and outline the position for each plant. For greater precision, mark out beds and borders with a string line (a piece of string stretched between wooden stakes) or, for a curved edge, use a flexible garden hose (see page 84). When you finally position your plants, be prepared for slight adjustments. In real life (as opposed to on plan), tweaking layouts may improve your design.

Preparing the soil for planting

Begin by removing any sod or plants on the soil. You will save a lot of time if you remove weeds in the garden before you re-plant it. Add weed-free compost, well rotted manure or similar organic matter to improve your soil structure. Some clay soils will benefit from added gypsum, while some acid soils may need added lime at this stage. Water-storing crystals, water penetrants or surfactants and slow-release fertilizer are also useful additions in areas where the soil may be lacking or the rainfall irregular. Always dig a hole twice as wide as the plant you are putting in, and a little bit deeper. This will ensure your new garden can grow easily into the soil.

Easy ways to do hard work

You don't have to be a Herculean heavyweight to be able to complete some of the hard landscaping tasks. In fact, brains can be more useful than brawn. Whether a job involves digging a hole, making a trench or lifting heavy weights such as rocks and cement, there is always a smart way and a hard way to go about it.

Tools of the trade

For paving you'll need a metal rake, screed (a 4 x 2 ft piece of timber or a steel with spirit level), rubber mallet, string line, chalk or pencil for marking cuts, masons hammer or scutch chisel, stiff bristled broom, trowels (for pointing, for example), a section of hose for pointing joints, and a hose with a plate compactor, also known as a 'wacker packer'.

Laying turf

1 Rake the prepared soil to form a fine tilth.

2 The supplier will deliver the turf in rolls like this. Do not store them for more than a few days or the grass will yellow.

3 Set up a string line or use a plank to lay the first row of turf. Each time you lay a piece, push the end against the previous piece.

The first step is to work out where your goods should be delivered. Always have a plan so that your stockpiles need to be moved only once and are as close to their final resting place as possible. It is very disheartening to lug 100 bricks to one position, only to discover that you have to move them again because they're sitting on top of the drainage pit you have to dig!

Machinery

The second step is to look at where and how machinery can help. A bobcat may sound scary and expensive, but often it will do in an hour what it could take you weeks to do manually. Check out the list of equipment available from hire companies, and ask friends to recommend plant operators who will be sympathetic to your needs and careful with any existing plants.

Post-hole diggers, conveyor belts and mini diggers are all useful pieces of equipment for major garden renovations.

Wheels

The most useful piece of equipment is a wheelbarrow. Buy a decent one, with a rubber, pneumatic tyre. This will make manoeuvring around so much easier, especially if the load is heavy.

A hand trolley is another great way of transporting heavy plants to difficult spots, as you can slide the carrying platform underneath weighty objects without lifting them off the ground. Simply tilt the trolley, then push or pull it to its destination. It should be narrow enough to go down most pathways or into areas with poor access. These days trolleys often have special wheels that even allow them to go up and down stairs without too much difficulty, so research what's available.

A bricklayer's barrow is useful for loads of bricks and pavers as it can help you to move up to 50 bricks at a time, depending on how strong you are. Even a platform on castors, which you can easily make yourself, makes it significantly easier to carry heavy, small objects.

Levers

Finally, a lever, such as a bar or a heavy piece of timber, is useful for moving rocks, stumps and other irregular objects. Just make sure that the fulcrum, the object that you lever against or are propped up by, is strong enough to support the weight that will be applied to it.

Did you know? American artist Margaret Kerr designs garden tapestries with bricks. She cuts the bricks into various shapes and sizes, then combines them into various geometric patterns, like masonry rugs. Some are garden 'runners', others 'prayer rugs', but all use the different textures and colours of bricks as the 'fabric'.

how to...
Move a heavy object

Moving heavy objects can be a relatively simple task if you employ some simple physics principles and reduce the amount of friction. Wheels may not always be convenient for the site, so create a roller from iron piping used in a series about 30 cm (1 ft) or so apart. This will make the job of dragging much easier. Or you could make a ramp, or use a heavy-duty piece of material such as hessian or carpet underlay to move something from A to B.

Furnishing your garden 'rooms'

Once you have designed the 'rooms' in your garden and settled on a style or palette that suits you, it is time to start the fun part. Furnishing your garden and adding the features and details will transform your space into a cohesive 'look'. Besides, shopping for seats, table settings, benches and the like is a welcome change from the hard grind of landscaping, and is the perfect solution for bad weather days or when you lack inspiration.

Of course, this detail can come from lots of places — recycling yards, bric-a-brac places, op shops, plant nurseries, hardware shops, homeware shops, the local classifieds and even garage sales. Keep an eye out for anything that will give your space its own individual stamp.

Carefully consider your key pieces, such as focal points like items of sculpture or water features, as these will of course attract the most attention and need to be worked into the overall scheme.

Items such as dovecotes may suit one style of garden, such as a country or cottage garden, but will look out of place in a contemporary setting. A modern piece of ceramic ware or stainless steel sculpture may complement this style better, while a group of totem poles may be the most suitable statement for an eclectic garden with ethnic influences.

Water features

Water features come in all shapes and sizes, from pools of still water to tumbling cascades, from wall spouts to rills, which are narrow channels of water inspired by Islamic gardens. Water features are undoubtedly attractive, but do consider the amount of work they require — for example, ponds need cleaning, pumps need servicing and plants need dividing. Also, the larger the body of water, the easier it is to manage, as it tends to find its own natural equilibrium. Covering the surface of still ponds with aquatic plants will help control algal blooms. and the more oxygenating plants you use, the better.

See page 172 in 'Water gardens' in 'Wild palette' for more details.

Sculpture

Sculpture is often relegated to the bottom of the 'to do' list. But if your garden lacks the 'wow' factor, maybe it's an option worth considering. Sculpture can be thought provoking, witty, challenging or classical. It can set the tone as well as showcase someone's talent, even your own.

Sculpture can be made out of many materials, including stone, metal, glass, wood, shell and plastic. It can even be an ephemeral or temporary piece, known as installation sculpture, and is a great way to experiment.

Or you could try living sculptures. Varieties of agave and yucca have such striking colourations and forms that they act as the botanical equivalent of modern art. Clumps of grass, some succulents, mossy rocks, mounds of *Scleranthus* sp. or a sea of baby's tears (*Soleirolia* sp.) can also be living artworks, although these too can be emphasized by the careful placement of figures. The ultimate version literally involves moving mountains, like the ancient Chinese gardens, or sculpting the earth, like a swirl of grass and water.

Brick tips

1 Bricks that are low in salt are less susceptible to efflorescence, that white chalky residue that sometimes appears on clay pavers, pots and bricks.

2 Bricks with chamfered or rumbled edges don't show up chips as easily, and they also slow down the water, directing it to seep into the sub-base rather than run off.

3 When ordering bricks for floors, allow for 35 bricks per square metre (12 bricks per square foot) if you lay them with their standard face up and with regular mortar joints.

In Scotland, The Garden of Cosmic Speculation, designed by Charles Jencks, is a modern sculptural earthwork. Here, a sinuous 120 m (394 ft) long terraced swirl wraps and warps around two crescent ponds. This culminates in a snail-like mound from which visitors can view the garden. This garden is a landscape expression of a fractal, which in mathematics is an irregular curve produced by repeated subdivision.

Final touches

This is the most neglected aspect of many gardens. While the absence of items such as soft furnishings, lighting and decorative detail may not be missed in terms of design, these are often the things that help create the ambience of your garden. Lighting in particular — whether it's custom-made or simply candles — adds the extra dimension of night-time use and can highlight your focal points or create a unique mood.

In fact, as gardens increasingly become outdoor rooms, it is these extra details that will become more diverse and popular. They can often be ephemeral touches too, such as paper Chinese lanterns used to dress up a setting for a party or coloured curtains of gossamer-thin fabrics draped over pergolas to add a sense of mystery and intrigue.

These inexpensive items may be the very things that transform your space into a magical arena in which drama unravels, perfect for special occasions or entertaining.

Below left: These cantilevered pools of still water reflect the sky and trees like a mirror, adding an illusion of extra space.

Below: Dressing your outdoor space as you would a room in your house is an integral part of personalizing your design.

Fundamentals

Guiding principles. Foundations. Rules of thumb.
Elements of design. Insight. Building blocks.

Opposite: This arched doorway is perfectly balanced by the
three-tiered topiary. Not only does the plant echo the curve of
the lintel, it also has enough height to look in scale.

Above: The Alhambra garden in Granada, Spain, comprises a number of garden rooms. This one features roses and severe cypress hedges.

Centre: A curved brick wall in a suburban garden acts as a backdrop for the garden on one side, and keeps the walkway clear on the other.

Far right: This old fireplace, once part of a house, has been incorporated into the garden wall.

Did you know? The word 'garden' comes from the same root word as yard – the Old English word *geard*, which meant an enclosure or garden.

Principles of garden design

If you think of designing your garden as you would a set of rooms in your house, the human scale of each garden 'room' and the personal touches you add to it can easily be translated into any outdoor space.

The first step is to decide how many garden rooms you need, the functions they perform and how they relate to each other. Then you should choose the paving for the 'floors', materials for the 'walls' and what structures, if any, you need.

Finally, the planting and decorating phases establish your personal style. The various elements of design (discussed on pages 101–19) are your visual tools. Start thinking about them early in the design process, especially in terms of some of the bigger concepts — what plants you'll use, how their forms relate to one another, how their colour will affect the mood of your garden and, indeed, how the various textures of the materials play off against each other.

If you compile a scrapbook of ideas and a mood board of materials, these will help you to clarify and visualize which components are important to you, and perhaps which ones you may have overlooked. But first, consider the rooms themselves and the materials you can use for building and decorating them.

The garden room

Your garden has a floor, walls, doors or entranceway, roof or ceiling, and it can be furnished with both decorative and practical objects. But probably the most important feature of any room is its function; relating this concept to the outdoors makes the space a really useful, valid area, not just a garden. For example, in your home there are hallways, bedrooms, bathrooms, a kitchen, dining room and living room. Dividing your garden into different areas according to function is a sensible basis for garden design.

The basic garden room can be broken down into its component parts.

Walls

Garden walls frame a space, but they also define boundaries, provide privacy and block out undesirables, such as wind and pollution. They can be either completely solid or transparent to various degrees, made from anything you like — living, organic or mineral. Trelliswork, perspex or glass, brick, hedging, rock walls, timber fencing and temporary panels like curtains are just some of the choices available to you.

Walls lend a garden a feeling of permanence. From ancient times walls have been used to close out the world, providing a safe, sheltered space in which to garden. Nowadays we don't need garden walls to keep out invading armies, but they are still useful for obscuring unattractive views, creating a sound barrier, securing property or creating a pleasant microclimate. Seats, barbecues and shelves can be built into a wall, along with alcoves and niches, water features and planters. Your garden walls can be either freestanding or retaining, and can complement your home. Low walls are ideal for internal boundaries, as small retaining walls and for levelling slight slopes into terraces.

Finial and wall **ornaments**

Over the centuries, ornaments and finials have been used to add further decoration to fences and walls. Various finial designs — from simple balls, rampant lions and urns to elaborate pineapples — can be found marking entranceways or capping fence posts. Walls can be embellished with plaques and sconces (wall brackets for holding candles), useful for breaking up large expanses of masonry or for decorating enclaves.

An elaborate metal frieze decorates an otherwise plain brick wall (above left), while a cherub wall plaque embellishes a garden entrance (above right).

Patterns for stone walls

The pattern you choose for building your stone wall should reflect the style of your garden. A haphazard pattern is appropriate for a wild garden, while a regular course suits a formal garden style. Also, not only the type of stone but also the pattern you choose may give your garden a sense of place: for instance, some areas are known for a particular type of walling, such as drystone or Cornish verticals.

Above: A drystone wall, topped with what is called 'up-ended coping', contrasts with the formal brick pillars marking the entrance to the property.

Above: This selection of bricks includes machine-made extruded bricks (the ones with holes), hand-made bricks and pressed bricks, which have a 'frog' or indentation for mortar.

Solid walls can be made from masonry, timber and stone. The smaller the unit size of your chosen material, the greater the scope for flexibility in form. For example, you can easily create curves and sinuous lines with bricks, while railway sleepers (or railroad ties) are best for long, straight walls. The lower the wall and the larger the unit size, the easier and faster construction will be, and vice versa. Any wall over a certain height — the height will depend on the local government ordinances in your area — will need a footing and engineer's details as well as local government approval before construction starts.

Stone

Stone has its own history, inherent charm and life force. These qualities seem to be transferred to any construction using it. Local stone is most commonly used for walls and landscaping; it can lend a garden a sense of place. Construction can be dry or mortared, random or dressed, and even gabions — metal cages filled with stacked stone, designed for industrial soil retention — are now popular for gardens. Popular types of stone for walls include limestone, sandstone, slate and bluestone. A cheaper and easier option is to purchase stone 'skins' that you glue onto a block wall. (See page 400.)

Bricks

Bricks come in all sorts of colours, textures and materials. Some have a high clay content, while others are made from concrete. There are weathered and rustic bricks, reclaimed and extruded bricks, engineered and facing bricks, clinkers and commons. Oxides can be used to colour the mortar, and there are various patterns of laying and styles of finishing or jointing brick work. Other ways to customize a masonry wall include paint effects, tiled feature borders and mosaic.

Timber

Timber is an extremely versatile material for retaining walls, solid walls, fences and semitransparent screens. Its character can vary, depending on the design, treatment and finish. The weather-beaten texture of railway sleepers lends a chunky, durable effect, while dressed and sawn timbers, painted and erected horizontally, comprise a slick, modern interpretation, which differs again from a palisade wall of treated pine logs.

Fences define boundaries and mark out spaces. They are also invaluable for preventing children or pets from wandering and for excluding livestock or intruders. Furthermore, they can provide privacy and delineate internal spaces.

The simplest type of wooden fence is the post and rail. Popular for dividing acreage, it can also add a touch of country charm to the urban environment. Arris fencing, fashionable after World War II, uses square timber rails set on an angle, and is a suburban twist on the same concept.

Picket fences, a decorative type of post and rail fence, are a great way to complement details on your house, such as the woodwork on your veranda. They were common in the early twentieth century, and a huge range of styles — from arrowheads to hexagon tops, dressed and undressed pickets — is available. Until the early twentieth century, hardwoods such as jarrah, tallowwood and brush box were common.

Below: The colours used in the mosaic wall are complemented by the autumn tonings of the trees and creepers.

Laying a low brick wall

The following step by step sequence is for a low garden wall only, no more than four or five courses high, in colonial bond, also known as 'English garden wall'. This pattern is a fast method of construction because the walls are laid in stretcher bond, with every fourth course having a header course that ties the skins together.

Once you have decided on a pattern, measure the length of the wall and work out exactly how many bricks will form the base course, taking into account 5 mm (¼ in) for each mortar joint so that you won't have to cut bricks to fit on every course. A good rule of thumb is to lay a concrete footing twice as wide as the width of the wall and as deep as the wall is wide. This entails digging a trench. A sloping site will need stepped foundations, so formwork will also be necessary in order to stop the concrete from finding its natural level. Also, if a wall is in a damp position, add a damp-proof course after the second course of bricks to protect it from rising damp from the earth.

But first you will need to mark out a trench and pour concrete into it. Allow the concrete to set overnight and then keep it wet for a few days while it cures.

1 Once the foundation has been laid, chalk the line of the wall onto the concrete. Set up the first two bricks, one at either end. To do this, place each brick on a mound of mortar and tamp it down until the brick is level and the mortar is about 10 mm (½ in) thick. Run a string line from end to end, holding it in place with a spare brick, so that the top of the string line is at the top level of the base course and at the front face of the wall. Double check that the string line is level as you lay the first course. With a rippling action, trowel some mortar onto the foundation between the two end bricks to create a bed for your first course. Run the bases of your bricks along the string line, buttering the inside of each brick with mortar as you go, and tamping it into position with about a 5 mm (¼ in) gap between each. Work on about five bricks at one end before doing the same on the other, continually checking that the course is level and plumb with your spirit level.

2 Buttering the end of a brick.

3 To lay the second course (as shown), in this case a header course, cut a 'queen' closer (that is, a brick cut in

half lengthways) and lay it over the joint. Then continue with the header course, linking both skins to each other.

4 Using a bolster and club hammer to cut a brick.

5 To lay subsequent courses, start first with the corners, building them up to the height of the wall, then joining the bricks in the centre one course at a time. Constantly check that your wall is plumb level and matching your guiding line so that the front is always even. Using a trowel's blade across the brick face, clear away excess mortar as you go. If you are left with dried mortar on the brick face when the job is finished, scrape it off with a trowel or wire brush.

6 The last step is called pointing the joints. You need to do this before the mortar has completely hardened. The most sensible finish for a garden wall is a weatherstruck joint. First, run along the vertical joint with the point of your trowel and then along the horizontal, pressing down at an angle so that rain will easily run off.

Above: A bamboo screen is an easy way to disguise an ugly fence (see page 196).

Right: Willow wands, planted in such a way as to form a diamond pattern, have taken root, forming a living trellis.

Timber fences dwindled in popularity from the 1930s onwards, as the Art Deco style favoured mild steel and brick combinations. Eventually, aluminium and brick fences became popular due to the ongoing maintenance required for timber, but the ease with which modern machinery can manufacture pickets and the advent of treated wood, coupled with a renovation and restoration frenzy, has led to their renewed popularity in recent times, especially for front boundaries.

Wood panel, paling (or close-boarded) and privacy fences are often used for side and rear boundaries. These may be painted and adorned with finials, post details and the like. Prefabricated panels of brush, split bamboo or overlapping boards can be purchased, then just erected *in situ*.

However, for fences with a little more panache, try experimenting with lath screens, made up of horizontal or vertical dressed timbers, with a gap between each one to let light and air through the fence. Horizontal slats, interwoven fences and open-boarded or 'neighbour-friendly' fences all offer some degree of privacy and separation without making you feel totally enclosed.

If you prefer boundaries that don't block views, consider trellis- and latticework, or even wattle and willow woven fencing. Just as open shelves can divide a large room into smaller spaces, semitransparent fences are a great way of doing the same in the garden. You could even plant a living willow fence in a 'wild' garden.

Another interesting idea is the palisade fence, where saplings of tea tree, tree fern trunks, chestnut and hazel poles, bamboo lengths and even tomato stakes are 'planted' vertically, at either staggered or even distances, to create a screen.

Perforated **concrete blocks** and **Hebel**

Rendering (or plastering) walls is another treatment for masonry. Old and new walls alike can be given a new look with a coat of cement render. You can transform a cheap and unattractive wall, such as one made from cement blocks, with a new 'skin' of render, applied either roughly for a bagged finish or carefully to achieve a smooth coat. The more textured the finish, the more rustic the effect; for a crisper, urban touch, smooth out the render with a sponge as you apply it. Rendering can now be done over special fibrous cement sheets, a cost-effective method that reduces the thickness of a wall (useful if space is a consideration). Another worthwhile product is an aerated compound called Hebel. It is similar to a cement block and is very light and soft but strong, and can be carved into shapes, then painted or rendered over to look like a traditional wall.

The planter box breaks up this brazen rendered wall (above left). A roughly rendered wall is a suitable backdrop for a Mediterranean-style garden (above right).

Glass

Whether used as panels or glass bricks, the transparency of glass provides a solid barrier while providing access to light and a view. This can be a huge advantage if the aspect is working against you — for instance, if you live in the southern hemisphere and your fence faces south — or if clear vision is required for supervising children, as with pool surrounds.

For added interest, glass can also be coloured, stained, slumped, reinforced or laminated. If it is silvered to create a mirrored surface, it will reflect light and create the illusion of depth in the garden.

An alternative to glass is perspex, a thermoplastic resin.

Right: This sand-blasted glass screen offers privacy, yet still admits light. The smooth face of the glass, the most reflective side, should face the main part of the garden.

Finials and pickets

Twentieth century techniques in bending metal encouraged new styles of fencing: manufacturers experimented with many different designs, from arrowheads and fleur-de-lis to scrolls, stars and twists and swirls. Colours were typically deep Indian red, bronze, green and black, sometimes with gilt added to define detail. Timber pickets with a range of finials – such as acorns, pineapples, spheres, points and balls – have also become popular.

Above: A traditional timber picket fence, with finials to embellish the gate posts.

Above: Metal lattice admits light and allows air to flow.

Below: Espaliered fruit trees can be used as a striking hedge, even in winter.

Iron, metal cladding and mesh

Since the Industrial Revolution, the permanence of metal has made it a popular choice for boundaries. The fact that metal can be as malleable and flexible as chain wire (or chain link) has also given it scope to be used in a variety of ways. From spiked wrought iron spears, popular from the late nineteenth century for forming boundaries to key gardens and terrace frontages, to the simple post and chain fence sometimes used to support rose swags, there is a style of metal fence for almost every application.

One of the major drawbacks of iron is that it needs regular painting to stop it from rusting; however, these days the availability of galvanized metals reduces the need for maintenance. Metal hoop edging, woven wire and wrought iron panels or lace work are other ways of adding historic character to your fencing.

Of course, modern techniques such as laser cutting have led to new options. A metal screen with leaf relief can be an attractive work of art as well as a barrier. The same cannot be said for solid metal sheets such as powder-coated corrugated iron fences that, although long lasting and virtually maintenance-free, retain so much heat in hot climates that plants are almost repelled by them. They can also reflect so much light that the effect can be dazzling.

Plants

Planting is often a much more economical way to create a barrier, especially if you can buy the plants when they are small or as bare-rooted specimens. You can even strike cuttings or propagate them at home *in situ*. A bonus is that — unlike stone, for example — a hedge or plant screen doesn't need to undergo a weathering process before it sits easily in the landscape.

Suitable plants for **hedging**

Above: Flowering hedges, such as these azaleas, add form as well as seasonal colour to the garden.

Given the number of plants you need in order to create an effective screen, it makes sense to choose the right plant for your hedge at the planning stage, as mistakes can be expensive. If you choose a plant that is too big for the job, you'll have to constantly prune it during the growing season and it will have unsightly 'legs' as a result. On the other hand, if you use a plant that is too small, your hedge will take a long time to grow or, worse still, the plants may never join, resulting in a row of plants that will look like broken teeth.

For a low hedge at 1 m (3 ft), choose from English and Japanese box (*Buxus* sp.), lavender (*Lavandula* sp.), rosemary (*Rosmarinus officinalis*), azaleas (*Rhododendron* sp.) and box honeysuckle (*Lonicera nitida*). These are also available as dwarf cultivars, so you can select still smaller growing varieties for borders.

Plants for a middle-sized hedge – about 3 m (9 ft) – include some lovely flowering plants such as *Camellia sasanqua* and orange jessamine (*Murraya paniculata*), as well as variegated-leafed shrubs such as *Pittosporum* sp., *Photinia* sp. with its new red growth, *Euonymus* sp., *Coprosma* sp. and privet (*Ligustrum ovalifolium*). Laurustinus (*Viburnum tinus*) and *V. odoratissimum* are both suitable for a plain evergreen hedge.

In a large garden you can get away with a towering hedge up to 5 m (18 ft). Plants suitable for this scale are cypress (*Cupressus* sp.), lilly pilly (*Syzygium* sp.), cape honeysuckle (*Tecoma* sp.), bull bay magnolia (*Magnolia grandiflora*), lime (*Tilia* sp.), beech (*Fagus sylvatica*), hornbeam (*Carpinus betulus*), holly (*Ilex* sp.), hawthorn (*Crataegus monogyna*), bay laurel (*Laurus nobilis*), English yew (*Taxus baccata*) and *Escallonia* sp. Planting alternatives of two coloured types, such as purple-leafed (*Fagus sylvatica* 'Riversii') and green-leafed beech (*F. sylvatica*), can also be attractive, creating what is sometimes called a motley or tapestry hedge.

Hedging, or clipping a row of plants into shape, has become popular again in recent years, probably because the electric clippers now available make trimming fast and easy. Also, the emphasis on formality in many garden designs has meant that hedging is back with a vengeance. Hedges can be of all shapes and sizes, from a small border up to 1 m (3 ft) to a towering 5 m (15 ft) screen or a pleached hedge, effectively a hedge on stilts.

Some suitable plants for pleaching are lime (*Tilia* sp.), hornbeam (*Carpinus betulus*), lilly pilly (*Syzygium* sp.), evergreen alder (*Alnus acuminata*) and coffee (*Coffea* sp.), while prickly plants that are great for keeping out intruders include *Hakea* sp., *Berberis* sp., *Pyracantha* sp. and *Rosa rugosa*.

The major drawbacks with a hedge are the time it takes to grow to a screening height, and the ease with which children and pets can still get from one side to the other. If these factors are of great concern, consider a cheat hedge, sometimes called a 'fedge', a cross between a fence and a hedge. For instance, chain wire makes an economical and secure boundary. It can be quickly concealed with evergreen climbers, such as ivy, native ivy (*Muehlenbeckia* sp.) and creeping fig. Just clip them to give the impression of a hedge.

Ideally a wall or fence should stand on its own merits, but sometimes plants add to the picture, like accessories to an outfit. Also, sometimes you inherit the wall, or budgetary constraints limit your options, and you simply have to work with what you have. Planting invariably softens the structure, while the structure can support or delineate the planting. In fact, one embellishes the other. Combining the two is an opportunity to link the built environment with nature, a key factor in creating a comfortable outdoor space.

There are various ways of planting walls and fences: climbers can grow on the surface, ground covers can spill over the top, wall plants can grow in crevices and wall shrubs (espalier) can grow against your fence. Suitable self-clinging climbers include Boston ivy, climbing hydrangea, ivy and creeping fig, while clematis, passion fruit, hops, ornamental grape, climbing roses, Chinese star jasmine, jasmine, honeysuckle and wisteria remain popular choices provided they are attached to the wall or fence. Great spillover plants such as *Cotoneaster dammeri*, snow-in-summer, *Convolvulus mauritanicus* and ivy geraniums work well cascading over a wall. Rock roses, valerian, *Corydalis lutea*, *Campanula* sp., fleabane, toadflax, *Alyssum* sp., thyme, lady's mantle, lobelia, rock cress and *Sempervivum* sp. will all grow happily in a wall, especially if sown by seed or planted in small earth pockets during the construction process. Suitable shrubs for espalier on walls include pyracantha, ceanothus, *Abutilon* sp., flowering quince, camellias, forsythia, *Euonymus* sp., *Michelia yunnanensis*, *Magnolia grandiflora* and roses. Fruit trees — both deciduous ones such as stone fruit and evergreen ones like olives and citrus — are also suitable.

Floors

The importance of a sound floor — one that's easy to maintain, reliable underfoot and looks good — should not be underestimated. Whether it is a soft or a hard surface, a floor has a unifying effect, tying the whole garden together. It can be cool or hot, sharp or smooth, slick or rustic. Paving is just one of many options. Your garden floor could be a sea of lawn, decking or a gravelled clearing. Other options include decomposed granite, mosaic, tile, living ground cover or simply mulch — anything from bark chip to shell grit.

Opposite: A gate left propped open invites the visitor to go in and wander.

Above: If you use the appropriate timber, decking is a good-looking and easy-care surface for your garden 'floors'.

A combination of materials is often an effective way of creating utilitarian surfaces. Just as your home might have carpeted bedrooms, polished floorboards in the living areas and tiles in the bathroom, you can mix and match elements that successfully combine function and aesthetics in your garden.

High traffic areas need a surface that copes with wear. Shaded, moist areas require a slip resistant and adequately drained surface such as aggregate, and children and pets may have different requirements again. So plan carefully to ensure that the result is practical and pleasurable.

Different floor types vary in their ability to let water seep into the ground. This is an important consideration, as the more surfaces you cover in impervious materials, the more runoff you'll create. You'll need to install drainage. This leads to greater costs, both economically and environmentally: rainwater from drains goes into the stormwater, wasting a valuable resource. (For more information on drainage, see pages 37 and 38–9.)

Semipermeable surfaces, such as paving laid on a sand bed rather than on mortar and

Living mulches and **ground covers**

Plants that grow horizontally, or prostrate, are perfect for covering the ground. They are referred to as living mulches. Wherever you can, cover the earth with something, otherwise weeds will grow there soon enough. You can use paving or mulch, but plants will also keep weeds down, especially if you choose the right ones for the right spots.

Living mulches suitable for the shade include bugle (*Ajuga* sp.), baby's tears (*Soleirolia* sp.), Corsican mint (*Mentha requienii*), dead nettle (*Lamium* sp.), golden moneywort (*Lysimachia nummularia*), pennyroyal (*Mentha pulegium*) and periwinkle (*Vinca* sp.).

For sunnier positions try chamomile (*Chamaemelum nobile*), saxifrage (*Saxifraga* sp.), rock roses (*Helianthemum* sp.) and creeping thyme (*Thymus* sp.).

For positions where you want lots of cover and heaps of vigour, try ivy (*Hedera* sp.), shore juniper (*Juniperus conferta*), prostrate grevilleas and African daisies (*Dimorphotheca* sp.).

Above: Small-leafed English ivies will cope with foot traffic, even in an outdoor dining area.

concrete, and those incorporating vegetation into their design, are both good compromises. Plastic turf cells (which hold earth for lawn yet take the main weight of cars parked on grass), gravelled areas, decomposed granite and compacted, hard earth are also floor types that can withstand greater wear and tear.

Turf

Grass is the most popular ground treatment in gardens, although its appearance varies, depending on factors such as sun and shade, pets and children, size and scale. It is relatively cheap to buy, can be laid easily, absorbs runoff, feels soft underfoot and unifies garden beds. It also copes with medium levels of foot traffic admirably — just look at the turf surfaces at sporting grounds — and will survive drought; although it browns off, grass does revive after rain.

On the down side, grass needs mowing, weeding, watering and feeding. It can become worn if there are no paths or when pets wreak havoc. It is also difficult to trim grass around the trunks of trees without damaging them. In addition, grass competes very heavily for water and nutrients with them. If you have grassy areas planted with trees in your garden, clear at least 1 m (3 ft) around each trunk and mulch well.

If your plot is small, carefully consider whether the effort required to mow, edge, weed, feed and water is worthwhile. Other ground covers may be more appropriate. See the box on 'Living mulches and ground covers' opposite.

Decking and timber

As it is a natural product, wood looks great in the garden. It can be useful in difficult sites, such as rooftop gardens and balconies where heavier materials are not always suitable.

It can even be laid over outdated concrete patios and save you the trouble of lifting and removing the original surface. Decking tiles are a quick and easy option (see below).

Installing decking tiles

Any level surface that needs a facelift can be transformed using decking tiles. You can buy ready-made timber squares. Simply clip them together to form the basis of a timber deck. Awkward gaps can be filled with decorative pebbles.

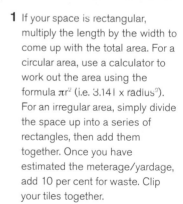

1 If your space is rectangular, multiply the length by the width to come up with the total area. For a circular area, use a calculator to work out the area using the formula πr^2 (i.e. 3.141 x radius^2). For an irregular area, simply divide the space up into a series of rectangles, then add them together. Once you have estimated the meterage/yardage, add 10 per cent for waste. Clip your tiles together.

2 Place them face down and use decorative pebbles to fill any gaps.

3 Alternatively, you could remove some sections and plant these squares with some small-rooted plants, such as ornamental grasses or succulents.

Tip

- Regularly oil the decking squares with an outdoor decking varnish. Marine-grade strength is best for areas that may receive runoff or rainfall.

Opposite: This outdoor table is perfectly positioned. The floor is stable and level, the ceiling is open to the sky yet partly shaded by trees, and there is ample space around the table so people can move about in comfort.

Wood also works well where levels are an issue, as decking can easily be laid on bearers at the desired height, even level with your home: the gaps between boards allow water to drain and therefore won't cause flooding in your house. This makes it particularly useful on steep blocks and can give a wonderful treehouse effect where you feel part of nature, yet separate from it.

One drawback of timber is that it can become slippery. If wet weather is common in your area, make sure that you lay the grooved surface of each board side down. The grooves provide air circulation under the decking; if you lay the grooved side up, then the grooves become full of decaying matter and eventually very slippery. Treated timber or Western red cedar will last longer in humid conditions. Teak and other hardwoods look great, weathering over time to a beautiful silver–grey, but they are more difficult to work with and often more expensive. If you are choosing hardwoods, make sure the timber is seasoned (either air dried or kiln dried), or it will shrink and buckle.

If you intend to coat your timber with oil, paint or a stain, then you'll need to wait at least twelve weeks (up to six months for slow-drying timbers) for it to weather and lose its tannins. Once your timber deck is stabilized, thoroughly clean the surface with a solution of 100 g (3½ oz) of oxalic acid to 1 L (1¾ pt) of warm water, then apply your chosen treatment according to the manufacturer's instructions. Your timber decking will last longer.

Combinations of timber and gravel, such as log rounds with loose aggregate or bitumen-impregnated blocks laid with sand, can be interesting too. Decking tiles and pebbles can also comprise a nice textural contrast (see page 83).

Laying flexible garden edging

Keeping loose aggregate or grass runners away from your garden beds can be very time-consuming unless you have suitable edging. It can be difficult to get the right arch for a curved edge without it seeming a bit contrived. Try using some electrical conduit for the job and your bend will flow evenly and not be too severe.

1 Simply peg one end in (or ask a friend to hold it) and flex the plastic gently, then place a peg on the other end to hold it in place.

2 Next, trace over with spray paint or lime to mark your line.

Tips

• If you don't have any conduit, use a garden hose. A long hose is perfect for large areas.

• Flexible plastic edging is another option (see page 390), which can look fine if the grass is grown almost at the same height as the edge and the bed is kept slightly lower, keeping the edge out of sight. Plastic pegs for pinning the edge in place are sold with it.

Loose paving

Aggregate comes in many different forms, from stone-based products like river stones, decomposed granite, gravel and shingle to organic products such as woodchip, fruit stones, nut husks, seashells and bark chips. Even coloured glass is now sold as a rumbled product with no sharp edges, suitable as a decorative surface.

project

Making gravel pictures

Gravel is available in so many exciting colours and shapes these days, so why not create your own miniature gravel parterre? This could be used as a feature in a broader area of paving, or even as a centrepiece under glass for an outdoor coffee table. A simple design will provide the most impact. Once you've worked out what 'picture' you want to create, follow these steps.

1 As concrete and mortar are fluid when wet, lay some formwork for this project. If your design is small enough, a timber box is perfect for the job. Just line it with heavy-duty plastic to protect it from the mortar.

2 Mix up the mortar with roughly 3 parts sand and 1 part cement. This is a wet, not dry, mortar bed, so add water until the materials are just combined.

3 Spread mortar onto the plastic, then use a wooden float to smooth it out and bring the liquid to the surface.

4 Position the pavers and cobbles on the mortar. Tamp them down slightly to embed them.

5 Cut flexible plastic (such as plant tags or ice cream tubs) into strips and use them to divide the areas of different-coloured gravel. Carefully spread the first of the decorative gravels, pressing it into the mortar base before topping it up.

6 Add the second of the decorative gravels. Remove the plastic divider strips when the mortar is still wet.

Top: Brick paving laid in a simple basketweave pattern.

Centre: Slate pavers should be laid on a concrete slab, then set with mortar.

Above: This stretcher bond pattern has been laid with wide gaps, which have then been filled with gravel.

Above right: The brick pillars on this pergola give the walkway a feeling of stately formality. Laying the bricks across the path makes it feel wider.

As aggregate tends to drain quickly, it is useful for a shaded site that tends to be damp, but it is not suitable for slopes where heavy rain can easily wash it downhill. A major disadvantage of using aggregate is that it migrates into other areas and can be thrown around by children. If the aggregate is too small, you'll walk it into the house on the soles of your shoes.

Some people tout gravel as the new lawn. It is true that it absorbs water, and therefore won't add to runoff problems. It copes with root competition from large trees, doesn't mind the shade and only needs raking to keep it looking good, so it may yet become the number one surface. If you do choose aggregate, bear in mind that it will need to be retained in some way; you will also need to weed it regularly and top it up every few years. Also, resist the temptation to use plastic underlays, as water can't penetrate the sheeting. This can turn the soil sour (acid) and end up trapping soil on top where weeds root in any case. However, for areas that will never be planted, it is practical to use weed control mats and geotextile materials.

Bricks and other unitary pavers

These come in all shapes, sizes and colours. They can be interlocking, salvaged or new, and can be clay-based or cement compounds. Because they are of a uniform size and shape, you can use them to create patterns, mixing colours and other paving materials through as highlights. Generally, the larger the unit, the faster the paving can be laid. If you live in a cold and frosty area, choose pavers that will tolerate temperature extremes. Check with your supplier about tolerance levels.

Pavers need to be laid on either a sand and road base layer, suitable for foot traffic, or onto concrete with mortar, an impervious, more stable layer capable of withstanding heavy loads. In both cases, the preparation of this sub-layer will make or break the finished surface.

Brick-sized pavers and bricks can be laid in many patterns (see above left). Larger units, such as concrete slabs, can be laid like rectangular flagstones. Using a mix of materials is also an effective way of adding interest, and is easy to do when dealing with regular shapes. Simply remove a unit or two and replace it with the desired feature — a tile, mosaic work, loose aggregate or a creeping plant, such as thyme.

Stone

Stone makes a durable garden surface. It is strong, long lasting and full of character. There are, of course, many sorts of stones and many ways to use them. For example, marble slabs make an exquisite landing, cobblestones a charming patio and flagging a wonderful terrace.

Many different patterns are possible with stone. Rectangular flags, such as Yorkstone or sandstone, can be butt jointed and laid in regular coursing. Irregular stone such as slate and sandstone crazy paving is best laid in a random pattern without coursing but with a mortar joint. Cobbles, or egg-shaped round stones (for example, large river pebbles) can be coursed or uncoursed and set into a bed of mortar. Setts (square or rectangular granite or basalt pavers) look great in a circular pattern, a fan shape or combined with gravel in geometric shapes such as diamonds.

Because of the high cost of stone, use local stone or secondhand material if you can. Adding stone as a feature section or combining it with other materials is an economical compromise. Other drawbacks of stone include the difficulty of handling its weight, and a risk of it staining, especially when it comes to porous or light-coloured stones. For some surfaces, a sealant can be used to protect it from the weather, spills and oil drips.

Below: Mixing paving materials has become a popular trend in recent years. Concrete slabs laid in a concentric pattern are softened by gravel (below left), while sandstone pavers have been combined with bricks and plants (below right).

Edging and trims

Edging acts as a barrier between one material and another. If installed properly, edging will stop areas of loose material from blending into each other, or grass from running into a garden bed. It can also define a section by way of a decorative border, trim or feature.

In its simplest form, edging is simply a cut grass edge, maintained with a sharp spade. This works reasonably well in the right conditions – when the soil is dense enough to keep its edge and the grass so tame that weekly cuts are not necessary. However, with stoloniferous grasses – such as kikuyu, buffalo, couch, bluegrass, zoysia and creeping fescue, grasses that spread rapidly via stolons – you may need a more permanent option to prevent your garden beds being invaded.

Edging is another way of emphasizing the style of your garden or visually linking materials. For example, many brick paths are improved by a header course, also known as a border course, and a larger stone border can highlight a gravel path. Period items, such as terracotta edging tiles or basketweave edging, add a touch of authenticity to the character of a landscape. Metal edging can add the crispness needed in many modern gardens, while timber remains a useful edge for curved garden beds and can disappear into the background of a design if required.

From left to right: Terracotta tiles and bricks; a mortared brick edge; and sleek metal trim.

In situ poured surface

Ready-mix concrete, asphalt-laying machines and even quick-lay curbing have to some extent revolutionized the way many commercial landscapes and more hardworking areas such as driveways are treated. Over the last twenty years or so, techniques have improved so much that these surfaces, which used to be utilitarian but not very creative, can now be individualized and tailored to suit your place while remaining comparatively cost effective.

Concrete

Concrete is a mixture of sand, cement, aggregate and water that is poured into a mould or formwork, then allowed to dry. This results in a hard, durable surface that is perfect for driveways and suspended terraces. Its thickness depends on what it's being used for. It is also permanent and, if laid correctly, needs very little maintenance. Slow curing, expansion joints and removing air bubbles all help prevent cracking.

However, concrete lacks some of the character of stone and can easily look like the poor man's substitute. Surface treatments can improve the appearance of concrete, so consider adding exciting elements such as exposed aggregate, bottletops, terrazzo finishes, brushed surfaces, oxide finishes and stencilled patterns. Polished concrete can result in a marble-like finish that has an industrial, chic look.

Left: This rustic, open-roofed structure can be covered in hot or inclement weather, or left as it is when the weather is perfect.

Bitumen or asphalt

Bitumen is a mineral pitch, or oxygenated hydrocarbon (as napha, one of the heavier hydrocarbons that comes out of the earth after gas and before petroleum). Asphalt is actually a smooth, hard, bituminous substance made of bitumen, pitch and sand, similar to coal tar and sand. You can add colour to asphalt, which is useful for children's cycle paths. Also, a rubberized and coloured mixture is available as an alternative soft fall for children's playgrounds.

Ceiling

The word 'ceiling' implies some sort of structure, but this need not be the case when it is applied to the garden. A superb sky can also be the roof to your garden. However, climate often dictates against this simple notion. For example, if you live in a hot, sunny climate, you'll need a canopy of trees,

Great **shade trees**

Above: For drought tolerance and autumn colour in a wide range of climates, it's hard to beat *Pistacia chinensis*.

Looking through the canopy of a tree into the sky is truly one of the most wonderful sensations — a link with nature that is uncluttered by the modern world. Trees also impose some human scale on the vast expanse of the sky. All gardeners should have a tree of some sort to connect with, even if it is just a bonsai. Choosing the right tree for your space will give you years of pleasure.

Some beautiful small deciduous trees, ideal for a compact garden, are *Catalpa bignonioides*, *Cercis siliquastrum*, *Cornus florida*, *Fraxinus angustifolia* 'Raywood', *Lagerstroemia indica*, *Magnolia denudata*, *Malus ionensis*, *Melia azedarach* and *Pistacia chinensis*. If you have plenty of space for a large deciduous shade tree, choose from *Gleditsia triacanthos* 'Sunburst', *Liriodendron tulipifera*, *Nyssa sylvatica*, *Paulownia tomentosa*, *Platanus* sp., *Pyrus calleryana*, *Quercus palustris*, *Q. robur*, *Sorbus* sp. and *Ulmus parvifolia*.

If you have views that need screening or inhospitable conditions you want to lock out, evergreens may be more suitable for your space. Suitable small evergreen trees are *Arbutus unedo*, *Eucalyptus ficifolia*, *Fraxinus griffithii* and *Michelia doltsopa*, while *Magnolia grandiflora* and *Schinus molle* are stunning large evergreen specimens.

whereas if you live in a wet climate you may need an actual roof in order to have a useable, all-weather outdoor room. Pergolas, shade sails, tents, pagodas and summerhouses are all interpretations of the garden ceiling, and can help make small gardens seem bigger, as floor space always appears larger when there is an overhead enclosure.

Doors and windows

You need to be able to enter and exit your garden room just as you would any room in a house. A 'door' can be a gate or archway, a flight of steps or a humble footpath. 'Windows' can provide glimpses of views or frame focal points.

Gates

When you approach a house, the gate is usually the first thing you encounter. It may make a statement about what and who lies beyond. Gates are definitely status symbols in the garden, so choose your materials carefully; ideally, you should incorporate architectural details that complement both the house and the fence.

Door hardware

Whether it's iron studs in an oak door for a Santa Fe look, or twisted wire latches for a cottage gate, door handles, hinges and latches are a great way to accent a particular style you have chosen for your garden.

Right: An elaborately carved door from the Alhambra palace in Granada, Spain.

Gates have a language of their own. They signal whether or not you are welcome to enter. Some gates are kept closed; they are tall and imposing and form a solid panel that stops you from seeing what lies beyond. But not all gates are so secretive: a lichgate actually invites you to stop and shelter, while a woven wire gate allows you to see through and over it to the garden beyond. It may even be left ajar in a welcoming gesture. Timber picket, bar and brace, and wrought iron gates offer security and a sense of enclosure while still inviting you to enter.

A gate can also be used to lead from one garden room to another. This type of gate should be a simple affair that invites you to see more and reinforces the style of a garden.

Arches and lichgates

Arches are simply curved entranceways that help delineate areas and invite you into the next room. Walking under an arch adds drama and anticipation to an entrance. The effect of blocking out the sun, even for a few paces, gives the impression that a secret is about to be revealed.

An arch can be engineered from iron, simply bent from a sapling or willow, clipped out of a hedge or created by bending or training two conical plants to meet in the middle. Depending on the purpose of the arch, you can add a gate or just leave the opening as it is. An arch should not be less than 2 m (6 ft 6 in) high or you'll feel the need to stoop when walking through it.

Lichgates, on the other hand, offer shelter for entranceways, and some even have built-in seating. The roof above them helps define their place along the fence line, clearly marking the entranceway.

Moongates are the oriental interpretation of an arch and, as the name suggests, form an almost completely circular arch, framing views and enticing the onlooker to enter.

Other entranceways

Cars now feature so much in our lives that many homes no longer have a footpath. Instead, a driveway leads from the gate to the front door. If this is the case in your garden, the flooring material will obviously have to be strong enough to hold the weight of a vehicle without cracking or buckling. It's a good idea to keep any plantings low and slightly back from these driveways, so that the driver can easily see pedestrians.

Overhanging branches that cast a pattern of light and shade without obscuring the driver's view will encourage the driver to slow down. Narrow roads and driveways also encourage slowing down, although this safety benefit may be outweighed by inconvenience if the parking area is restricted, making loading and unloading difficult.

Did you know? The Chinese believed that when you walked through an arch you left any evil spirits behind. Often there was a wall behind the moongate, forcing you to turn left or right, leaving the evil spirits behind as they can only walk in a straight line.

Opposite: The simple geometric pattern on this metal gate is typical of the Art Deco period.

Left: The azaleas and flowering cherries along this driveway enhance the journey from the gate to the house.

Don't forget to leave enough space for turning the car and allowing its occupants to get in and out easily. As a rule of thumb, a driveway only needs to be about 2.4 m (7 ft) wide as long as plants are kept at a distance of 0.9 m (3 ft) from either side of the car. A curved driveway needs to be wider than a straight one so that cars can handle the curve safely. Generally, a curve in the driveway should be one-third wider than the car using it, but 3.6 m (11 ft) is a safe estimation. Allow extra width (about the equivalent of a car's length) at the entrance to a double carport so that the driver can square up the car before entering. If your home fronts onto a busy road, and you can afford the space, a circular driveway is ideal.

Garden windows

Garden windows make your space seem larger by lending the impression that there is still more to see. One great advantage of windows is that the view may not even be of your own garden — it may be a view of a borrowed landscape (see page 44) or a distant vista. It could even be a reflection of your own garden glimpsed in a mirror.

Specific features can also be framed effectively by a *clairvoyée*. Typically, this is a round, porthole-style gap that has been strategically placed in a wall to highlight what lies beyond. It may be a simple clipped reveal in a hedge or a circular hole in a brick wall. You can even have timber and glass sash windows or porthole windows like the ones used in your home. If the view is poor, use frosted glass, mirrors or stained glass to disguise what lies beyond. These work particularly well in a hedge, as the contrast between light glass and dark foliage, and between the built and organic is accentuated.

Above: Things are not always what they seem. This trompe l'oeil is designed to fool you into thinking there is another garden room beyond the wall.

Right: A *clairvoyée* offers a tantalizing glimpse of the view behind a high hedge.

Trompe l'oeil

Trompe l'oeil literally translates to 'trick of the eye', a perfect inclusion for a small garden, as it will make it seem larger. This is done by fooling you into thinking there is more to see, or by playing with perspectives so that views may appear further away than they actually are. A painted mural, a lattice frame, a mirror or a mounted door are all applications of this trickery, and if plantings are included, the effect can be very realistic.

Connecting the rooms

Hallways, staircases and transitional zones such as lobbies and anterooms are all links between the rooms in your home. Using pergolas, verandas, patios, stairs and paths to connect your garden rooms can be both practical and inspiring.

Paths

Pathways are for foot traffic but still need to be wide enough to accommodate wheelbarrows. They really come into their own in a garden where one purpose is to wander around and enjoy the plants. As well as allowing you to get from A to B, paths should also add something to the landscape and character of a garden.

To build an effective path, first look at your 'desire' lines closely. At the planning stage work out where you'll be walking and why. Is

there a track to the clothesline? Is the front door accessible? How will you get groceries in and out of the house? Are people likely to walk side by side down the path? If so, a 1.5 m (5 ft) wide path will be necessary. Once you've worked out what you need, track where you want to go and how fast you need to get there, and build a path to suit. A curved path may be appropriate for the route from the gate to the front door, for example, but not between the backdoor and the clothesline if you're carrying a basket of wet washing.

By placing paths where they are needed, you'll eliminate unnecessary damage to lawns, shrubs and garden beds. On the other hand, in a larger garden, wandering paths add a sense of journey, anticipation and expectation well worth the effort and expense required in installing them.

Above left: A garden 'hall', created by a series of rose-covered timber arches, leads you from one garden room to another.

Above: The changing direction of this path creates an atmosphere of intrigue and discovery.

Above: Shallow semicircular steps add a sense of grandeur to a garden.

Opposite: A garden pavilion can be both a shelter and a stylish entertaining area.

Suitable materials

A path may be a simple mown strip of grass through longer turf, a trail of stepping stones or some wooden rounds in mulch. The type of path you choose may enhance the journey from one part of the garden to another.

Loose materials — gravel, wood chips, pebbles and coarse sand or grits, such as decomposed granite — are all useful for medium traffic areas and only need to be 1 m (3 ft) wide for single file, comfortable use. Their main drawback is that the material can easily disperse in heavy rains, so you need to install appropriate edging in susceptible locations. Although organic surfaces will be the most economical paving material available, they will break down, so allow for the cost of replacing them every few years. Bear this in mind when you are doing your initial costing.

Driveways

Many of us are so dependent on cars that accommodating them, even in a small city property, has become commonplace: in some areas driveways and carports occupy a great deal of the available land. A driveway may be the only entry point to a property. If this is the case in your garden, take care to choose an attractive ground treatment, and clearly mark the point at which you deviate for the front door with another focal point.

Changing level

Level changes add another layer of interest to your garden. You can use either steps or a ramp, or a hybrid of the two versions — a stepped ramp — to make level changes. Steps are best for steep slopes, as they can rise quickly over a short distance, whereas ramps, necessary for disabled access, need more distance to travel the same height.

Steps can be winding, circular, square, floating, enclosed within a wall, parallel or projecting, include landings, be two-way or unidirectional. If the flights are long, consider allowing for extra seating space. Examine all the possibilities to find one with the style that suits your garden design and site, then marry it with an appropriate material, such as wood, stone, brick, turf or concrete.

Covered or semicovered structures

Covered areas are great for climate control. In hot climates, properly roofed areas are essential for blocking out the hot midday sun. Verandas and porticos, porches, patios, colonnades and galleries are all useful additions to the main building and they have the added advantage of shading the house walls and keeping the interior somewhat cooler.

For aspects that are protected from the full force of the sun, especially in climates where it is less intense, consider permeable overhead structures: they still let light in but give a sense of enclosure. For these positions, pergolas and arbours are ideal. Climbing plants can be used to soften the structure. A deciduous climber reduces the impact of the summer sun but lets in winter light, while flowering and perfumed creepers can smother your structure in blossom and perfume.

Site formulae

Here are some helpful formulae for working out steps and ramps as well as combinations of the two.

In order to calculate how your steps are going to work out, you'll need to calculate the height they need to rise and the distance that they have to travel. Risers shouldn't be more than 15 cm (6 in) high, otherwise your calf muscles won't cope, and treads shouldn't be less than 30 cm (1 ft) deep, or your feet won't comfortably fit on the step! Treads can be more, however, even a landing or ramp, but a comfortable medium is about 38 cm (15 in) for a standard step. Landings are needed every fourteen steps or less, otherwise the flight will be daunting. Like paths, steps need to be about 1.5 m (4½ ft) wide if traffic both ways or side by side is expected, and about 1 m (3 ft) wide if not.

Of course, some areas need not have a roof at all. A terrace is the perfect example of an anteroom open to the sky; the roof is implied by means of a different floor treatment, such as paving.

The functions of garden rooms

To ensure your garden is properly utilized, consider not only access and comfort but also the purpose or function of each 'room'. More than just a sanctuary, your garden can be used as an extension of the living areas of your house.

The bathroom

Since ancient Roman times, bathing in the garden has been regarded as a desirable and opulent experience. Today's backyard may boast a pool or spa. In beachside suburbs in warmer climates, outdoor showers, hose-down areas and private baths are also becoming popular.

Roman baths and drinking fonts as well as the elaborate cooling rills of the Moors provide much of the inspiration for water features in gardens today (see page 226 for details). These days the water feature rarely has a practical function — it is an adornment only, more like an item of furniture.

The kitchen

Most cooks want to be where the action is. If you like to entertain outdoors, nothing beats an out-of-doors kitchen. That could be a portable barbecue, a wood-fired stove, a simple hungii (or pit oven, used in the Pacific islands) or a stainless steel cooktop incorporated into its own annex, with hot and cold running water and a bar fridge to service the proceedings.

The living room

Often a garden is used for simply relaxing. You might have a hammock strung up in a tree or even built-in chaises for lounging on. Whatever the style or size of your garden, clever use of space will enable you to include a relaxation area, even if it's a nook on a flight of stairs or a garden bench in its own quiet space.

The dining room

Dining out is a great way to enjoy your garden, and indeed, fresh air sharpens the appetite while delightful surroundings enhance the taste of food. Siting tables and chairs appropriately is a vital part of setting up an outdoor dining area: any furniture should be in a not too hot, not too cold place, sheltered from draughts, close to the house and, above all, on a stable surface. Portable furniture — for instance, trestles, card tables, directors' chairs and folding café chairs — will make this garden 'room' a lot more versatile.

Opposite, top left: A pizza oven is the focus of this outdoor entertaining area.

Opposite, top right: For those who live near the beach, a garden shower is a practical addition.

Opposite, bottom: This timber deck has a cleverly integrated bench.

Above: A shabby chic dining setting combines elegance and ease.

The space required for **table arrangements**

It's easy to underestimate the space you need for an outdoor table setting. If space is limited, consider constructing built-in furniture, such as banquet seats, that will help keep the area tight. If you have a little more space and are considering freestanding pieces, remember that furniture needs more room than it actually occupies. People need to be able to walk around the table and pull out chairs in order to sit down, so this should all be possible on the terrace or patio. Allow a minimum of 1 m (3 ft) from the edge of your table to the edge of your paving. Oval tables are ideal for fitting the maximum number of individual seats for the setting, while rectangular tables will accommodate bench seats, which also save space.

Above: Simple to install, candlelight is one of the cheapest and most romantic forms of outdoor lighting.

Centre: The benchtop on this gardening trolley folds out to reveal a work area with a recessed container for holding potting mix.

Lighting is another factor worth considering here, especially if dining out at your place is likely to occur after the sun goes down. Another important consideration when planning an outdoor dining area is insect control. Mosquitoes, flies and moths can make your al fresco dining experience unpleasant. Some strategies to combat this include keeping fish in your water feature to keep larvae under control and using citronella oil burners and candles. Or you could try planting some insect-repelling plants — such as pennyroyal, tansy and the citronella geranium — in a spot where their leaves can be easily bruised by passers-by, releasing their essential oils.

The playroom

'Go outside and play' is a common parent's catchcry. Providing safe places in which to explore, discover and learn is an important aspect of designing a garden for a family. Sandpits, play equipment, treehouses, quiet areas, perfumed plants, sensory walks and hard surfaces for balls, bikes and other rolling and bouncing things are all worth considering. The trick is to design the space so that it grows up with your children, becoming multifunctional. Storage is also well worth including in your design, so the children can pack away their toys when they are finished with them.

The garden closet

Storage is a critical element in your home's interior, and it should also be part of your garden design. Indoors, good-looking closets, boxes, hidden cupboards and furniture stash away all your bits and pieces, so it makes sense to translate these same options to the outdoors, using weatherproof products. If large, bulky items such as compost bins,

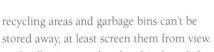

Above: A treehouse can be a child's favourite retreat, the focus of hours of happy playtime. Unlike other play equipment, it frees up the garden floor.

recycling areas and garbage bins can't be stored away, at least screen them from view.

Smaller items such as hand tools and gloves may end up in a shed if you have space, but a trolley that can house the lot and be wheeled to various areas as needed can fit the bill. Storage boxes located beside sandpits, hooks for tools, and benches with hinged seating that double as storage areas are all useful.

The elements of design

The elements of design are the building blocks of art. The main elements of garden design are line and pattern, scale and proportion, masses and voids, shape and form, texture, colour and tone. These are the tools you need to create a style in your garden. Always keep them in mind, from the planning stage onwards.

A breathtaking garden carefully balances light and shade, and uses uniformity, rhythm and scale. Colour is the icing on the cake. By studying all these elements, you can manipulate them to create different effects. The end result should please the senses.

Your garden may look indecisive if it doesn't have an overall theme that unifies all these elements. One way to achieve this is to restrict yourself to a theme, but you could also repeat a plant, colour or shape, such as circular areas of lawn and paving combined with a series of round ponds. Even using the same type of stonework, edging or mulch throughout your garden can help unify your design.

Line and pattern

When you first draw up your garden and start experimenting with the placement of garden beds and the like, you are really playing with the lines and patterns of your garden. This basic grid becomes softened once plants grow, but a strong design will remain the backbone of your garden all year long.

Line

In the garden, lines are much more than the edges of a path, or the curves of a garden bed. By running lines away from the viewer, you can make a site seem deeper; by making them converge, you can accentuate this even further. You can also make a site seem wider by running a line horizontally across it.

To direct the viewer to a focal point, the lines should head in that direction. The most obvious use of line in the landscape is the avenue, but other lines include garden edging and water rills.

Avenues

Although avenues originated in ancient times (see page 18), today they are still useful for creating a sense of anticipation and occasion, whether it's for roadside plantings, commercial landscapes or domestic use. This modern translation could be a simple repetition of species along a driveway, a pleached avenue to screen out neighbouring properties or a means of framing a view or other focal point such as a piece of sculpture.

Below: The paving detail and the repetition of the lavender plantings both help to emphasize the length of this path. The colour purple recedes into the distance, making the garden seem deeper.

Some suitable deciduous trees for an avenue include rowan (*Sorbus aucuparia*), hornbeam (*Carpinus* sp.), elm (*Ulmus* sp.), lime (*Tilia* sp.), plane (*Platanus* sp.) and oak (*Quercus* sp.). For an evergreen avenue, choose from *Ficus* sp., cedar (*Cedrus* sp.), paperbark (*Melaleuca quinquenervia*), cotton palm (*Washingtonia filifera*) and plum pine (*Podocarpus* sp.). In domestic settings, smaller trees are more appropriate (see page 110).

Pattern

If you repeat a line often enough, it becomes a pattern, and patterns are essential to the overall character of a design. They can be static, dynamic, straight, curved, symmetrical or asymmetrical.

Some patterns create movement — such as herringbone or stretcher bond patterns in paving — and are dynamic, while others appear static — a chequerboard pattern, grid or circular detail. Recognizing these patterns can help you choose the right one for the job.

If there is no focal point in your borrowed landscape — for instance, you have a walled garden that has no outside interest or views — a patterned layout that will hold the eye within the site, such as a chequerboard, may help to create interest and stop your eye from wandering, looking for something to focus on.

Conversely, a dynamic pattern may be appropriate if you are trying to direct the visitor's eye — for example, a herringbone pattern along a path or a spiral pattern towards a central feature. Patterns can be varied endlessly, so be creative with them. You can create patterns with manufactured materials or with natural materials, such as woven willows or pebbles, cut grass and trimmed plants.

Above: Pear trees trained into an arch over an avenue draw attention to the house beyond.

Plant patterns

You can use plants for garden pattern making, either by themselves as parterres and knot gardens (see page 349) or in combination with pavers and other landscaping materials such as gravel. A popular choice is to plant a grid of short clumping grass such as mini mondo between large format paving squares to help define a grid-like imprint on the ground level. This is very effective in small areas and helps to soften solid paving.

Different **paving** patterns

Different paving patterns include running or stretcher bond, grid or soldier courses, basketweave, herringbone (either 45 or 90 degrees), bedding faces (with either half or whole bricks), circular, repeating unit or diminishing squares.

Cobbles, or large stones, can also be used to create a pattern — whether it's a spiral of stones on the lawn (see page 295), or a more intricately laid pattern in a mortar bed. See the black and white cobbled surface on page 267.

Left: Mix and match paving materials to make your own interesting combinations.

Above: Here, colour, form and texture have been cleverly combined to create layers of plantings.

Centre: Combining a variety of leaf shapes — such as those of the cut-leaf maple (*Acer palmatum*), cream clivia and *Sagittaria atropurpureum* shown here — provides additional visual interest.

Scale and proportion

Scale is important. Your home and any other buildings on the property should ideally be in proportion to the block size. Broad, sweeping lawns planted with large trees will make a small cottage seem pokey, while a small bed of annuals planted in front of a grand home will fail to anchor the building to its surrounds.

Other tricks with scale can make a garden seem bigger or smaller. Planting the foreground with large trees, and the middle ground and background with trees that gradually reduce in size will make your garden seem larger. In many Japanese gardens the same effect is achieved by placing large-leafed plants in the foreground, and smaller-leafed species in the background. Likewise, by having the foreground in sunlight, and the background in the shade, you can create the illusion of a deeper garden.

Another method is to place rectangular garden beds, paved areas or pools in diminishing sizes in a line so that the largest one is nearest the observer and the smallest one is furthest away. This tricks your mind into believing that they are actually all the same size, and that the garden is deeper than it is. But do use these methods carefully, as the converse effect is created when you look at the garden from the other direction.

The easiest way to create an intimate space is to create a series of enclosures or 'rooms'. By planting or building 'walls', and even creating a roof from overhanging branches or vines, a space can feel more intimate. Hidcote, a garden in the United Kingdom (see page 22), employs this technique very successfully. It has a series of garden rooms, and even includes an outdoor ballroom.

Above: The best plants for pergolas are ones that have pendulous flowers, such as wisteria and laburnum, drooping through the structure itself.

Scale also affects features in the built landscape. You need to consider the width of paths and whether there is enough space for people to walk abreast comfortably. A wider path will make a garden look broader, while a narrow path with overhanging trees can create a sense of enclosure. Likewise, a sweep of steps should be considered carefully. Not only is the riser to tread ratio important for comfort in ascending or descending, but also a well designed flight of stairs can be a feature in itself. (See page 97.)

Garden structures such as pergolas also need to be in proportion to the house. Take into account what the structure will be used for as well as the number of people who will be likely to use it. If you are planning to hold large dinner parties in your chosen structure, allow enough space for guests to move about freely.

Masses and voids

The lines drawn on a garden plan really start to work when they are transferred into the third dimension. The siting and growth of trees, shrubs and smaller plants can mould a space. Masses — trees and tall shrubs — divide and emphasize the voids around them — low plantings and lawns, even pools, for example. Masses lend a garden solidity and weight, while voids allow you to see above them. Fundamental to a satisfying design is the contrast between masses and voids, and between shape and form (see page 106).

These three-dimensional effects largely create the shape of your garden. Another example of a mass and a void is the pergola. The structure itself is the mass, while the space between the ground and the pergola is the void.

Masses and voids are allied to scale, because these are the basic means by which the scale of the ground plan of a garden and the thousands of cubic metres (or feet) of sky above ground level can be divided and defined.

Shape and form (habit)

Shape and form are terms that describe the outline of either a plant's leaf (shape) or silhouette (form), also called habit. By contrasting the two, either at the leaf level or with silhouettes, you can create visual interest in your garden.

See also page 52 and the photocopiable silhouettes on page 438.

Below, from top to bottom:
Cynara cardunculus, Amaranthus sp., *Eucomis autumnalis* and *Epimedium* sp.

Leaf shapes

Various leaf shapes can play against each other to make beautiful plant associations. Round leaves, spiky foliage and fan shapes all contrast to make interesting plant pictures. Reed-like plants and grasses also have a shape or habit that is worthy of inclusion in the garden. Small-leafed plants like violets, baby's tears and ferns really contrast well with broader-leafed plants such as bird's nest ferns. Strap-leafed plants such as poa, iris and mondo grass in turn highlight hearts and rounds, such as hosta leaves. Large leaf shapes — from enormous gunnera leaves to the ragged banana — add that 'wow' factor to a garden.

Plants for certain **leaf shapes**

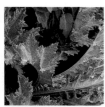

Large leaf
Acanthus sp., *Asplenium* sp., *Cortaderia* sp., *Cynara cardunculus, Ensete ventricosum, Fatsia* sp., *Macleaya* syn. *Bocconia, Mahonia* sp., *Livistona* sp., *Monstera* sp., *Musa basjoo, Philodendron* sp., *Rheum palmatum, Trachycarpus fortunei*

Reed shape
Acorus sp., *Amaranthus caudatus, Arundinaria* sp., *Arundo* sp., *Carex* sp., *Cyperus* sp., *Dierama* sp., *Iris* sp., *Lomandra* sp., *Miscanthus* sp., *Phyllostachys* sp., *Restio* sp., *Typha* sp.

Rosettes
Aeonium sp., *Agave* sp., *Aloe* sp., *Arthropodium cirralum, Bromeliad* sp., *Cycas* sp., *Echeveria* sp., *Eucomis* sp., *Sempervivum* sp., *Yucca* sp., *Zamia* sp.

Hearts and rounds
Asarum sp., *Bergenia* sp., *Brunnera* sp., *Catalpa* sp., *Cyclamen* sp., *Epimedium* sp., *Hosta* sp., *Ligularia* sp., *Petasites* sp., *Petiphyllum* sp., *Plantago* sp., *Tropaeolum* sp.

Form

Form reflects the growth habit of plants and can harmonize the walls and floors of your garden. Each plant has a natural form and silhouette, which may change as the plant matures, and which can often be manipulated by pruning. These forms can be combined to achieve interesting effects and contrasts.

For example, many shrubs and perennials have a rounded, bun-like outline, which may be contrasted with a different form, such as a columnar tree or a prostrate ground cover. A shrub with bare, basal stems may need to be planted among rounded bushes that will hide its base, while plants with weeping habits may need some simple box-like hedging for effective contrast. Trees with this habit — for example, silver birch, maples, cherries and grafted conifers such as *Cupressus macrocarpa* 'Greenstead Magnificent' and 'Saligna Aurea' — were particularly popular throughout the twentieth century. Some shrubs — such as *Cornus controversa* 'Variegatum', *Viburnum plicatum* 'Mariesii' and *Loropetalum chinense* — have this habit naturally. These days grafting techniques have improved so much that many spreading plants can be grafted on top of a standard stem to create a weeping plant. Grevilleas, roses and fuchsias have all been used successfully in this way.

Below left: The shape and colour of the trees are the main features of this garden.

Below: Tall spires of pea flowers in a glorious range of colours make lupins a favourite vertical element in the cottage garden.

Globular shapes could be shrubs clipped into tight balls. This shape is commonly featured in Asian gardens using azaleas, and in Italianate gardens using English box. Hebes, Japanese box, *Pittosporum tobira* and cypress are also suitable for clipping into this shape.

Spiky forms vary from tiny grass tufts to the giant forms of yucca. Dragon tree (*Dracaena draco*), *Cordyline* sp., iris, *Kniphofia* sp., *Euphorbia* sp., *Echium* sp., *Phormium* sp., *Sisyrinchium* sp. and gymea lily (*Doryanthes excelsa*) are just some examples of dramatic spiky plants.

Vertical plants with columnar or conical shapes can be used like botanical punctuation marks to break up the rhythm of many shrubs. They can also create balance if they are placed symmetrically — for example, on either side of an entrance. Many conifers, such as the famous *Juniperus* 'Skyrocket' or *Cupressus sempervirens* 'Stricta', work well, as does clipped topiary obelisk-shaped box, especially when it is used to define a parterre. *Prunus* 'Amanogawa' is a columnar, flowering plum, useful for both its flower and form. The tall spires of lupins, foxgloves, *Agastache* sp., hollyhocks and larkspurs complement a cottage garden filled with frothy flowers, and even the humble vegetable garden can be transformed with vertical growers like beans, peas, tomatoes and other vines that require support.

Many plants have a striking architectural or sculptural impact. Structural plants such as *Acanthus* sp., cactus and even artichokes can be used as focal points, and form an excellent link between hard features, such as a house, and the 'soft', such as plantings. Architectural shapes can be anything, from plants that mimic a built feature, such as topiary plants that have been clipped into roofs or walls, to plants that have natural architectural forms, like the agaves, the plant equivalent of the Sydney Opera House.

Using the contrasting form of flower shapes is particularly important in perennial and cottage gardens. (See page 263.)

Texture

Texture is literally how something feels, but in the garden it is also taken for granted that when you see a surface you imagine how it feels without

Below: A combination of various leaves showing different shapes and textures.

needing to touch it. So much can be achieved with just texture. All sorts of tactile elements, from plants to surfaces, can be surprising and exciting to look at. Weatherboards with blistering paint, smooth round stones, the glassy surface of still water and the bristle of twigs are just a few materials that form the fabric of outdoor living.

When it comes to plants, texture involves the contrasting foliage rather than shapes. For example, the lacy fronds of a tree fern accentuate the linear and sharp-edged foliage of libertia, or branching flag iris (*Libertia paniculata*) and vice versa. Similarly, the glossy foliage of the camellia looks even shinier next to a fine-textured conifer. And a broad, sweeping planting of grasses like *Miscanthus* sp. can look magical against the flat and small texture of an expanse of lawn.

To heighten the contrasts in your garden, use plants with different textures together. Mix and match glossy with furry, spiny with smooth, and feathery with succulent.

Texture is not limited to foliage: look at the bark on tree trunks, or the spines on a cactus. Many seed pods, husks and the like have wonderful textures that can be used to create interest.

Beautiful bark

To plant for bark alone requires courage. To resist the seductive and ephemeral pleasures of foliage, flowers and fruit can be hard, but consider the benefits — year-long interest rather than six weeks of glory is just the start. Many trees, of course, have become popular for their bark alone.

Right, from top to bottom: *Pinus canariensis, Asplenium australasicum, Arum italicum, Stachys byzantina, Mahonia ilexifolia, Sedum rubrotinctum* and *Miscanthus* sp.

Plants with different **texture**

Linear and fine
Cotoneaster salicifolius, Hippophae rhamnoides, Ozothamnus rosmarinifolius, Pinus strobus 'Nana', *Pyrus salicifolia* 'Pendula', *Sambucus nigra* 'Laciniata'

Glossy
Acanthus sp., *Arum* sp., *Aspidistra* sp., *Asplenium nidus, Bergenia* sp., *Camellia* sp., *Euonymus* sp., *Hedera* sp., *Hosta* sp., *Ilex* sp., *Prunus laurocerasus, Viburnum* 'Emerald Lustre'

Ribbed or pleated
Alchemilla mollis, Asplenium crispum, Corylus sp., *Licuala* sp., *Livistona* sp., *Ricinus communis, Rodgersia* sp., *Sambal* sp., *Trachycarpus* sp., *Veratrum nigrum, Viburnum davidii, Vitis coignetiae*

Furry/velvety
Artemisia sp., *Correa* sp., *Cotyledon* sp., *Lavandula* sp., *Potentilla* sp., *Hieracium lanatum, Helichrysum petiolare, Lychnis coronoria, Salix lanata, Salvia argentea, Salvia officinalis, Senecio cineraria, Stachys byzantina, Vitis vinifera* 'Purpurea'

Spiny/prickly
Acacia verticillata, Aciphylla aurea, Argemone mexicana, cactus, *Chorisia speciosa, Cynara cardunculus, Desfontainia spinosa, Eryngium agavifolium, Morina longifolia, Onopordum acanthium, Mahonia* sp., *Silybum marianum*

Succulent
Aloe sp., *Crassula* sp., *Echeveria* sp., *Kalanchoe* sp., *Lampranthus* sp., *Sedum* sp., *Sempervivum* sp., *Senecio* sp.

Strap
Ornamental grasses such as *Astelia* sp., *Crocosmia* sp., *Hemerocallis* sp., *Iris* sp., *Lomandra* sp., *Miscanthus* sp., *Phormium* sp., *Sansevieria* sp., *Sisyrinchium* sp.

Above: Detail of crepe myrtle bark (*Lagerstroemia indica*) showing its smooth patina and streaky colours.

Right: Plants that produce seed pods, berries and cones provide texture and seasonal interest.

Four superb small trees for this purpose include *Luma apiculata* syn. *Myrtus luma*, which has cinnamon-coloured bark that peels off in patches, exposing a cream inner surface. The crepe myrtle (*Lagerstroemia indica*) is renowned for its streaky tan, red, brown and cream bark, a real feature all year, as well its crepe-like flowers. Gordonias (*Gordonia axillaris*) have a similar bark with age, and are adorned with large, white, camellia-like flowers. A similar effect can be created with the Australian native water gum (*Tristania laurina*), which also has canary yellow flowers in spring.

The silver birch (*Betula pendula*) is a perennial favourite in gardens: in summer the shimmering white trunks contrast with the dappled shade underneath, then in autumn they play against golden leaves and delicate catkins. There are other birches that are equally deserving of a place in the garden. The paper birch (*Betula papyrifera*) and red birch (*B. nigra* 'Heritage') both have stunning peeling bark, the first white and papery, the latter shaggy and pinkish orange.

Many gum trees with ghostly trunks or unusual markings can be featured in the garden. Those most suited to garden situations include the lemon-scented gum (*Eucalyptus citriodora*), Wallangarra white gum (*E. scoparia*) and the river peppermint (*E. elata*), all known for their white trunks. The scribbly gum (*E. haemastoma*) has a beautiful white trunk curiously marked with scribbles, which are caused by an insect tunnelling through the bark. Another favourite is the spotted gum (*E. maculata*). Its trunk peels in various stages, leaving leopard spots of varying shades of grey, green and cream.

Other spotted trunks worth contemplating include the plane tree (*Platanus* x *hispanica* syn. *P.* x *acerifolia*), which has a dappled trunk of cream, grey and tan. It will grow to quite a size, so it is best for large gardens or farmlands. The leopard tree (*Caesalpinia ferrea*) is great for tropical areas. It is fast growing, and quickly develops the spotted grey, white and beige trunk for which it is named. The added bonus with this gorgeous small tree is the feathery mass of yellow blossoms that cover its top in late summer.

For papery bark, try the paperbark family (*Melaleuca* sp. and *Callistemon* sp.), from the huge spreading broad-leafed paperbark (*M. quinquenervia*) to the daintier snow-in-summer (*M. linariifolia*). Others — such as the paperbark maple (*Acer griseum*), Tibetan cherry (*Prunus serrula*) and Manchurian cherry (*P. maackii*) — are the unlikely bearers of superb, polished, copper-like flaky bark and the usual display of leaf colour or blossom appropriate to the genus.

Finally, some bark can be especially interesting, and fun for children. The cork bark from the cork oak (*Quercus suber*), used to plug wine bottles, has a spongy texture that makes it great to touch. The ironbarks (for example, *Eucalyptus sideroxylon*) have such thick, black bark that they can withstand fire, while the longleaf pine (*Pinus palustris*) has jigsaw-like, red–orange, papery bark, a feature in itself. Even some shrubs, such as the spindlebush (*Euonymus alatus*), have textural bark that invites you to touch it. Chinese elm (*Ulmus parvifolia*) is also beautiful in this way.

More bite than **bark**

Above: *Robinia pseudoacacia* in flower.

With its thorn-like protrusions all over its trunk, the kapok tree (*Chorisia speciosa*) will discourage the most ardent climber, but the display of pink orchid-like blooms and seed pods filled with silky threads, once used for stuffing pillows and mattresses, will easily compensate. For the ultimate in spiny bark, however, it's hard to go past the honey locust (*Gleditsia triacanthos*): although the pods are filled with sweetish pulp that is used as drought stock fodder, the trunk and branches are so thickly covered in thorns that only a starving person would dare climb this tree. Robinias usually have a pair of spines on the branch at the base of each leaf.

Below, from left to right: Some different textures in the garden: glorious barks — silver birch (*Betula pendula*), bottlebrush (*Callistemon viminalis*) and cork oak (*Quercus suber*) — as well as a weathered tabletop with blistered paint.

Tips for using colour in the garden

1 Colour outside should be used to back up the function and feeling of the garden, the flower colour adding to the effect of the foliage, form and texture of the shrubs, trees and ground covers.

2 Colour has a big effect on mood. Use bright colours in lively environments and softer, subtle tones in restful areas.

3 Locate the strongest colours in the foreground, and allow the colours to become paler with distance. Too much strong colour at a distance foreshortens the space.

4 Work with any surrounding colour schemes, from the house out, and from the boundary to distant views.

5 Grey foliage 'cools down' bright colours, and white flowers help contrasting colours blend effectively.

6 Colours change, depending on the time of day and intensity of sunlight. Pale colours look soft and gentle in the morning and evening light, but can seem bleached and washed out during the day. Conversely, colours that work in the heat of the day can appear garish in softer light. Similarly, seasonal changes affect the strength of light and colour. Red is the first colour to 'disappear' at dusk.

7 Colour is often used to attract the visitor or viewer's eye. If you want something to stand out and be noticed, a loud splash of colour nearby will hold the eye. Red is eye catching, powerful and has an 'advancing' quality that can make spaces appear smaller and more intimate. All hot colours are dynamic and attention grabbing. Some can even be alarming.

8 Select a range of colours that suits your home and personality, but do deviate from this range to allow contrast into your garden.

9 Try working with foliage colour as a backbone to your garden design. Darker foliage allows colours to seem more pronounced.

10 Larger flowers are harder to blend successfully than smaller ones.

Right: Orange Mollis azaleas contrast well with purple iris.

Opposite: The white climbing roses and white alyssum carpeting the edges of the walkway make the pergola seem longer than it actually is. The purple echium flowers and grey foliage have the effect of making the bed in the foreground deeper, while the yellow flowers of euphorbia, purple's complement, add drama to the scene.

Tone and colour

Over the last 100 years or so, colour has become an increasingly important design element in gardens. This has coincided with the development of new flower colours thanks to breeding and hybridization in the modern era. Colour can be introduced into the garden in many ways — foliage, fabrics, paintwork, tiling and even food can all be effective ways of adding colour, whether temporary or lasting, to your garden.

The colour wheel

To use colour effectively, you need an understanding of the colour wheel, and how one colour affects another.

The three primary colours are red, blue and yellow. The three secondary colours of green, violet and orange are mixtures of the primary colours. Together, they make the colours of the rainbow, which is an excellent natural guide to colour. Shadings or hues of individual colours vary, depending on the strength and intensity of each primary colour, while tone is a measure of the black and white component in each colour. Black, white and grey are inert colours, which means only the brightness, not the colour, changes.

The colour wheel can be divided into halves — the 'cool' colours of green, grey, blue and mauve, and the 'warm' colours, such as yellow, red, orange and hot pink. Colours adjacent to each other, or nearby, are called harmonious colours, while colours opposite each other are called complementary.

You can use this knowledge as a tool in garden design. For example, when using contrasting colours, make a cool colour the base and the hot colours highlights to intensify the effect of both colours. Alternatively, hues next to each other harmonize, and pure colour gardens can also be very restful. See page 252 for more details on the colour wheel.

Above: Dozing off in a comfortable garden room, surrounded by varieties of salvia in bloom.

Opposite top: Daphne lends its exquisite perfume to the chilly winter air.

Other design considerations

Unlike other schools of art and design, gardening allows you to create a feast not just for your eyes but also for your other senses. Paintings, after all, just hang on a wall and decorate a room, but you can 'live' in a garden.

Perfume, taste and other delights

When designing your garden, try to consider all your senses, not just sight. A garden is more than a picture to be looked at and admired. The crunch of leaves underfoot, the smell of mown grass and the coolness of shade are just some of the sensations that make being in a garden a joy.

Smell, from the perfume of both foliage and flowers, is probably the most common sensation after sight, but touching gnarled bark, stroking furry leaves, listening to birds and tasting the fruits of your labour are equally rewarding. Creating a garden is not just about 'how to do it', but also 'how to enjoy it'. Remember light, shadows, atmosphere and wildlife all play a part.

Fragrant plants

Fragrance in the garden is so important that whole books are devoted to the topic. Who can resist the smell of an old rose or the wafting perfume of daphne, so pervasive that it can be detected some distance away?

For many people, a flower is only desirable when it has a perfume. But in terms of gardening 'pizzazz', often perfumed plants lack a little in the colour department. The reason for this is simple: most perfumed plants use their scent, not their colour, to attract insects. White, cream and soft yellows are the most common colours of perfumed plants, and their perfumes usually intensify at night, dusk and dawn when insect activity is at its height.

Some favourites are the frangipani (*Plumeria* sp.), sweet olive (*Osmanthus* sp.), paper whites (*Narcissus papyraceus*), angel's trumpet (*Brugmansia* sp.), *Choisya* sp., jasmine (*Jasminum* sp.) and moon flower (*Ipomoea alba*), although the perfumes of luculia, boronia and daphne are so exquisite that it is worth persevering with them in spite of the difficulties in growing them.

Delicious ornamental plants

Tasty plants aren't confined to the vegetable garden or orchard. Many ornamentals have tasty fruit or aromatic leaves as a bonus. There are the usual candidates — such as olives, persimmon, strawberries and citrus — as well as other, less obvious plants. Berrying plants like blueberries, gooseberries, lilly pillies, crabapples and strawberry guavas (*Feijoa* sp.) make great jam; the allspice tree (*Pimenta dioica*) and lemon myrtle (*Backhousia citriodora*) are wonderful for herbal teas; and edible flowers — such as rosemary, salvia, nasturtium, calendula and chives — will enliven any salad.

Fragrant leaves

The perfume of a flower is only one example of scent in the garden. Crushing an oil-rich ground cover underfoot, standing underneath a tree with pungent leaves or bruising the leaves of a favourite aromatic shrub can all yield unexpected pleasure. Some favourite aromatic herbs include lavender, rosemary, creeping thyme and mint, while scented-leaf geraniums, lemon-scented tea tree, camphor laurel and eucalypts will also provide unexpected pleasure. After a morning rainshower, when the children kick a ball around the garden or during a quiet reflective moment, these scents will brighten your day.

Above: The leaves of the lavender have a strong aromatic scent.

Sound

Trickling water, crunchy gravel, birdsong and rustling leaves are all sounds that enhance your time in the garden. Plants with whispering voices include lemongrass (*Cymbopogon citratus*), zebra grass (*Miscanthus* sp.), *Arundo donax*, *Bambusa multiplex*, Central and South American bamboo species such as *Chusquea aileon*, pampas grass (*Cortaderia selloana*), beech, giant rhubarb (*Gunnera* sp.), black bamboo (*Phyllostachys nigra*) and kuma zasa (*Sasa veitchii*).

Light and shade

Balance is the key with light and shade. Shade is essential in hot climates, as direct sunlight can be overwhelming. However, too much shade can be gloomy and depressing, especially in cold climates. One of the joys of having a garden is sitting in the shade of a tree on a hot day, looking out at the sunlit area. An important feature of light and shade is not so much the different effects in isolation, but experiencing the transition from one to another. Moving through successive areas of light and shade can give the viewer great pleasure, but it needs careful orchestration.

One such effect is the cooling sensation of a tree planted near a drive or entranceway. As you pass through the shade, it is shady and welcoming; viewing the house in a sunny clearing as you approach it heightens this sensation. Another example could be a shaded tunnel or avenue of trees that leads on to a bright and lively clearing with a fountain as its focal point. The play of light on water droplets also has a cooling effect.

Above left: Young fruit on an apple tree can be ornamental.

Left: A breeze rustling the leaves of bamboo is one of its lesser known attractions.

If the natural light is strong, position plants or architectural features where they will cast dramatic shadows on surrounding surfaces. A pergola's horizontals, for instance, can be constructed in such a way that when the light shines through them it produces a strong, geometric pattern of shadows. Or position plants with an architectural form, such as dracaenas, in front of a plain background, such as a wall, so that their shadows create an interesting backdrop.

Light can also be important in ponds. A small pool of water, however shallow, will make your space appear larger. You can use a light-absorbing lining, such as black plastic, which will make the water reflect its surroundings like a mirror, creating an impression of infinite depth.

Light-reflecting surfaces, such as a large mirror mounted on a wall, will add the illusion of space by increasing the amount of light in your garden.

Time and seasonality

Unlike other design schools, garden designers deal with the fourth dimension of time. Plants grow and mature, and seasons change. It's important to consider not only how a garden will look in spring, or in five years' time, but also how it will change in winter, and grow in twenty years' time.

'Think not of spring, she will look after herself. Plan for the others and be rewarded with a truly great garden', is a wise saying worth noting. What this in effect means is that nature is normally driven towards a flurry of blossom in spring, so by carefully orchestrating displays at other times of the year, you will ensure year-round garden pleasure. Concentrating on your winter garden will not diminish your spring garden to a bland non-event; it will just make winter a pleasurable surprise.

Above: Dogwood (*Cornus* sp.) has fine flowers in spring and glorious coloured leaves in autumn.

For many people, planting a garden is a weekend adventure. One fine day in spring you too are awakened from your winter spell and venture to the nursery, buy up big on a range of flowering pot plants, to return home again and fill up odd spots. By planning either a monthly visit year round to the nursery, or by planning a garden for year-round pleasure, you can create ever so much more, and enjoy your garden for so much longer.

The changes in a landscape over time are indeed what make garden design so challenging and fulfilling. Having a picture grow, change and rework itself can be both a frustrating and joyful element. Just as you think the garden is looking perfect, a plant may outgrow its space or a flower might fade. Embrace these changes. New flourishes of growth have long been associated with hope and rebirth, and gardeners should look upon them as opportunities for new plant pictures.

Choosing plants that have two seasons or transform from one display to another is a practical way of getting more for your money. For example, the dogwood has showy white bracts that look like a spring snow shower before they break into leaf, then in autumn

the display of red and orange leaf colour will set your garden ablaze. Oak leaf hydrangeas are the summer-flowering, smaller-growing equivalent, with its reliable autumn show. Many berrying plants, such as viburnum, rose bushes with hips and hawthorn reward you with not one but three seasons: first, spring blossom, then the summer fruit and finally an autumn leaf finale.

The ephemeral nature of both leaf colour and blossom is indeed part of its charm, to be breathed in deeply while a display is in full force, then exhaled as the next begins. These changes also give rise to microclimate manipulation that makes our lives so much more comfortable. The deciduous vine-covered pergola is just one of many such examples.

Some gardens are short lived — for instance, a garden makeover prior to sale day or the possibility of extensions encroaching at a later stage may both affect the sustainability of a landscape. Plants can still be used to effectively tackle many problems, such as weeds, erosion and unattractive views. Fast-growing shrubs that are quick to reach maturity, such as grevilleas and barberry, are ideal for screening possible rooms, and climbers that rampantly cover structures will quickly take the rawness off a new building. Turf, of course, is an instant carpet of green for a comparatively low cost, and annuals are the ultimate 'throwaway' high impact plant.

However, curb any desire you may have to plant trees without careful planning. A tree is an enduring landscape feature, and the trouble it can cause due to inappropriate planting — be it too close to buildings, under wires or on top of drainage pipes — in a decade down the track is not something you would want to inherit or pass on.

Opposite: A wonderfully colourful leaf display in autumn.

Right: This bare deciduous vine affords a sense of enclosure while admitting the winter sun.

Wild palette

Inspired by nature. Meandering. Set free. Spirit of the earth. The sensual pleasures of breeze and birdsong. Whimsy. Impulsive.

Opposite: This garden epitomizes the free spirit of the wild garden, where plants grow in their own way, in their own time.

Above: A stone terrace reached via a flight of fancy —
lady's mantle (*Alchemilla mollis*) has self-seeded in all the
cracks and crevices.

Right, from left to right: Grasses and pretty flowers on
delicate stems, a birdbath under a canopy of star jasmine
(*Trachelospermum jasminoides*) and a rose-tangled
porthole all suit the whimsical nature of the wild garden.

Wild design elements

Gardens can be interpreted in many different ways, and for some the ultimate garden is one that mimics nature — free, wild and unfettered. A garden that can lift your spirits.

Of course, natural gardens vary, from woodland gardens, alpine rockeries and seaside gardens to desert gardens and meadow grasslands. The key is neither the plant material nor the location, but rather the mood this type of garden evokes. It is a carefree, frolicking sort of space, having what Edna Walling once described as 'an air of wildness'.

A key element of this informal style is its free-flowing lines. A wild garden takes full advantage of the climate and natural level changes, low spots and rocky outcrops. Blending the built environment with a wild garden is a bit tricky, as you don't want to take anything away from the romance of nature itself. There is a reliance on natural materials such as timber, stone and water, and these are used in a simple, raw way. Unsealed stone is randomly stacked without mortar and allowed to weather, water is allowed to cascade naturally, and timber remains undressed and untreated.

Curves, soft materials and loose composites characterize paths. There is also a limit on manufactured products such as steel, concrete, glass and plastic, although these may be used effectively as contrasting focal points.

Texture is also a dominant element. It may be found in rugged surfaces, weathered timbers, gnarled bark, crunchy gravel or scattered seashells. In the natural garden, colours are muted, with seasonal highlights or small dashes of intensive colour. The shadows of winter or the play of light through treetops are part of the character of a wild garden.

Pitfalls

The novice may think that wild gardens are maintenance-free, hassle-free, plant-and-forget places. But while nature has an incredible knack for creating checks and balances, that doesn't mean your own attempts at re-creating a natural garden will be as successful. In the garden, pruning replaces the wind, mowing the wild animals, mulch the leaf litter and weeding the perfect combination of plants. While it may not be as time-consuming as a formal style that requires regular clipping, it still requires effort and input.

Mimicking nature is not as easy as you might think. Even an experienced garden designer like Gertrude Jekyll has noted: 'No kind of gardening is so difficult to do well, or is so full of pitfalls and of paths of peril'; and it 'should never look like garden gardening, or, as it so sadly often does, like garden plants gone astray'. Getting stone to look as if it has always been there is a difficult task, and planting randomly is an underestimated skill.

Meadow gardens

A field of flowers and soft grasses may be your idea of the perfect garden, or at least a feature of your ideal weekend getaway. From as far back as medieval times, this sort of garden or 'mead', as it was referred to then, was considered the closest thing to heaven on earth. In fact, it doubled as a graveyard in those days for that very reason.

An uninterrupted view of waving, billowing wildflowers that smell gently of honey and sway hypnotically with each breath of wind could be your vision of paradise. Imagine lying down on a fragrant green sward, dotted with flowers, as you watch butterflies hover and clouds float against a perfect blue sky. There may be a rough path mown through the grass, and there is probably a soft picnic rug and a basket full of treats to satisfy your hunger.

As meadows occur naturally in grasslands throughout the world, there is bound to be a combination of plants to suit your climate and taste.

Places suitable for a meadow garden

Meadows consist of annuals and grasses. These plants often have an annual life cycle that developed because their growing period was restricted by drought, sudden cold or extreme heat. For this reason, try to plant annuals in areas that can lie fallow for a spell without offending the eye; you should also be able to tolerate browning foliage.

On the plus side, meadows are perfect 'instant' gardens, worthwhile planting in degraded areas where you need a quick fix, or if you are planning a special occasion and you need a cheap and fast remedy for a neglected spot.

Below: A picnic in paradise.

Opposite: A dream meadow of flowers and rustling grasses.

Plants that **dance** in the breeze

Fine foliage and the seed heads of many grasses add a dynamic quality to the wild garden, as they dance in the smallest breeze. Some favourites include the delightful angel's fishing rod (*Dierama pulcherrimum*) and the vigorous flowering perennial known as willow herb (*Epilobium* sp.). Ornamental grasses are also beautiful for their dynamic effects. The genus *Miscanthus*, which includes silver banner grass, zebra grass and eulalia, is particularly useful, as are the various spear grasses (*Stipa* sp.). For height and colour, try moor grass (*Molinia caerulea*) or, for a lower effect, the precocious quaking grass (*Briza* sp.) is lovely but can seed readily.

Willow herb (above left) will bend and flex, as its name suggests. Zebra grass (above right) waves and rustles in the slightest breath of air.

A meadow planting can tolerate unusually poor soil; indeed, sometimes rich soils or too much water after germination can result in lank, top-heavy growth that can't support itself.

The ideal spot for a meadow is in the sun, with at least eight hours of direct light so that your plants will flower prolifically and the stems will be sturdy. Plant trees to punctuate a large drift of flowering meadow, but take care to use them only to add interest, as overplanting will create too much shade and your meadow will not thrive.

Materials for a meadow garden

For the meadow garden, the trick is to use materials that add to the essence of the meadow. This might be to either catch the sun or mimic it in some way, or to draw inspiration from the tiny creatures that inhabit a meadow.

The effect of sunshine might simply be a honey-coloured feature planter filled with wildflowers or a glazed birdbath, which is perfect for encouraging wildlife, as are seed dispensers. Simple details that capture the beauty of the 'birds and bees', such as wire sculptures of dragonflies or fabrics printed with these motifs, can also be fun.

Hard materials can also add to the mood. Yellow and gold in glass mosaic borders around paved areas of sawn sandstone, which shows the grain to its advantage, will add a glint of light. Blond timbers such as ash and pine left to bleach out in the sun could also suit this scene, and are useful for observation decks, birdhouses and pergolas.

Left: White delphiniums, the delicate blooms of aquilegias and alliums like coloured pompoms make a pretty combination.

Mood board for a meadow garden

Shopping list

- pea gravel
- grasses (seeds or sod)
- meadow flower seeds such as Californian poppies and field poppies
- straw mulch
- willow wands for woven boundaries, a feature wall and garden edging
- blond-coloured sawn sandstone for paving
- rush seats, pine table and cushions
- golden glazed item, such as a pot or dish to use as a birdbath
- water feature essentials, perhaps still water surrounded by long grass
- signature piece, such as sculpture, old harvest machinery, a pitchfork or a scythe

Above: Soon the clematis crown adorning this cherub's head will be a mass of wispy seed heads.

Flaxen mulches such as straw make the perfect cover for garden beds. Rough mown grass paths are also appropriate for areas that don't receive high traffic, and are great for encouraging wandering ways and discovering new vistas. Pea gravel and pebble-mulched paths can blur the boundary between garden and passageway. Some stones even look like speckled birds' eggs.

Try to have seamless boundaries between the garden and beyond. In country areas a ha-ha is perfect for keeping out stock and yet retaining the views beyond it, and a woven sod and willow wall has a touch of whimsy perfect for this style in any garden, large or small. For a more 'traditional' fence, you could try growing a living willow lattice.

A meadow garden in twelve weeks

If a meadow is your idea of Eden, as it was for monks in medieval days, you can create one in your own backyard.

Did you know? A ha-ha is like a sunken fence, an invisible retaining wall in a ditch, which is a wonderful way to create a boundary where you want the countryside to merge with the garden in a seamless line.

The first step is to clear your site. Make sure the planting bed is completely free of weeds, as once you have sown a meadow garden, weeding can become difficult and maintenance arduous. A good idea is to weed a spot, then allow it to lie fallow for a few weeks so that any seeds that were lying dormant can germinate. After these have sprouted, lightly hoe over the area to dislodge them, and then rake the soil to a fine tilth — that is, soil that is clear of rocks, boulders and lumps of clay.

Next, choose your collection of seeds and sow them directly into the soil. You can either sow them as a shaker mix, or plant individual species in wavy lines. Your selection should be true to type self-seeding annuals, not F1 hybrids, as these will not set seed and continue the desired effect in seasons to come. A shaker mix is easy to make up. Just use a container such as an

Above left: For a unique twist on the garden wall, try growing your own, like this sod and willow wall.

Above: A meadow garden with a warm colour theme.

Left: The juxtaposition of this sleek water feature and the waving grasses around it has a simple but inspirational effect.

empty salt dispenser and mix seeds and fine, dry sand or vermiculite together, combining them well. The result is a haphazard application of varieties. For wavy lines use a long stick as a dibble, and plant seeds into the shallow furrow it leaves behind.

Press the seed lightly into the surface and water gently. Keep the soil moist for 6–8 weeks until germination is complete.

After about five weeks, hoe or hand weed to remove any stray weeds that may have germinated with the meadow seeds.

Plants for a meadow garden

Meadows occur naturally in grasslands around the world. You may choose to stick to plants from your region, or mix them up to make a meadow of your own design. Popular European flowers include the field or Flanders poppy (*Papaver rhoeas*), love-in-a-mist (*Nigella damascena*), Queen Anne's lace (*Anthriscus sylvestris*), corn cockle (*Agrostemma githago*), ox-eye daisy (*Leucanthemum vulgare*), red campion (*Silene dioica*), cornflower (*Centaurea* sp.) mixed with rye grass (*Lolium* sp.), meadowsweet (*Filipendula ulmaria*) and meadow cranesbill (*Geranium pratense*).

Also from the northern hemisphere are the prairie flowers from North America. The range is enormous and many have become popular bedding plants, making charming cut flowers. Choose from New England aster (*Aster novae-angliae*), ox-eye sunflower (*Heliopsis helianthoides*), *Cosmos* sp. (white and pink), lupins (*Lupinus* sp.), *Clarkia* syn. *Godetia*, coneflower (*Rudbeckia* sp.) and *Eustoma* syn. *Lisianthus*. More carpeting flowering varieties include baby blue-eyes (*Nemophila menziesii*), Californian poppy (*Eschscholzia californica*), scorpion weed (*Phacelia* sp.), flax (*Linum* sp.), poached egg flower (*Limnanthes* sp.) and tickseed (*Bidens* sp.), while evening primrose

Below: The golden colours of sunshine and harvest can be found in the flowers of Californian poppies, blanket flower, kangaroo paws and Sturt's desert pea.

(*Oenothera* sp.), spider flower (*Cleome* sp.), blanket flower (*Gaillardia* sp.) and tickseed (*Coreopsis* sp.) are fabulous self-seeding annuals for spring and summer colour.

The southern hemisphere has its own beauties. Veldt flowers for an African-inspired savanna incude many of the daisy family, such as African daisy (*Dimorphotheca* sp., *Osteospermum* sp. and *Arctotis* sp.), Livingstone daisy (*Dorotheanthus bellidiformis*), blue daisy (*Felicia* sp.) and treasure flower (*Gazania* sp.). Australian wildflowers include kangaroo paw (*Anigozanthos* sp.), Sturt's desert pea (*Swainsona formosa*), pink mulla mulla (*Ptilotus exaltatus*) and a range of daisies, including flannel flower (*Actinotus helianthi*), golden everlasting or strawflower (*Bracteantha bracteata*), paper daisies (*Rhodanthe* sp.), pink paper daisy (*Helipterum roseum*), daisy bush (*Olearia* sp.), snow daisy (*Celmisia* sp.) and Swan River daisy (*Brachyscome iberidifolia*).

Planting a meadow

A meadow can be planted in a number of ways. The cheapest option is to seed the whole thing with annual grasses and flowers (see page 128), but you can also plant up a perennials meadow or blend annuals with perennials. For this, you'll need to buy plugs or seedlings of grasses and perennials. After flowering, allow the annuals to set seed before cutting them back, then lay the refuse back down as a mulch. Treat grass seed heads in the same way to ensure you have a steady supply of seed source, and keep weeds down.

1 First, make sure the area is devoid of weeds, then simply plant out the seedlings in random clumps. We've used a combination of the Australian native grass *Lomandra* 'Tanika' and the grey-leafed *Festuca glauca*, mixed with self-seeding annuals such as *Cosmos* sp. and the prolific seaside daisy (*Erigeron* sp.).

2 Plant rye seeds in the gaps.

3 Use a shaker mix of seeds and vermiculite, then tamp down lightly. The vermiculite acts as a mulch.

4 Water lightly and weed regularly until the meadow is established.

Above: Encourage bees to visit your garden. Never spray chemicals when they are nearby.

Below: A rough mown path can change direction on a whim next time you mow.

Beneficial insects

One bonus of a meadow garden is the insect life it attracts. Butterflies, bees, hoverflies and many other beneficial insects are attracted by the nectar-rich flowers of a meadow in full bloom. Not only will these beneficial insects attack pests, they will also pollinate your flowers. Such a symbiotic relationship makes a meadow garden an ideal understorey for orchards or a fine nurse crop near plants that need pollination or protection.

Maintenance

If you want your meadow to continue year after year, you must allow the flowers to completely die down and wither so that their seed is dropped as a source for the following season. Use a brush cutter to cut the old plants down, and leave them as mulch. Alternatively, shake the plants to dispel the seeds, and then remove them, or cut down the faded flowers with a mower on its highest setting and allow the grasses to take hold. Don't use a catcher to collect the clippings or you'll also remove the seeds.

Make sure you weed during the preparation stage and after the meadow has died down. Use clumping grasses such as rye to fill the gaps. Mulching with chopped up meadow plants will also reduce weeds.

Water your meadow consistently for the first few weeks, while germination is taking place. After that, ease off and only water in very windy or extremely hot conditions.

A path roughly mown through your meadow will help you access and use the space, and a mown border will keep the effect tidier. Remember, however, that the more you mow, the fewer wildflowers will appear.

Opposite: Rustic chairs woven from willow complement the soft grasses in this garden.

project

Planting a willow tunnel

Willow wands can be used as living structural elements in lots of ways. They are most often used to build a living fence: the wands are planted into the ground on the diagonal and then tied together with string to form a lattice, which actually sprouts leaves. Other inventive ideas include growing an overhead structure, such as a gazebo, out of four tall stems joined together in the centre as a 'roof', or using two stems in a similar way to grow an arbour.

This living willow tunnel project is for children to have fun with and explore. The open-weave structure is really just the essence of a tunnel, with plenty of air and light showing through so there is no danger of anyone suffering claustrophobia, but still enough of a 'roof' to make running through it an adventure!

1 Buy a bundle of willow wands from your florist or specialist supplier. Check that they are still fresh and green inside, otherwise they won't strike (that is, form roots). Using dots of spray paint as a guide, mark out your tunnel. Space the wands diagonally opposite each other, so that when they are joined at the top, they will form a series of crossed over archways.

2 Using a bulb planter, scoop out a plug of soil at each mark.

3 Willow strikes very easily provided it is kept moist. To ensure that this happens, incorporate some water crystals into the soil. Once hydrated and swollen, these will act as a reservoir of moisture for each stem until it grows its own roots and can fend for itself.

4 Place a wand into the plug and secure it with a small stake and tie. Use budding tape as this will hold as it flexes sufficiently for the stems to grow and bend in the wind. Firm the soil down around each wand.

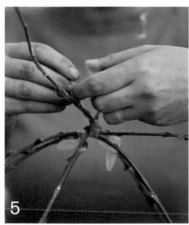

5 Use budding tape again to tie the tops of each willow stem together in a diagonal arch pattern. Water in well and keep moist until the wands have struck and leaves are sprouting freely. Trim off excess growth to keep the tunnel in shape.

6 The children will enjoy it even more when it is covered in green growth.

Woodland gardens

As the name suggests, a woodland garden has a canopy of trees and overhanging foliage; light filters through to the forest floor, creating a sheltered microclimate for growing delicate ferns, interesting perennials and drifts of bulbs. These grow in layers, with carpeting ground cover plants and bulbs in the more open areas, and shrubs, ferns and perennials on the perimeters.

The contrast between light and shade is an important element in the woodland garden. Shafts of sun light up a clearing or glade; the further into the woodland, the darker it becomes, with only dappled hints of sun reaching the forest floor. As you walk through this garden, dank smells and damp rise up to greet you.

A woodland garden evokes the enchantment of the forest. You can almost see fairies, gnomes and goblins among the mushrooms that grow on pockets of thick leaf humus and the decaying logs, which are also covered with velvet mosses and lichens. The trees drip with Spanish moss, and the air smells like moist earth.

In the distance a brook may trickle quietly, or birds cry 'whippoorwill'. It is a garden for the imagination, and for tranquillity, meditation and calm.

Places suitable for a woodland garden

A shady garden with an existing canopy of trees obviously lends itself to the creation of a woodland garden. Otherwise you'll need time and patience to create one.

A garden requiring some protection from the elements can also be a prime candidate for a woodland. When you plant trees you modify the climate and create a microclimate below that helps provide shelter from both wind and sun.

Below: Lichen is part of the forest's rich tapestry of interconnected relationships.

Opposite: This stately tree creates a shaded microclimate where woodland plants thrive.

Maidenhair thrives in a damp position. Even an artificial water course like this little brook (above) can look natural with the right plants growing around it. Ferns love the gloom of the forest floor, but some flowers, such as certain irises, will still flourish (above right).

Larger gardens, with plenty of space for trees planted en masse, or a block with surrounding trees that can be included in your landscape, are ideal candidates. If privacy is an issue in a medium-sized garden, trees are ideal for hiding boundaries, creating the illusion of space and screening out the neighbours.

Of course, there are many different types of woodland — some are deciduous forests, some coniferous, others are eucalypt. If you live in a temperate area you can create blossoming woodlands out of flowering fruit trees, like those found in Asia. Subtropical countries can adapt plants from South

America, such as *Jacaranda* sp. and trumpet tree (*Tabebuia* sp.), which have wonderful flowers in late spring before leaf growth.

As varied, then, as the canopy of trees is the understorey of shrubs, ground covers, perennials and bulbs that grow in the dappled light below. For a truly accurate woodland, you would have to emulate the correct species below each type of forest; however, it is possible to simply mix and match plants from regions around the world.

Mood board for a woodland garden

Materials for a woodland garden

Woodland gardens are made up of layers — layers between the canopy and the forest floor in the forest itself, and layers in the materials you use, adding depth and interest to the built landscape.

Mossed-over rocks and stones show the layers of time and age. These are perfect for paths that lead you around the trees from the house or to utility areas. For tip-toe paths that you might take on a journey of discovery, try more informal materials such as strewn pine needles, wood chips, pine fines or leaf litter, with tree rounds making the perfect 'stepping stones' and wooden slabs or logs ideal for walls or steps. In some countries, tree fern 'logs' are used as stair risers, and they can last outdoors for many years before succumbing to rot.

Naturally, timber is the perfect material for woodland boundaries. It is readily available, renewable, versatile and fairly simple to work with. Fences, gates and retaining walls can be easily built with wood. Staining or oiling timber will help preserve it and still show the natural grain, so this is the preferred treatment method for this style. Keeping the timber rough sawn (undressed) will also add to the effect.

Always let your supplier know what you intend using the timber for, and check the rating of your material for outside use before exposing it to the weather. The rating will relate to whether or not the timber complies with the standard for in-ground use, for example. Some types of wood rot easily and need to be treated, while some hardwoods, such as old railway sleepers, will cope happily outside for many years.

Eucalypts, such as jarrah and ironbarks, have been used for centuries around the world and are noted for their natural strength. Turpentine has long been sought after because of its tolerance to submersion, both in salt and fresh water. Softwood such as pine will need to be C-C-A pressure treated in order to be used in contact with the ground, while Western red cedar is renowned for its ability to cope with wet weather. However, if it is used outdoors it will need staining to retain its colour. It is perfect for an outdoor deck.

Details should be evocative of the forest. A rustic birdhouse, perfect for encouraging birds to nest, acts as a focal point. Seating should be natural and casual — a wooden plank resting on stone boulders, or even a log shaped into a bench. For an outdoor dining setting, choose fabrics that are

---

An **Australian** native garden

Many Australian gum trees make a wonderful woodland when planted en masse. White, ghostly trunks are a feature of many. Those most suited to garden situations include the lemon-scented gum (*Eucalyptus citriodora*), the Wallangarra white gum (*E. scoparia*) and the river peppermint (*E. elata*). Mottled gums are another interesting choice, with spotted gum (*E. maculata*) looking fabulous en masse.

These eucalypts are fast growing and evergreen, and they make fine stands of timber within a generation. Underplant them with exotics, such as bulbs and azaleas, or with natives such as *Boronia* sp., *Crowea* sp., dog rose (*Rosa canina*) and *Blechnum* sp.

Above: This *Boronia pinnata* has fragrant pink flowers and strongly scented fern-like leaves.

Did you know? The algae and lichen that grow on tree trunks are harmless.

Above: Boughs decorated with lichen by Mother Nature.

Far left: Mondo grass softens both the edges of the path and the stair risers.

Left: A palisade fence imitates tree trunks, and helps blur the boundary between the built landscape and the natural forest.

Shopping list

- selection of trees, such as silver birch (see 'Planting a woodland garden')
- shrubs for screening such as Japanese pearl bush (*Pieris japonica*)
- self-seeding annuals for shade, such as fairy primula
- perennials, bulbs and ferns
- suitable loose mulching material for under trees – pine needles, leaf litter or woodchip
- steppers, such as tree rounds or mossy flat rocks
- a signature piece, such as a rustic birdhouse or log bench
- safe and discreet lighting that doubles as an insect repellent, such as citronella candles or oil burners

layered and textured too, such as heavy velvets and embroidered linens. Tiles that have a deep, dark reflective surface or hidden fossil-like secrets embedded in their surface, such as limestone tiles, will add an air of intrigue and surprise to even the most ordinary landscaping feature.

Planting a woodland garden

Planting a woodland is easy, as long as you carefully select your trees and care for them well in the initial stages. You will then have the right framework for planting an understorey, which will grow into a living carpet.

Limit your selection to two or three of any species and repeat them to create copses or groves of trees. A nice combination could be *Cercis canadensis* 'Forest Pansy', with its dark purple foliage and pink blossom, and silver birch (*Betula pendula*).

Plant your trees in unordered groupings, with some lying in close proximity to each other and some with more space in which to spread. Scattering a handful of stones is a good way of deciding how to place them, or throw different types of potatoes to the ground to represent different species of tree.

Once the canopy has grown sufficiently to provide some protection beneath, you can plant the understorey of annuals, ferns, perennials, shrubs and bulbs. For this example, a combination that picks up on the white and purple tones of the trees could look good. Try a combination of white anemones, white nerines and autumn crocus for autumn flowers, and purple-leafed bugle flower, purple-leafed wood violets, white dicentra, white daffodils and snowflakes for a spring and summer display.

Left: The leaves of golden ash glow like falling embers as they fall to the ground.

Plants for a woodland garden

Trees are obviously your first consideration.
They are the largest living element in your
garden and will dominate its landscape. They
provide shade with their canopy and beauty
with their form. Bark and flower will add
interest and seasonal change, but most
significant of all is the dappled light and
shade they cast beneath them. This will vary,
depending on the shape and density of your
choice. Evergreens like spruce (*Picea* sp.) and
gums (*Eucalyptus* sp.) will block out light
consistently all year, while deciduous trees
will allow winter sun to filter through the
tracery of branches to the forest floor. Popular
deciduous trees for woodlands, copses and
the like include *Acer pseudoplatanus, Betula*

Above: White nerines guide the
visitor to a clearing at the end of
the woodland path.

Left: Magnolias form part of the
woodland canopy in their native
habitat in Asia, but will happily
bloom in any temperate garden
provided they are sheltered from
drying winds in summer.

Naturalizing bulbs

Bulbs look magical planted in drifts below trees. To create this effect, choose hardy bulbs that will naturalize — that is, come up by themselves each year without cold storage, division or special treatment. Depending on your climate, crocuses, bluebells, *Sparaxis* sp., *Babiana* sp., snowdrops, cyclamen, freesia and *Narcissus* sp. are just some of the choices available.

Most bulbs are on sale only in autumn when they are dormant, but do look out for easily germinated varieties, such as freesia, which you can sow directly into the soil as seed.

1 Scatter bulbs where you want to plant them. This will give a more natural effect.

2 Wherever each bulb falls, twist the bulb planter into the ground to the correct depth for the type of bulb you are planting, and then pull it out again, still twisting.

3 Place the bulb in the hole in an upright position.

4 Replace the plug of soil so that the soil is level. Press it into place with your foot.

pendula, *Crataegus* sp., *Fraxinus* sp., *Pyrus* sp., *Quercus* sp., *Sorbus* sp., *Cercis* sp., *Cornus* sp. and *Magnolia* sp.

Shrubs can be useful for enhancing the permanency of your woodland, both for screening utilities such as sheds and fences and also as a backdrop for smaller perennials. Japanese pearl bush (*Pieris* sp.), azaleas and rhododendrons, Japanese snowbell (*Styrax japonicus*), *Berberis* sp., *Euonymus* sp., hydrangea, holly (*Ilex* sp.), *Philadelphus* sp., *Spiraea* sp., lilac (*Syringa* sp.) and *Viburnum* sp. are all suitable.

Annuals like heartsease (*Viola tricolor*), cowslip (*Primula veris*) and honesty (*Lunaria annua*), which tolerate some shade and self-seed easily, are great for woodland gardens, as they quickly fill up any gaps left by other plants. They also spread in a haphazard and natural way, lending the garden an uncontrolled, wild element.

As long as the canopy has established itself, providing shade cover, use ferns to provide a delicate contrast with some of the broader-leafed perennials and the more upright, rigid growth of trees and shrubs. Hardy and popular choices include buckler fern (*Dryopteris* sp.), hart's tongue fern (*Asplenium scolopendrium*), hard fern (*Blechnum spicant*) and lady fern (*Athyrium filix-femina*).

When planted en masse, swathes of perennials will knit together like a patchwork quilt as they grow, with each perennial distinguished by its own texture and pattern, its own river of foliage. Some hug the ground as they grow, to form a mat — bugle flower (*Ajuga reptans*), creeping Jenny (*Lysimachia nummularia*), sweet nettle (*Lamium* sp.) and *Pachysandra* sp. — while others will contrast with spears of flowers — foxglove (*Digitalis purpurea*), valerian (*Valeriana* sp.) and *Euphorbia polychroma*.

Still others use delightful foliage as their mark — *Rodgersia* sp., *Hosta* sp., *Brunnera macrophylla* or yellow flag (*Iris pseudacorus*). For flowers that enchant, look no further than bleeding heart (*Dicentra* sp.), Japanese windflower (*Anemone* x *hybrida*), hellebore (*Helleborus* sp.), wood anemone (*Anemone nemorosa*), meadow rue (*Thalictrum* sp.), blue phlox (*Phlox divaricata*), cuckoo flower (*Cardamine pratensis*), columbine (*Aquilegia* sp.), bellflower (*Campanula carpatica*) and Solomon's seal (*Polygonatum* sp.).

Bulbs are like the finishing flourish for your woodland. You must choose varieties that are self-sufficient, suited to your climate and happy to remain in the ground for years to come. The range is huge, and includes hoop-petticoat daffodils, daffodils and jonquils (all *Narcissus* sp.), grape hyacinths (*Muscari* sp.), snowflakes (*Leucojum vernum*), snowdrops (*Galanthus* sp.), bluebells (*Scilla* sp.), *Cyclamen hederifolium*, nerines, nodding onion (*Allium cernuum*), autumn crocus (*Zephyranthes candida*), English bluebell (*Hyacinthoides non-scripta*), *Erythronium* sp., *Fritillaria* sp., *Ipheion* sp. and wood lily (*Trillium* sp.).

Maintenance

Trees in a woodland can be cared for in three ways: do nothing to them other than remove damaged and diseased wood; crown lift them, by removing the lower branches, so that there is more room at the ground floor level (see page 146); or reduce their height by either pollarding or coppicing.

Coppicing and pollarding are traditional ways of managing deciduous forests in order to produce stems for firewood, fencing material and ornamental growth in gardening, such as a thicket of brightly coloured willow or dogwood stems (see the photographs on page 146).

Top left: Pinecones are like ornaments in the forest canopy.

Top right: Blechnum ferns thrive in the dim light of a woodland.

Above: Hostas adorn the forest floor with their blue–green variegations and textures.

Left: Fritillarias grow well in cool temperate areas.

Pollarding (above left) and coppicing (above right) will keep these trees producing new growth.

Coppicing involves cutting back trunks to ground level, so that the canopy is opened up. Light is then able to filter down to the lower storey, allowing plants that would otherwise die off to thrive. This technique, along with crown lifting and branch thinning, can stop your woodland from becoming too thick. Trees that have traditionally been coppiced include hazel, beech, ash, willow, sweet chestnut and dogwood.

Pollarding is when a tree is cut or polled in order to produce a close, rounded head of young branches. The main difference between this process and coppicing is that it leaves the trunk and branch stubs in place. Plane trees, crepe myrtles, willows and some eucalypt species, such as silver dollar gum, can be treated in this way.

To pollard a tree, work around the tree from the outside in, cutting back each stem on an angle away from the crown so that water runs off towards the roots and not towards the centre, where it could create rot. Depending on the variety of tree, repeat this process either annually or every seven years or so.

Watering trees to establish them through their first summer is another crucial step. Once trees have put down their roots, however, they are usually able to cope with most dry spells, although you will need to water them during periods of wind and drought.

The best mulch for a tree is its own leaf litter, which turns into nutrient-rich humus as it breaks down, feeding the tree in a very gentle way. For an extra boost, place slow-release tree pellets around the drip line (that is, the foliage perimeter) in spring. These can be organic, such as chicken manure tablets, or inorganic (that is, made from chemicals). Both feed adequately, but organic methods are better for encouraging beneficial soil organisms such as worms and 'good' bacteria.

Crown lifting

Many trees naturally shoot branches from low down the trunk. This may be just the look you're after, but in most gardens, you'll need access to under the canopy, so you'll need to lift the crown.

1 To encourage a tree with a single trunk and plenty of head room, cleanly remove any side shoots as they appear on the trunk.

2 Remove lower branches with secateurs (or use a pruning saw on thicker limbs), but leave the ridge collar (the skin-like fold of bark at the branch junction) intact as a small stub to reduce the chance of bacterial infection entering the tree. Trees naturally compartmentalize at these junctions to protect themselves, and you should respect this when pruning. Any shoots that develop on your cleaned trunk can be rubbed off as they swell, which is by far the least disruptive way to tackle undergrowth.

Left: Fallen leaves provide a thick humus as they rot down.

Above: Naturalized snowdrops.

Did you know? The word 'coppice' comes from the French word *couper*, 'to cut'. Today the word means a small wood of underwood and small trees, grown especially for periodic cutting. A copse is a group of trees treated this way. The word 'pollarding' comes from the Middle English word *poll*, meaning 'to take off'.

how to...
Stake a tree correctly

You may need to erect shelterbelts, simple temporary barriers of hessian to protect your trees from severe wind. Staking is generally not recommended for trees, as it makes them dependent on a crutch instead of becoming self-supporting; however, occasionally this is unavoidable, in which case a three-stake method is best. Drive in three stakes out from the trunk of your tree. The distance will vary depending on the present size of the tree you are planting; however, you should never encroach on its rootball. Use hessian webbing or budding tape to hold your tree in place, tying it securely to the stakes using a figure 8 pattern so that it can still flex in the wind and strengthen naturally. After your tree has grown into its new position, remove the stakes.

Rock gardens

Many plants have adapted themselves to grow successfully in what seem to be appalling conditions — extreme temperatures, poor soils or rocky outcrops. These plants are commonly called 'rock plants', and they can be easily categorized into those that cope with heat, and those that can endure extreme cold.

Below: These succulents will cope with hot, dry conditions, neglect and poor soil.

Opposite: A living tapestry provided by a range of colourful rock plants.

The first group evolved in the desert and arid regions of the world. They include cacti with spines and succulents with fleshy foliage, even *Tillandsia* sp. (a type of bromeliad), which live off mists that come in over the desert in some areas in the morning. Other plants, such as lavenders, have oil-rich, grey or hairy foliage — all adaptations to drought, heat and wind. As precipitation is so low in these areas and soils tend to be sandy or gravelly and therefore drain rapidly, these plants can't cope with wet feet.

The second group of plants is the alpines — plants that can cope with altitude, wind, cold and often bleak conditions. Again, drainage is normally the key factor for their success as their natural habitat is on scree, the technical term for a mountain slope covered in small rocks and stones, so replicating this with gravel soils or eroded rocks in the garden is essential.

These inhospitable locations have resulted in a diverse range of horticulture. Plants have become specialized to particular conditions — tiny crevices, fissures between rocks, windswept plains and salt-laden dunes.

Rock plants are often ephemeral in their beauty, putting on a brief show when the conditions are right, so that they can reproduce before the snow falls in alpine areas, or after rain in arid climates. These plants also tend to have a striking form and interesting textures.

Imitating these extreme environments can be difficult. Nevertheless, artificial rock gardens continue to be popular. When they are executed well, rock gardens can be exquisite. The range of species that grow in these conditions is enormous and the overall effect can be similar to a carpet or tapestry, luxuriant with colour and texture. The trick, to paraphrase Alan Titchmarsh, the celebrated English garden writer and presenter, is not to let your garden look like a miniature Mount Etna in a tiny garden.

Places suitable for a rock garden

Naturally sloping sites that have rockeries built into the slope are ideal, and allow a better range of species too. Pockets of free-draining medium can be easily incorporated into the retaining rocks, artificially replicating what would occur in nature. In their natural habitats, rock plants grow in places with rock fragments, small amounts of soil and organic matter.

The key to creating a rock garden is to provide good drainage. Rock gardens are also a good method of gardening for stopping soil erosion on steep sites, as it is actually like creating miniature terraces and slows the water down after rain, allowing it to soak into the embankment rather than slide over the top, taking precious top soil with it.

Victorian **rock** gardens

Rock gardens were very popular in the late nineteenth and early twentieth centuries, when it was fashionable to display a collection of any variety of plants – ferns, rock plants, orchids, begonias or geraniums. Often buildings such as hot houses, ferneries and glass conservatories were needed to grow them effectively. There were even specially made glass enclosures built into drawing room windows so that enthusiasts could grow and display cacti.

Above: Raised beds are perfect for succulents, as they thrive where the soil is well drained.

Plant trophies, such as these orchids (above left) and begonias (above right) were prized and displayed with enthusiasm in Victorian times.

Mood board for a rock garden

Heavy soil needs added organic matter to help it become freely draining. The organic matter binds with the clay, helping to coagulate into round balls, called peds, which allow water to pass through easily. Often, added grit and a raised position will also help. Sandy soil may benefit from added organic matter, but it is better suited to this sort of plant material. Even areas that seem useless for plants, such as mounds of bricks and rubble left by builders after a house renovation, may in fact be ideal habitats for rock plants, as they mimic their steep, inhospitable homelands.

You don't have to grow rock plants in a traditional rock garden. You can achieve terrific effects by growing them in shallow, trough-like containers, called sink gardens (see the project on page 158), or in tiny terracotta pots under glass to stop them rotting in wet climates. Incorporating rock plants into stone flagging or concrete slab patios is a great way to visually soften hard surfaces and link them to the garden, merging the built landscape with the soft.

Materials for a rock garden

Local stone will always suit your place better than imported stone. It is also the most cost-effective material to use, as the cartage of heavy materials, such as stone, is expensive. The best idea is to try and locate a nearby quarry. Not only will they mine local stone and gravels, but also you'll be buying at the source rather than through an intermediary, saving you money.

Choosing rocks that have some relationship to the area is the first step, but also consider linking these to your home and built features elsewhere. Does your house feature stone foundations or walls that can be linked visually? If not, you could build stone capping into a wall or pillars at the gate, and so integrate the garden with its structures.

For garden paths, try ones built from irregular shapes of split stone. These are great for slowing you down, ensuring that you stop and linger at the ephemeral delights of your rock garden, and walk carefully enough so as not to tread on low-growing plants that are in pockets of the stone path itself. For faster paced areas or high traffic zones such as entertaining areas, replace the earth and plant-filled gaps with mortar joints, or lay the stones carefully together on a bed of sand so that they knit tightly with small joints.

Stone is obviously the ideal choice for walls and boundaries. Whether placed

Below: This rock garden is planted with bulbs, alpine perennials, cranesbills, thyme and cottage pinks.

Shopping list

- a selection of specimen rocks, such as split stone or sandstone
- a mulch for top dressing – suitable scree, gravel or chipping
- water-retaining soil additive such as peat moss or coconut fibre
- perennials, bulbs, alpines and dwarf conifers
- flagstones or paving stones for footpaths and patio areas
- ground covers for growing in crevices in rock walls
- signature piece, like a carved stone statue
- water feature, such as a rock cascade

Above: A potted *Graptoveria* 'Debbie'.

Left: A terraced rock garden incorporating shallow steps.

Top: A relatively new rock garden.

Above: Bend your knees and keep your back straight when lifting heavy objects like rocks.

naturally or coursed, built wet or dry, the effect is stunning. If your site is sloped, try using a series of low retaining walls, each with its own terrace suitable for planting, instead of one sheer drop. Not only is it less likely to topple over or need heavy engineering, it can also be a great opportunity for gardening with rock plants with perfect drainage and growing conditions.

Building a rockery

Dropping barrow loads of rocks onto a flat piece of land and then planting into the resulting mess is simply not good enough, either for the plants or your effect. Spending just as much time and thought on a rock garden as you would with any other style will pay dividends in the future. If your site is flat, the first step is to excavate down slightly, then backfill with rubble so that your bed will drain freely.

Choose some large pieces of stone, each with a good face. Arrange these pieces with the good face out, with about a third of each stone firmly bedded into the ground. Running each stone slightly backwards into the slope will make the overall effect more natural.

Arrange smaller rocks around the larger, key rocks. Keep the grain of each running in the same direction and tilt them in the same way as the larger rocks in order to create a natural-looking group.

Add soil and grit to the crevices between the rocks. If you are worried about your soil quality, mix equal parts of soil (sandy loam is best) with humus or peat and sharp river sand or gravel fines. Next, if you can, bury any newly cut or broken edges. To encourage mosses and lichens, paint on watered-down manure or yoghurt to the remaining newly exposed edges.

Plant your rock plants into crevices, nooks and crannies. Buy small specimens, as they will be easier to squeeze into tight places. Make sure they are weed-free before you plant them so that you don't create future maintenance nightmares.

Mulch with grit, and water well. Keep your garden regularly watered until the roots take in their new positions.

Plants for a rock garden

If you think of a rock garden as a miniature landscape, you'll see that choosing plants with a range of shapes, colours and forms is equally as important here in order to create a rich and varied garden scene, not just one that looks like a haphazard collection of plants.

The absolute classic rock plants include stone cress (*Aethionema* sp.), rock cress (*Arabis* sp.), rockfoil (*Saxifraga* sp.), stonecrop (*Sedum* sp.), houseleek (*Sempervivum* sp.), alpine phlox (*Phlox condensata*) and rock roses (*Helianthemum* sp.). Then there are the collector's items for those who like to grow something challenging — choose from bitter root (*Lewisia* sp.), edelweiss (*Leontopodium* sp.) and gentians (*Gentiana* sp.).

Spreading ground covers such as snow-in-summer (*Cerastium tomentosum*) and the carpeting pink (*Dianthus deltoides*) are best for large areas or borders, as they can grow quite large. For trailing over rock walls, the intense blue of gromwell (*Lithodora diffusa*) is hard to surpass, but the mauve *Convolvulus mauritanicus* is a good alternative if your climate or soil isn't suitable. Spurge (*Euphorbia myrsinites*) and the alpine form of nasturtium (*Tropaeolum polyphyllum*) are two other options. They both feature attractive grey foliage, which can look great teamed with stone.

Permanent plantings of perennials such as candy tuft (*Iberis* sp.), chamomile (*Chamaemelum nobile*), *Arenaria* sp., *Aubrieta*

Above: Lewisia is a subalpine plant from North America.

Left: Houseleeks (*Sempervivum* sp.) are so-called because they used to be thrown onto thatched roofs where their waxy leaves would help stop root leaks.

Right: Yellow heather (*Calluna* sp.) among a mass of ericas. Both provide colour over winter and spring.

Far right: Pink dianthus edges this rock garden.

how to...
Plant a mini rock garden

Planting up a mini rock garden is easy, providing the planting mix is right. Make sure it drains freely by adding plenty of grit or gravel to a peat-based potting mix. You could also cover the base with a layer of stones or gravel first. Next, plant out your selection of rock plants, then mulch with more gravel and a stone or two for effect if you wish.

sp., *Diascia* sp. and wallflowers (*Erysimum* sp.) will form the basis of your pockets. Dotting about dainty annuals — such as violas, columbines (*Aquilegia alpina*) and alpine poppies (*Papaver alpinum*) — is a good way of filling up gaps quickly and growing plants in trickier nooks, as these plants readily seed into stonework and seemingly grow out of nothing.

Bulbs will also make a sensational impact each season. Rosy posy (*Rhodohypoxis* sp.), miniature cyclamen, *Ranunculus* sp., dwarf and hoop varieties of daffodils, ornamental onions (*Allium* sp.), *Crocus* sp. and rockery tulips (*Tulipa greigii*) are all suitable.

Small-growing conifers and shrubs are also useful for giving your rockery a more permanent structure. Ericas, heaths and heathers are the typical rock garden shrubs, as are rock rose (*Cistus* sp.), bog rosemary (*Andromeda* sp.) and brooms (*Genista* sp.). The dwarf stone pine can also be used for this purpose. Conifers are generally used as vertical exclamation marks in the horizontal landscape, with *Chamaecyparis obtusa* 'Nana',

Chamaecyparis pisifera 'Nana', *Juniperus communis* 'Compressa' and *Picea glauca* var. *albertiana* 'Conica' favourites in this garden.

You can also use grassy tufts as vertical accents. The blue fescue and blue-eyed grass or satin flower (*Sisyrinchium* sp.) are both useful here. For adding moss-like mounds, select from *Sagina* sp., *Mazus* sp., *Oxalia* sp., *Pratia* sp. and cup flower (*Nierembergia* sp.).

Maintenance

Weeding is usually an easy task in the rock garden, with annual weeds easily coming away from the loose soil. The main problem is when perennial weeds with underground bulbs or corms get a hold, as these can put their roots down under rocks, making them difficult to remove properly. When this happens, an application of a weedicide such as glyphosate is usually the only course of action. For easy maintenance gardening, check all new plants carefully before introducing them to your garden, and weed thoroughly before planting.

Because of the free-draining nature of the raised beds and coarse planting mediums in rock gardens, watering should be a regular practice in summer during periods of drought. Naturally, watering will be eased off to virtually nothing in winter. Succulents and cacti, of course, will cope easily with summer drought, but do benefit from some light watering in spring to promote flowering.

The only other on going maintenance is pruning, which in the case of alpine plants is really just dead-heading and trimming, but for coastal plantings of shrubs may involve more shaping of plants to emulate the effect of winds. The occasional liquid feed is also recommended to produce extra good displays of flowers.

Some countries utilize succulents for freeway plantings and the like where maintenance is virtually zero from the day they are put into the ground. You have to be tough to hang out on the streets, after all.

Propagating **alpines**

Alpine plants can be reproduced or propagated in a variety of ways, but the most suitable methods are by cutting, division or layering. Some people also like to raise plants from seed. This method, however, really should be left to the enthusiasts, as many alpines take up to three years to emerge, and many need cold frames or mini-glasshouses for propagation to be effective.

Taking cuttings, normally of a stem section about 8 cm (3 in) long with the lower leaves removed, is by far the easiest method of propagation, especially if you are trying to build up a quantity of plants. Dip these cuttings into cloning gel or rooting powder, pot them into small pots of sand and peat, and then keep them moist and shaded until they grow roots.

Some people like to enclose their pots in clear plastic bags to keep the environment humid, but check every few days that your cuttings aren't rotting away.

Herbs and woody plants such as *Cistus* sp. strike better if a small amount of older wood is left on the cutting. This is known as a heel, and literally forms the 'foot' of your cutting as you tear it from the main plant.

Layering is a suitable method for plants with low or creeping stems, such as alpine strawberries. Covering these stems with soil and nicking them slightly with a knife will encourage them to take root, at which point they can be separated from the parent plant.

Division is the best method to use on all clumping plants. Spring and autumn are the best seasons to 'operate' on your plants. Simply lift the clump with a spade, and then cut it up using a knife and secateurs, ensuring all parts have a root and stem. Discard any tired or woody portions.

Two trowels are needed to divide this clump (above left). Pinning down the stem of some plants encourages them to put roots down (above right). This technique is called layering.

project

Making a sink garden

Miniature landscapes are very appealing. Micro rock gardens work particularly well due to the small size of many alpines. They also need perfect drainage, so this suits container culture where you can specifically tailor your mix to suit each plant.

The style of container can vary enormously, providing it's shallow. Typical candidates include porcelain sinks (which is why these gardens are often called sink gardens), carved stone such as sandstone or tufa rock — a calcium carbonate deposit with a naturally aerated texture that looks aged instantly and allows mosses to colonize quickly. A hand-made conglomerate, sometimes called hypertufa, can also be applied to a mould. It looks effective once it weathers slightly.

1 Paint the outside of a foam box with a bonding agent.

2 Mix 2 parts of sphagnum moss or peat, 1 part sand and 1 part cement together to make up a mixture called hypertufa, which looks like a firm mud.

3 Pat this onto the still tacky bonding agent, kneading it into place.

4 After a few days, if you want to roughen up the surface further, scrub the half-dry mixture with a brush. This is also a good time to punch holes for drainage into the base. We used an old metal pipe.

5 Leave to dry for a couple of weeks. Keep the inner foam layer in place for extra stability. Fill it with grit and potting mix. Plant into this, and mulch with a layer of fine gravel to protect the plants from collar rot.

Seaside gardens

Gardening by the sea offers many challenges and opportunities. The first benefit is the ever-changing view provided by the sea itself. Watching the moods transform and the ambience shift is a sight few people ever grow sick of. Whether or not your piece of the coast is a windswept peninsula, a sun-baked bay or a briny estuary, there is always something to look at in the greater landscape — boats on the water, sparkling water droplets or, indeed, the white froth of a violent sea.

Below: Scallop shells are perfect for lining a seaside rill.

Opposite: Not only are these plants salt tolerant, they can also cope with a constant breeze, which keeps them low.

Undoubtedly, the main design element for a coastal garden is the play of light and water, the feeling of exposure and the tactile nature of the materials. The squeak of sand, the crunch of stone and shell, the sound of wind through foliage are all part of the experience. It is with these huge benefits in mind that you take on a landscape by the sea. And it is at your own peril if you try and fight these elements instead of working with them.

The first priority in planting a seaside garden is to find plants that cope with wind, salt spray and sandy soils. A garden must also have shelter from these elements, as too much of a good thing can become tiresome, and finding a place out of the wind and sun to eat or read is vital for the success of your garden.

Places suitable for a seaside garden

Naturally, being by the sea is the key ingredient for creating a seaside garden. Like the real estate agents say, it's all about location. Without the right location the degree of difficulty in pulling off such a look increases, but it is possible to create a garden of fantasy seaside, like a stage set. The problem here is, however, that unless it is exercised with extreme skill, it may look like

the poor man's version. Remember, you won't have the other components necessary to create the right ambience, such as the sparkle of water, the sound of waves, the taste of salt in the air or the wind, and these can't be replicated.

Materials for a seaside garden

When selecting a palette for your seaside garden, always look for local materials. You may have shale stone, seashells, sand or rocks in abundance, so use what is around your area for inspiration.

Useful floor types include decking, which is great for creating a nautical feel. Decking

tiles may also be useful, especially when used in the intermediary zones between the garden and entertaining area. Combined with pebbles or shale chippings as a border or at the garden boundary, they can work really well. Alternatively, try limestone slabs (which originated in the sea) or travertine pavers, which can also be used outdoors and have a wonderful texture, almost like coral, about them. Sandstone would also be appropriate.

Gabion walls, essentially metal cages filled with rocks, have long been used for bank stabilization and for breakwaters. They look great by the sea. High-tensile stainless steel

Above: Pebbles, chippings and shells are suitable mulches for a seaside garden.

Left: Pride of Madeira (*Echium* sp.) and lily of the Nile (*Agapanthus* sp.) grow happily near the seaside.

Mood board for a seaside garden

Building a gabion wall

Gabion walls are a low cost and relatively easy method of walling with stone. You simply buy the empty gabion cages, assemble them and start stacking!

1 Excavate down 10 cm (4 in) or so to create a firm base. Next, place your first cage onto this levelled area and open the lid.

2 You can cut costs by filling these cages with unwanted material such as broken bricks and rubble, and only facing them with quality stones. If you are going to do this, make sure that you place geotextile material behind the facing stones so that the other material doesn't wash forward.

3 Fill with neatly stacked stones (and rubble), then close the lid and seal it with a wire coil or ties.

cables strung between timber bollards will also give a maritime feel to boundaries. Other details might include chain links, especially rusted ones from salvaged yards, or rope edging.

For overhead, it is essential to provide some sort of sun protection in such a harsh environment, otherwise diners will have to cope with both sunburn and glare. Canvas awnings or shade sails provide the perfect link with the water, and if erected properly will cope with the wind, unlike beach umbrellas, which are likely to become airborne missiles.

Team deck chairs upholstered with striped fabrics with teak tables of faded grey or distressed painted finishes for the perfect look. Small touches — such as seashell tiles, fishing nets, blue painted walls or glass mosaic trims, shell-encrusted pots and driftwood sculptures — will complete the seaside scene. Even old boating or surfing equipment looks great when reinvented in the garden as art.

Did you know? Asparagus is native to coastal areas and should grow well by the sea. Other vegetables worth experimenting with in salty areas include sea kale (also known as silverbeet or swiss chard), sea beet and marsh samphire.

Opposite: Decking and a deck chair — two essentials for a relaxed holiday ambience in the seaside garden.

Shopping list

- scavenged items from salvage yards
- decking tiles and shale or similar
- canvas for chairs and awnings
- salt-tolerant plants
- water-storing crystals for retaining moisture
- stainless steel cables
- decking boards or paving such as sandstone slabs, travertine or limestone
- shells and driftwood
- blue paint or glass tiles for trim
- signature piece — perhaps a seagull statue or footprint sculpture

Working with what you have

Using what little vegetation is already growing is always a good starting point in vulnerable ecosystems such as cliffsides, seasides and beachfronts. Let larger shrubs protect younger plantings while they get established. Even if they are coastal weeds, such as bitou bush (*Chrysanthemoides monilifera*) or *Lantana* sp., cut them back as your new plants take hold, as they will stabilize the soil with their roots, even while they die!

If you have no existing flora, planting some taller shrubs that are extremely hardy and tolerant to take the brunt of the wind and salt will help you provide a microclimate behind them for smaller things.

A garden that is textural, with lots of grassy swathes, will always work well by the seaside, emphasizing the wind and its beauty as plants sway in the breeze. For more height, plant an undulating roll of shrubs, punctuated by sculptural plants to add interest. Significant plantings of succulents and a variety of silver foliage plants, glossy leaves and striking shapes will always look good and survive with minimum maintenance, leaving you free to enjoy the beach and take in the view.

In the dehydrating environment of the seaside garden, sandy soils need an artificial boost, so add some water-storing crystals as you plant so the soil will hold more water than it would otherwise.

how to...
Create a seaside mobile

Flotsam and jetsam and boating bits and pieces can be used for creating an outdoors mobile, which will jingle and jangle in the breeze. Use driftwood as a support, and attach fishing lines or net to use as a base for your collection. Drill a hole in each shell, as shown. Tie on interesting shells and the like, then hang it in a tree or from a pergola as a unique piece of garden art.

Above left: Canary Island date palms (*Phoenix canariensis*) are among the hardiest trees in dry and windy conditions.

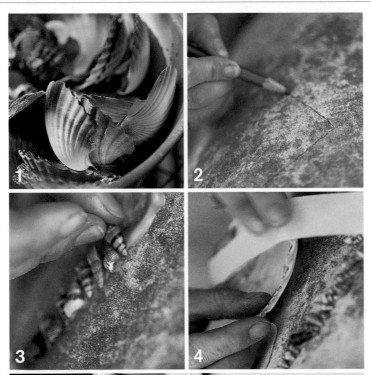

Decorating a pot

Decorating with shells, pieces of coral, pebbles and stones and other items from the sea is a time-honoured tradition. For a touch of whimsy, decorate your garden with seaside bits and pieces yourself. It doesn't have to be a cave or *grotto* from the Italian Renaissance. Give a concrete pot a face lift, hang decorative panels or tiles on walls, create a shell-encrusted basin for a water feature or even give garden edging this treatment.

1 Collect and clean an assortment of shells, stones and pebbles. Your local fishmonger can probably help you out here, especially with the more common shells such as mussels and oysters. Put them through the dishwasher to thoroughly remove the last fishy traces.

2 Practise with your design on paper, trying out a few patterns before finalizing your picture. Then trace this with pencil onto the surface of the pot.

3 Use a construction adhesive to hold the shells in place. Working on one small section at a time, press the shells, stones and other bits and pieces into the tacky adhesive.

4 Tape the larger shells to provide extra support while the adhesive dries.

5 Remove the tape. Plant up with salt-tolerant succulents, such as *Kalanchoe* 'Quicksilver' and *Aeonium arboreum* 'Zwartkop'.

Plants that cope with salt spray

Living by the seaside may be a great lifestyle, but for plants it can be tough going. Salt-laden winds buffeting constantly and chlorine or salty splash from either pools or the ocean have a desiccating effect on foliage, which can endanger many garden favourites.

The tough-as-Hades mirror bush (*Coprosma repens*) and New Zealand flax (*Phormium tenax*) are fabulous front runners in a seaside garden. All the varieties of New Zealand Christmas bush (*Metrosideros* sp.) and coastal rosemary (*Westringia* sp.) are terrific for creating windbreaks and screens. Many herbs, such as lavender, cotton lavender (*Santolina* sp.), rosemary (*Rosmarinus officinalis*) and common myrtle (*Myrtus communis*) grow easily, and can be clipped into formal hedges or left as informal shrubbery.

For colour, try bougainvillea, snake vine (*Hibbertia scandens*) and agapanthus for summer displays. Oleander (*Nerium oleander*), pink vygie (*Lampranthus spectabilis*), pig face (*Mesembryanthemum*), Veldt daisy (*Osteospermum* sp.) and buddleja (*Buddleja salviifolia*, *B. alternifolia* and *B. davidii* hybrids) are all reliable in extreme conditions.

Textural contrasts from plants like Japanese cycad (*Cycas revoluta*), sea kale (*Crambe maritima*), sea holly (*Eryngium* sp.), blue chalksticks (*Senecio serpens*), tamarisk (*Tamarix* sp.), giant lilyturf (*Liriope gigantea*) and sea thrift (*Armeria maritima*) will add to the diversity of the scene.

Left: Working with the wind can yield remarkably beautiful results. Here, a bank of grasses moves like breaking waves.

Below, clockwise from the top: As its name suggests, sea holly will happily endure a beachside location, providing interesting textural contrast; blue chalksticks has finger-like succulent leaves that are salt resistant; and New Zealand Christmas bush flowers each summer with a blaze of red puff flowers.

Right: This amazing fish mosaic has been fashioned from various paving materials with patience and skill.

Far right: Flowers for a seaside garden — the Veldt daisy, gold sedum and Canary Island daisies.

Below: If you live by the sea, make sure you set aside a quiet spot for time out. Nothing could be easier than a hammock strung up between two trees.

Maintenance

Creating a low maintenance garden is normally a key design aspect for the seaside gardener: after all, there are many distractions down by the water, so making a garden that looks after itself will be advantageous.

Here are some tricks of the trade for making the most of your seaside garden.

• When planting, use water crystals to help store precious water and release it back to the roots as plants use up soil water.

• Every season, apply a water surfactant that will allow water to break through the waxy coating on each sand particle and thoroughly wet the soil.

• Add plenty of organic matter to the soil as it acts like a multitude of mini sponges.

• Mulching not only reduces evaporation, it also reduces weeding. Seeds find it much harder to germinate in stones or wood chip than they do in bare earth, and it is also much easier to use a weedicide if mulch has been used in the beds.

• Don't choose messy plants. While palms may seem like the ultimate beach plant, bear in mind that they actually require a lot of work. The seed husks and old fronds constantly need removal and take ages to break down in the compost.

• Plants that have little leaf drop and are kept trim by the wind — such as pittosporum, rosemary and lavender — will minimize the time you need to spend on them.

Right: *Phormium tenax* and its cultivars lend a relaxed air to a seaside garden.

Water gardens

Water provides an instant connection with nature, and for this reason has a quieting effect. These days, however, real estate with a water view has a premium price tag. If you appreciate the calming force of water but will never be able to afford to live near it, creating a wetland, bog garden or natural pond on your own property may be a reasonable compromise.

Below: The water lily is an exquisite flower, and a treat for the water gardener.

Opposite: The reflective qualities of water are just one part of its charm. It can create the illusion of doubling the amount of space you have, as every flower is repeated in its reflection.

A water garden is a twist on the water feature concept, as in this type of garden the land elements become the feature and the water elements occupy the main area. Seating, a floating deck and even suspended walkways provide opportunities for enjoying the wet garden plantings.

A wetland or bog, on the other hand, is a marginal area. This is when the ground is constantly moist or marshy. It could be beside the sea (and therefore salty) or in a ditch or on the bank of a stream, or even in a spot where natural springs come to the surface. The definition of a wetland is simply where the soil is wet for at least a week in each year.

Naturally, this can be due to many factors, such as low-lying areas, heavy, non-draining soils or a water table that is within 30 cm (1 ft) of the surface. Artificially, this can be the result of you damming or lining an area, or even sinking some sort of vessel in the ground. In the future, and this is more likely to occur on larger properties, it may be the result of transpiration beds instead of a septic system being used for treating household effluent.

However, you don't have to devote yourself quite so wholeheartedly to this concept in order to dabble. Many gardens have been built on a moisture-rich soil where the damp conditions suit a variety of plants, such as *Astilbe* sp., *Ligularia* sp., *Arum* sp. and *Hosta* sp.

Places suitable for a water garden

Naturally, poor-draining sites or low areas in the garden make the best sites for bog gardens, but you can install a lined pool anywhere you like as long as there is access for digging equipment.

You can locate a naturally poor-draining area with the simple dig test. Dig 60 cm (2 ft) holes randomly around your property, looking out for heavy clay areas and low-lying spots. After two hours, go back and check if there is still water near the surface. If there is, the area is poorly drained and will be ideal for a bog garden, or you will need to install drainage in order to grow other plants effectively.

Ponds are generally full of still water, which creates a more contemplative, reflective mood. A livelier atmosphere can be achieved by constructing a stream. This water will have to recirculate, and for this you will need a pump and an electrical source, but such a water feature can be charming and worth the extra effort involved.

Remember that most moisture-loving plants require the water to be there in the soil during their growing season. If your soil is wet naturally in winter but dries up during summer, you will have to replenish the water supply during summer.

If you have a small garden, such as a courtyard in the city, you can create an artificial water garden in a disused water tank or other water-holding vessel. Just sink it into the ground or leave it exposed, then fill it with earth and plant it with bog plants.

Above left: A suspended walkway appears to float.

Left: The rowboat on this pond is used like a prop.

Mood board for a water garden

Materials for a water garden

If you're going to create a pool, pond or stream in your garden, then your first consideration should be a suitable lining material, such as butyl rubber, although precast concrete and fibreglass ponds are also suitable options for naturalistic water features.

Covering these up is your next priority, so that your feature will look natural. Rocks and stones are normally top of the list, as they not only give the weight needed for holding down liners but also weather well. They can be used in shallow ponds and streams as an attractive base layer.

Edges can be made of stone, or bricked for a more formal effect. Another traditional method of edging rivers and lakes is piling. A pile is a pointed stake or post, a timber beam driven vertically into the bed or edges of soft ground, such as beside a river. The piles used around the lake at Kew Gardens, near London, are about 15 cm (6 in) in diameter, and are closely packed beside each other, yet lie slightly proud of the ground in order to protect the pond edge and give a surface to work from when maintenance jobs need to be done.

Shopping list

- water plants, including oxygenating types and marginals
- bog plants
- some sort of liner (plastic, fibreglass or concrete)
- aquatic wildlife, such as snails and fish, if required
- duckboarding or timber for bridges, walkways and decks
- pulverized bark for mulching around the pond
- stone for edges and/or turf
- submersible lighting and pumps if necessary

how to...
Slip proof your timber paths

A boardwalk (or duckboarding) is often used as a footpath in damp areas or as a raised walk across a water garden. The problem is that the wooden boards can become slippery with moss. To save you from slipping off the surface, fix chicken wire to the boards with galvanized U-shaped nails so that your feet can get a good grip.

Opposite: A two-tiered water feature allows water to fall in an elegant sheet.

Left: This fabulous pontoon-like deck is the perfect viewing platform for a water garden.

Creating a pond

Ponds can be bought ready-made out of preformed material, but for a really naturalistic pond you are far better off digging a suitable hole in a free-form shape. Lining it with butyl rubber sheets to waterproof it, concreting and treating the pond or, in the case of larger ponds, lining it with clay as if you were building a dam, will make it capable of holding sufficient water. An overflow point so water can run off is a good idea if your area is prone to floods. Also, proximity to a water source for top ups during dry periods is advantageous.

1 Plan your pond as a free-form shape, make it as large as you can and place it at the lowest point in your garden. Creating shelves or ledges for various plant types will allow you the greatest flexibility in terms of plant choice. Start these off at about 20 cm (8 in) deep and 15 cm (6 in) wide, and then step them down to about 50 cm (1 ft 6 in) in depth. Mark out the shape with sand or spray paint first, then use pegs to indicate the different depths.

2 Excavate the pond, using the pegs as a guide to depth. Rake the flat areas, and line the base of the pond with sand to stop rocks or jagged edges from tearing the liner. Lay geotextile material. Next, cut the liner larger than the hole, and lay it in the pond.

3 Fill the pond with water and then trim away the excess. Use rocks, timber piles, turf or marginal plants to disguise the edges of your liner.

4 Plants can be planted directly into your pond if they are hardy and you are in an area where the water doesn't freeze over. To do this, simply place the root ball straight on top of the plastic and then weigh it down with rocks. For potted plants, however, make sure that each specimen is topped with gravel and lowered into the pond very slowly, otherwise the soil will lift out with the air bubbles as the pot reaches its destination.

The simplest edge of all, of course, is plants. Turf running right up to the water's edge is charming and natural. If it is combined with mosses, ferns and marginal plants, the effect can be devastatingly beautiful.

The paths in wetland gardens are normally raised, and are often built from timber, although sometimes stone is used too.

Plants for a water garden

Many plants happily grow in wet or boggy soil. You can choose from the ancient ferns, mosses, rushes and sedges to the more evolved species, including flowering plants and grasses. Weeds too grow happily, so dense planting is essential.

Grass and grass-like plants are the perfect companions for a waterside garden, as many species flourish with their feet in wet earth and even water. Club rush (*Schoenoplectus lacustris* subsp. *tabernaemontani* 'Zebrinus'), with its horizontally striped leaves, looks very striking, while the vertically striped zebra grass is also effective. Sweet flag (*Acorus calamus*) and Japanese rush (*Acorus gramineus*), both sedges, are perennials that like shady, damp spots. Some, especially those native to New Zealand, are fine in the sun, and include interesting coloured foliage types such as a cultivar called 'Bronze Curls'. Other grass like plants include papyrus (*Cyperus papyrus*) and umbrella sedge (*C. involucratus*), both of which will cope with complete waterlogging, and gardeners' garters (*Phalaris arundinacea* var. *picta*), tassel cord rush (*Restio tetraphyllus*) and New Zealand flax, which are better suited to marginal areas.

For flowering selections, the plume-like blooms of *Astilbe* sp. are hard to surpass as are the many colours provided by the wide range of water-loving iris species (for example, *Iris pseudacorus*, *I. laevigata*, *I. ensata*, Louisiana iris and *I. sibirica*). Less common are the

Above: The lotus flower (*Nelumbo nucifera*) is held in high esteem by many cultures.

Below: Pickerel rush (*Pontederia cordata*) is a frost-hardy water plant. Its glossy heart-shaped leaves make it an attractive addition to the water garden.

dazzling red blooms of cardinal flower (*Lobelia cardinalis*), swamp hibiscus (*Hibiscus coccineus*) and the amazing richness of Indian shot (*Canna* sp.). The spathe-like blooms of *Calla palustris* and arum lily (*Zantedeschia aethiopica*) are also elegant additions for the edges of your water garden.

Foliage plants are important too. For moist areas, try taro (*Colocasia esculenta*), giant rhubarb (*Gunnera* sp.), *Houttuynia* sp., leopard plant (*Ligularia* sp.), ornamental rhubarb (*Rheum palmatum*), *Rodgersia* sp. and skunk cabbage (*Lysichiton* sp.). Ferns are also perfectly suited to water gardens.

Completely aquatic, submerged selections include water hawthorn (*Aponogeton distachyos*), lotus (*Nelumbo* sp.), water lily (*Nymphaea* sp.), nardoo (*Marsilea* sp.), water milfoil (*Myriophyllum* sp.), pickerel rush (*Pontederia cordata*) and bulrush (*Typha* sp.), whose flower heads are great for cutting.

Maintenance

Despite what you might think, water gardens do require maintenance. The pond itself needs cleaning out periodically if it starts to silt up. Many of the plants will also benefit from grooming, such as dead-heading, dividing and trimming of dead foliage. Creating a pond with this in mind will help you from the outset, as you can make certain that access points are available. In cold climates where the water freezes over you may need to lift plants and store them until this risk is over.

A green alga can occur in pond water but it is only a problem if it causes excess greening of the water. The causes include excessively alkaline water or lack of oxygenating plants. If there are no fish in the pond, Condy's crystals (¼ teaspoon per bucket of water dissolved and then added to the pond water) can be used to treat infestations. Or simply use a

Above: Still water sometimes suffers from algae blooms. Use a scoop to remove them and, if there are no fish, treat the water with Condy's crystals.

Opposite: A timber boardwalk forms a bridge. The blue wood stain will help protect it against rot.

Did you know? A stool is a root or stump of plant from which shoots spring. An osier is a shoot of willow used in basketwork. Osier beds are traditionally grown in wetland areas, as are reeds and rushes for thatching roofs.

Right: Water lilies make beautiful cut flowers. Pick them when the buds are about to open and display them in a vase or bowl.

scoop and pull out excess strands. Floating aquatics that prevent sunlight from penetrating into the water will also help, as will submerged oxygenating plants, such as nardoo (*Marsilea* sp.) and arrowhead (*Sagittaria* sp.).

Keeping your water free of mosquito larvae will save your garden from becoming a mosquito-infested nightmare. A few goldfish in your pond will keep them under control, as will the many native fish that your local aquarium can advise you about.

Weeding, too, is an important part of maintaining a bog or water garden. Be careful not to introduce over-vigorous plants that may soon overwhelm your water garden. Water hyacinth (*Eichhornia* sp.), fairy moss (*Azolla* sp.) and duckweed (*Lemna* sp.) are particularly dangerous. Check with your local water authority as to which species may have been banned from your area. Keep pond perimeters mown or hand weeded to stop these from becoming weed havens.

Mulch your bog garden areas with pulverized pine bark or hardwood fines rather than with straw and peat. The latter were traditionally used in this sort of garden but they need to be replaced each year, whereas timber mulches last two or three years.

how to...
Plant a bog garden

Planting bog plants in a soil-filled container that has poor drainage can be a wonderful way to grow these moisture-dependent plants. You don't have to be too fussy about the potting mix — a rich garden soil is fine. You can block up any drainage holes with a silica gel. A combination of ferns, New Zealand flax and one of the stunning canna lilies that are now available makes a superb mobile bog garden.

Opposite: Slender, vibrant blue poles — waterside sculptures — are reflected in the patches of water between the water lilies.

Exotic palette

Journey as the destination. Voyage and culture.
Ancient artefacts and relics. Imagination.

Opposite: Horseshoe arches like this one can be found
throughout southern Europe and North Africa.

The scent of a rose may transport you to the walled rose gardens of the Alhambra in Spain (above), or a collection of cacti could remind you of the stark beauty of succulents in the desert.

Garden postcards

There are many ways in which a garden can reflect its owner's personality, and one popular way in recent years has been to replicate places that interest the gardener – like a garden postcard. This comes as no surprise, considering that global travel and advances in communication have made the world and its treasures more and more accessible.

Gardens can transport you beyond the confines of your backyard to a different world, to a landscape far away. This is normally achieved by creating gardens inspired by other cultures and ethnicities. The effect can be very real: with the senses of smell and memory located beside each other in the brain, it may only take a few fragrant plants, such as frangipani and lavender, to make a particularly evocative setting in your own garden.

It may be a simple souvenir from your own travels that reminds you of a favoured holiday, or it could be a makeover complete with artefacts, native plants and materials from another country. How far you go depends on whether or not you want to blend your outside environment into your 'destination' garden, or totally change this space into your secret escape oasis.

Whatever lengths you go to, this is a genre of garden design that is highly effective in creating a space where you feel relaxed and can unwind. Many people choose to replicate the garden of a tropical resort, but gardens that encapsulate specific cultures are especially exciting. Some larger gardens, or those of well travelled owners, may even be divided into smaller rooms, each showing a different location.

Pitfalls

Whatever your backyard destination, remember that this style of themed garden — by its nature — will not marry well with the surrounding landscape, and as such is best suited to introspective garden spaces that are walled or screened from their surrounds.

Another potential pitfall is the difficulty in linking your home's architecture with an exotic garden. A Victorian terrace will not marry well with an oriental garden, for instance. Even if the architectural style of your house suits your chosen 'destination' garden, you may need to add a colour treatment or some sort of covering to your walls, for example, which in turn may not suit the look of your suburb if they can be viewed from the streetscape. Creating this sort of garden will require careful skill and blending, particularly around the margins where it interfaces with the 'real' world.

Oriental gardens

The world of the Orient is so different from Western culture. In the Orient, the placement of every plant, rock, path and stray leaf is given careful consideration. Although oriental gardens often look like wilderness places, they are, in fact, carefully contrived spaces.

Below: Choose signature pieces like stone lanterns carefully. A cheap copy will spoil the ambience of your oriental garden.

Opposite: This garden of moss and azaleas, water and stone typifies the oriental landscape.

In some of the greatest oriental gardens, the 'mountains' and lakes are purpose built to help create the illusion of a natural landscape in miniature, with rocks, boulders, sand and water representing mountains and seas.

There is also an ancient philosophy that underpins all oriental garden design. In the Chinese style, which was developed first and has remained relatively unchanged for thousands of years, the four natural elements of earth, rocks, plants and water are all important: the rocks represent the bones, the water the blood, and the soil and plants are the 'flesh'.

Rocks form the 'skeleton' of a Chinese garden. They are the chief structural element, used to hold up volumes of soil to make 'mountains' and to build water cascades. Rocks are also often used as characters in allegories, placed in such a way that they tell a story. The more detailed, intricate and worn a rock is, the more precious it is.

Water courses through the garden like the blood pulsing its way around your body — cascading down rocks, forming reflective pools and walls of water. The effect is dynamic, as it creates coolness and quiet scenes in some places, raging and rapid cascades or dark and moody pools in others, only to change again into sparking silver ponds jewelled with fish and sunlight.

Plants and soil form the 'flesh' of a Chinese garden. Colour is subdued and

Above: Raked gravel becomes a
calm sea in this peaceful but
highly contrived landscape.

Right: Even flowering plants, such
as these azaleas, are clipped into
bun-like shapes. The flowers may
be sacrificed if the flowers
become unruly.

symbolic, with plants in the lucky colours of
orange and red (bananas, persimmon trees,
pomegranates and cumquats in a warm
climate, or red camellias, azaleas and
flowering cherries in a cool one) used
frequently. Often plants are trimmed into
shapes; rounded bun shapes are popular.

Oriental gardens are perfect for those
who want to create a little peace and
tranquillity in their lives, to have a place for
contemplation. Pavilions and temples
replace Western outbuildings as places from
which to view, reflect on and ponder the
garden. These also have the more practical
purpose of providing shade, shelter, tea and
music rooms. Zigzag paths, dragons, walls
and moongates also add to the *qi*
(pronounced 'chi'). This is like a river of
energy or life force that flows in your
garden, keeping out the bad spirits and
welcoming the good ones. Including
curved lines and eliminating corners will
help it to flow.

Above: A hand-bound bamboo gate and fence.

Japanese gardens have their own Zen-based interpretations. These include the *shimbumi* (the art of creating serenity and harmony in a garden); the *wabi* design technique (the master of understatement), seen at the world famous Ryoanji temple gardens (see page 198); and the *roji* (a stroll or walk through a garden to the tea-house, which is designed to still your mind before receiving tea).

Places suitable for an oriental garden

The key element of success in creating an oriental garden is a link with nature. This is all part of recognizing that the landscape itself is dominant and humans are just a small part of something much bigger. A space should therefore pay homage to this bigger picture, draw in elements of the borrowed landscape and incorporate the best of what's already there to highlight it.

Above: This white apple blossom is a twist on the traditional flowering cherry, so strongly associated with Japanese gardens.

Above right: Gates are an integral part of the oriental landscape: they make you pause and reflect as you wander through the garden.

Mood board for an oriental garden

Within this landscape will be a private place that provides gentle stimulation for all your senses. Carving your own niche in the garden is easier than finding a spare room in the house, and even rooftop gardens on city buildings would be good candidates for an Asian-inspired sanctuary.

how to...
Contain bamboo

To contain plantings of running bamboo, use a barrier. Sheets of fibreglass buried 60 cm (2 ft) in the ground, or sections of large plastic drainpipe used as bottomless tubs, are suitable. The root control barrier is only as strong as its joins, however, so overlap the barrier so that the bamboo can't force its way through a gap. Also, some rhizomes can travel over the top of the barrier, so make sure that yours extends above ground level to prevent this from happening.

Materials for an oriental garden

Rocks are obviously an essential element of oriental gardens, and Asian gardens frequently make a feature out of imported rocks that have special value or characteristics. Crushed white quartz is also essential for raked gravel gardens.

Bamboo is the other must-have construction material. Cladding is a simple way of transforming an ugly fence into an ambient boundary for your Asian-inspired garden, and bamboo is lightweight, waterproof, easily attached and cost effective. It looks terrific as an edging material, as a living element or as furniture.

An outside source of scent — be it incense, an oil burner or a float bowl of scented candles — helps with the scene setting. Add to this a wind chime or the slow gurgle of water and it is easy to imagine being lulled into a sublime state of relaxation. Using natural elements such as water, stone, metal, shell and timber adds to the effect. Other details — such as bamboo edging, granite setts, polished black pebbles, water bowls and rice paper lanterns — will all work well.

Setting the scene

The Japanese and Chinese saw their gardens as works of art, like poetry and painting, and held them in the same high esteem. For this reason, in addition to collecting materials that have an oriental feel, try and blend some greater depth of meaning into your garden design. This will add to its authenticity.

Overall, oriental gardens rely on the use of empty space, or a void, although it is easy to fall into the trap of emphasizing materials. Restrain your use of colour by playing off pale yellows, china blues and soft greens against black, white and small touches of red.

The first step towards having your own oriental garden is to buy or create a screen for the boundary. This is essential for stilling the mind, as it were, and shutting out all the distractions of the outside world, although your chosen screen should allow you to enjoy parts of the borrowed landscape (see page 44) that you have deliberately chosen to highlight.

Fast-growing running bamboo is perfect for large planter boxes or areas contained by a root control barrier as it will quickly provide a dense curtain of soft foliage. Alternatively, use clumping bamboo species or sacred bamboo (*Nandina domestica*). Panels of woven bamboo are another option (see page 196).

Bamboo

Above: The soft, elegant effect of this living bamboo screen is just part of its appeal.

Bamboo is one of the world's most versatile plants. It can be made into fences, fishing rods, water pipes, furniture, food, pots and even homes. It is a renewable resource (so you can use it without feeling guilty) and it is also beautiful and durable. Not surprisingly, its popularity is booming in the Western world.

There are varieties of bamboo in all shapes and sizes – from giants that can grow to over 30 m (100 ft) to pygmy varieties (such as *Arundinaria pygmaea*) that grow only 30 cm (1 ft) high but spread with fast and efficient rhizomes to provide excellent ground cover. Leaves can be variegated with white or gold, and the stems themselves can be black, gold, striped, white or grey; some even have a bulging stem that looks like a fat Buddha's belly.

Bamboo is useful for screens, as accent pieces and ground covers, and especially beside water features, where its graceful arching canes can be reflected in still water. Remember, however, to check whether the variety you choose is a clumping type (non-invasive) or a running one that will need a pot or barrier so that it stays within its bounds (see opposite).

If you do have a feral crop of bamboo that you want to eradicate, try these three simple steps.
1 Cut the bamboo down to the ground and then feed it with urea or sulfate of ammonia.
2 Water well and encourage new vigorous growth.
3 Paint new, susceptible growth with neat glyphosate. This works better the warmer the weather is and the more actively your crop is growing.

Opposite: Bamboo's durability makes it a popular construction material.

Above: A Japanese garden is full of pleasing textural contrasts — the delicate leaves of maples, fine swathes of grass, the smooth sturdiness of bamboo and the crunchiness of gravel.

how to...
Attach a bamboo screen

Bamboo screens can be bought just about anywhere now and are useful for giving an oriental look to rundown fences. Simply unroll your length of bamboo, then use a spirit level to make sure it is level, or rest it on an even straight edge or plank. Then staple it onto your existing wooden fence. Small U-shaped nails are ideal for this. Check the quality of your bamboo screen carefully before you buy it, however, as some are poorly put together with slack wires and uneven slats.

If you are incorporating any large pieces, such as a significant tree — a clipped stone pine (*Pinus pinea*) or maple, for example — or an unusual rock, you should place these next. Position stones onto a bed of coarse sand first so you can bed them down easily.

Then surround yourself with serene colours and soft, organic shapes. Moss-like plants such as little club moss (*Selaginella* sp.) or baby's tears (*Soleirolia* sp.) make a wonderful green carpet, as do low-growing grasses such as golden sedge grass (*Carex elata* 'Aurea') or mini mondo (*Ophiopogon japonicus* 'Kyoto Dwarf'); even a sea of maidenhair fern (*Adiantum* sp.) would look cool and calming, and help create that Zen atmosphere. The keys are simplicity and easy care.

Punctuate this massed green with a few focal points: a sculptural cycad or a granite

bowl filled with water and duckweed (*Lemna* sp.) is the sort of understated signature piece that works best.

Cover any bare earth with an attractive gravel mulch, such as crushed white quartz or smooth black stones. Rake it smooth, or into patterns.

Plants from the Orient

So many plants have travelled from Asia to Western gardens that it is almost as if they have always been part of our planting palette. Camellias, rhododendrons, magnolias, lilacs (*Syringa* sp.), liliums, many roses, some *Prunus* and Chinese aster (*Callistephus* sp.) all have their family roots in Asia, but their seeds have scattered across the globe. For larger plantings, contained bamboo, maples, Japanese cedars (*Cryptomeria* sp.) and pines (*Pinus* sp.) are all perfect. Other treasures from the Orient

Above: The placement of every stone or rock in your oriental garden requires careful consideration.

Above right: Keep the number of decorative pieces, like this stone bowl and scoop, to a minimum.

Japanese **stone gardens**

Ryoanji, a Zen temple in Kyoto in Japan and home to the most famous Zen rock garden in the world, is regarded as one of the pivotal works of Japanese garden design. Made of nothing but clay walls, raked sand and fifteen rocks, this ancient garden dating back to the late 1400s is said to have been designed by the famous painter and gardener Soami.

The garden is highly influenced by the ideals of *wabi* – honesty and understatement. *Wabi* is a powerful design technique that uses simplicity and understatement to allow the viewer's imagination to 'fill in the blanks'. Zen Buddhist monks still come to the temple today to meditate by staring into the blankness of the garden. Some have described the composition in colourful terms, such as 'a tiger crossing the sea with her cubs' or 'islands in the ocean'. The raked sand does resemble water lapping at the base of mystical islands, but it can be whatever your imagination makes it.

include *Mahonia* sp., *Akebia* sp., *Paeonia* sp., *Delphinium* sp., *Corydalis* sp., *Meconopsis* sp., *Weigela* sp., *Kolkwitzia* sp., *Buddleja* sp., *Jasminum* sp., *Euonymus* sp. and *Paulownia* sp.

Maintenance

The precision of oriental gardens requires regular maintenance. Raking gravel into patterns or even just keeping it clear of weeds and debris is an essential task that must be done regularly. Clipping and trimming plants into shape will also be a three times a year job in temperate climates, more so in warmer areas where growth is constant.

For step by step advice on how to topiarize plants, refer to the 'Cloud topiary' project in 'Organic gardens' on page 389, and see page 349 in 'Classical gardens'.

Flowering **quince**

Above: The flowering quince makes a lovely cut flower for winter. Prune off lengths in bud and place them in warm water to encourage early blooms.

In China they call japonica 'flower of 100 days'. It is one of the most delightful blossoming deciduous shrubs for gardens today. You may know it better as flowering quince (*Chaenomeles japonica*), or even recognize it from Japanese wood block prints, where it is often portrayed. The flowers are normally scarlet, although there are delicate tints of apple blossom and white if you prefer. It is a big shrub, forming a tangled thicket of prickly branches although it can also be a fine espalier specimen. It is one of the easiest shrubs to grow in any non-tropical climate.

Opposite, top: Peonies are native to Asia. This delicate pink cultivar is called 'Sarah Bernhardt'.

Opposite, bottom: In a culture where old people are honoured, even old trees are supported.

Left: Delicate flowers on one of the early bloomers, the Taiwan cherry.

Bamboo **deer scares**

Above: The gentle knocking noise of a deer scare contributes to the contemplative atmosphere of an oriental garden.

A bamboo water feature is a distinctive element of many oriental gardens, and the best known type is referred to as a deer scare. Water flows from the source along one piece of hollow bamboo pipe into a second piece of bamboo. The result is a carefully balanced water feature that tips like scales as the second pipe fills. Eventually this pipe empties completely and jumps back up, hitting the source pipe with a gentle knock (thus scaring away any deer).

Right: Placing oriental follies in the English landscape was popular from the seventeenth century. This pavilion and bridge are part of the 'region of China' garden at Biddulph Grange, England, created by James Bateman in the 1850s.

Santa Fe gardens

Gardening in one of the driest places on earth could be regarded as an impossible task, yet the gardeners of New Mexico have embraced their indigenous flora, perfectly adapted to suit these conditions. They have designed their gardens to suit the climate by using internal courtyards, blocking out the extreme heat and creating a shaded haven.

Below: Pincushion cacti (*Mammillaria* sp.) flower reliably and form large colonies easily.

Opposite: Too valuable a resource to be wasted on plants, water in a Santa Fe garden is restricted to a central pond and narrow rill, where it has maximum impact.

Mud brick, or adobe, is the most common building material in Santa Fe gardens. Its colour of faded earth and its smooth texture form a neutral backdrop for vibrant colour. Texture from cobbles, stucco and stonework underpins the whole scene. The lines are organic, echoing the adobe walls made of hand-packed mud and straw.

The Spanish, who introduced the use of ceramic tiles as they conquered South America from the fifteenth century, have heavily influenced the Santa Fe style. It embraces colour like no other garden style. Bright contrasting tones are placed in bold juxtaposition; no combination is too garish, so you can abandon all the rules.

In contrast to the earthen walls, colour is also often used as a feature on walls. It is splashed liberally over some rendered surfaces, resulting in buildings of pink, turquoise, marigold, indigo, lapis lazuli and yellow. Coloured tiles are also common, with ceramics often covering walls, floors, furniture, pots and water features. This creates a dizzyingly colourful pattern that is played off against a broader landscape of neutral colours, warm ochres and the bluest of blue skies.

Use plants not so much to provide colour, as the material world has that aspect well and truly covered, but as striking outlines. The most commonly used plants are native

succulents — such as mother-in-law's tongue (*Sansevieria* sp.) and agaves (*Agave* sp.) — and cacti with trees, palms and vines, such as bougainvillea, casting cooling shade wherever possible.

Places suitable for a Santa Fe garden

Inward-looking gardens or homes with wings enclosing a courtyard can carry off this style, but the warmer the climate and the brighter the natural light, the more convincing the effect. The climate also needs to be low in humidity (or the garden must be covered to protect it from regular rainfall), and the soil must be well drained for much of the plant life to grow well.

On the upside, succulents are easy to transplant and thrive on poor, low-nutrient soils and high pH, root-ridden, shallow soils or steep sites. They even cope with salt-laden winds. Succulents also refuse to burn, making them the best living fire retardant — ideal for fire risk areas.

The dryland or desert garden

Heat extremes and lack of water are the two biggest influences on the desert garden, but some plants are so clever that they have evolved to retain water, capture mists and reduce transpiration rates as a means of surviving such appalling conditions. Their forms are so elaborate that desert plants are some of the most striking plants in the world. There are rosettes, spikes, stars and many more shapes that will entice you. Providing some shade is available so you can relax and enjoy the scene, a desert garden can be a beautiful place to be.

Finally, a helpful tip: the poorer the soil, the brighter the colours and more intense effects you get with succulents, so ease off the fertilizer.

Did you know? A genuine adobe wall, which is made of individual sun-dried mud bricks, bonded together with mud mortar, is a technique that dates back at least 10 000 years to Middle Eastern towns such as Jericho.

Opposite: This collection of succulents was discovered under a veritable mountain of undergrowth generations after it was first planted, a testimony to the amazing endurance of these plants.

Above: Bougainvillea love dry conditions. They are ideal pot plants for hot, sunny positions and thrive on neglect.

Materials for a Santa Fe garden

River stones laid flat as paving, heavy beams or raw timber, baked clay pots and adobe walls, doors emblazoned with iron studs and walls with grille inserts form a muted, earthy, textural backdrop. This is a weathered style; everything should look as if it has spent centuries under the hot sun. To this add the jewel-like embellishments of paint and tiles.

For a genuine Santa Fe look, add architectural elements such as lintels, gates and fencing made from rough-sawn timbers. Leave them untreated and open to the elements so the weather will fade them and give them a great aged patina.

Keep the 'floor' treatments simple. Swept earth, rammed earth, flagging stones, sand, grit, scoria and compacted granite are all ideal for low use areas; use terracotta and ceramic tiles on higher traffic areas. Sisal flooring can also be effective in covered areas.

Above: These spherical cacti are the fabulous golden barrel cactus (*Echinocactus grusonii*), which may take years to reach this size. They are native to Mexico.

Above right: Handmade nails like these will add a touch of authenticity to your Santa Fe garden.

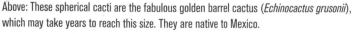

Mood board for a Santa Fe garden

Below: Chimineas provide both warmth and a focal point for outdoor entertaining.

Below right: The stunning leaves of felt plant (*Kalanchoe beharensis*) in the foreground. Although suitable for outdoors, kalanchoe will only tolerate light frosts. To overcome this, bury the pot with the plant still in it for the majority of the year, and then bring it indoors for winter.

Where to start

Designing a colour-filled Santa Fe garden requires not only a dry climate, but also courage: after all, you need to be brave to use the outlandish colours of this style as well as to handle a plant selection where the plants come with their own armoury.

The paint shop might sound an unlikely place to start creating a garden, but in the case of the Santa Fe style, it mightn't be such a bad idea. A good colourist will be able to advise you on the use of colours: creating a feature wall indoors is not so far removed from playing with colour outdoors, although the brighter the light, the more intense the colour can be.

The next step is to think about enclosure. If walls already surround your garden, then textured paint or a rendered effect could be used as a substitute for a genuine adobe wall. Alternatively, you could make a garden wall out of rendered straw bales (see page 211).

Make sure there is adequate drainage in the planting areas of your Santa Fe garden. If this isn't naturally the case, you may need to add grit to the planting medium and make up a garden with retaining walls and planter boxes. Alternatively, group together a series

Faking it with iron paint

Metal cladding can be expensive, but the look of rusted metal is undeniably suited to the Santa Fe style. Liquid iron can be applied to any suitably prepared wood, plastic or masonry surface — indeed, anything paintable. It is ideal for exterior use, and continues to improve with age and exposure to the weather.

1 As with all paint preparation work, make sure that the surface is free of dirt, grease, mould and loose material. Seal porous surfaces and sand back any that have been previously painted so that the new paint can bond properly.

2 Using a spatula, stir the mix really well to distribute the iron particles evenly throughout. Apply two coats, allowing twelve hours' drying time in between.

3 Once the base iron paint has been applied, speed up the rusting process with an application of hydrochloric acid (1.65 g per litre or $1/20$ oz per pint). (*Warning:* You must wear rubber gloves and eye protection, and keep your skin covered when handling the acid.) Within 24 hours of the final base coat application, apply the acid up to three times until you achieve the desired effect. Allow three hours between coats.

4 We planted our pots with *Sedum* 'Autumn Joy' and *Kalanchoe thyrsiflora* 'Bronze Sculpture'.

of pots for impact. Finally, select and plant some exciting cacti and other succulents.

Succulents and cacti as landscaping plants

The range of succulent plants is enormous, which means there really is one for almost every situation. The range of useful ground covers is vast, but includes *Aptenia* sp., *Echeveria* sp., *Sedum* sp., many euphorbias (such as crown of thorns, *Euphorbia milii*), *Graptopetalum* sp., *Kalanchoe* sp., *Sempervivum* sp. and *Mesembryanthemum* sp. The colours, shapes and character of these plants make them perfect for mass planting, and for planting into patterns or designs.

Single specimens that make a statement and add that 'wow' factor include *Agave* sp., *Aeonium* sp., *Yucca* sp., *Crassula* sp., *Cotyledon* sp. and *Aloe* sp. The architectural forms of these plants make them a favourite not only in a Santa Fe garden but also in a modern setting, such as in a minimalist or bold design (see pages 402 and 414).

For larger, tree-like succulents, consider the terribly named but divine clubfoot (*Pachypodium lamerei*), which has frangipani-like flowers with a heavy perfume and a spiky trunk. *Dracaena draco*, or dragon tree, is also striking. *Kalanchoe beharensis* is

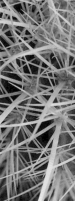

how to...

Build a straw bale garden wall

Fill a trench footing with concrete and insert vertical reinforcing bars to the final height of your wall while it is still wet (but check first with your local authority as you'll need approval before building a wall over a certain height, usually about 1 m/3 ft). Apply a waterproofing agent to this when it is dry, then 'lay' bales of double-stacked, completely dry straw in a stretcher bond pattern by impaling them onto the bars. When the desired height has been reached, enclose the straw with chicken wire and render it with coloured cement (which has an oxide added) to a thickness of 20 mm (¾ in). When this layer has dried, apply a second layer in the same way. You will then have a strong, chunky, weatherproof wall with the feel and flavour of Mexico.

Did you know? Sisal is made from the leaves of *Agave sisalana*, native to Mexico and South America.

popular for its felt-like leaves, and sea cucumbers (*Cereus* sp.) are great for their typical cactus look and the ease with which they can be cultivated. The desert rose (*Adenium* sp.) has lovely flowers, but it only likes tropical and subtropical zones, or else needs to be brought inside for the winter.

Plants from the Americas

A huge range of plants comes from the Americas, but without doubt a dominant genus is *Agave*, with about 300 species native to the southern United States. Many of these

Shopping list

- terracotta tiles for primary outdoor entertaining area
- crushed granite or scoria for secondary hard surfaces
- perforated concrete blocks, or straw bales and render for solid walls
- paint suitable for concrete surfaces outdoors, such as cement-based paint
- rusted iron relics, old tools and branding irons
- tezzoras — small tile details
- sisal flooring
- iron hardware, such as hinges and decorative nails
- secondhand timbers or rough-sawn sleepers for vertical structures, raised beds and garden edges
- selection of succulents and cacti
- suitable free-draining plant-growing media
- gravel or scoria mulch
- suede, leather and heavy linens for soft furnishings

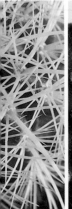

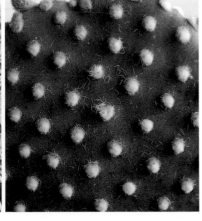

Opposite: The tall narrow forms of the silver torch cactus (*Cleistocactus strausii*) look fabulous when backlit by the sun. They grow to 1 to 2 m (3 to 6 ft), but may need support.

Left, from left to right: The flower-like form of echeverias; the straw yellow spines of the golden barrel cactus; and the dark green pads of *Opuntia microdasys*, which have bumpy aureoles, giving them the name teddy bear cactus.

Above: The ponytail palm (*Beaucarnea recurvata*) develops a large bole or trunk base for water storage.

have a peculiar life cycle, only flowering after 60–100 years of vegetative growth. This gives rise to common names such as century plant (*Agave attenuata*). Agave flowers are sometimes spectacular in size, with the spike reaching over 1 m (3 ft) tall.

Some 40 species of yucca as well as mother-in-law's tongue and cactus, such as the famous saguaro (*Carnegiea gigantea*), are also native to the United States and Mexico.

how to...
Compact crushed stone

Loose materials made up of a mix of differently graded particles are perfect for a compacted, more solid surface or comfortable 'floor'. Decomposed granite road base mixed with fines, known as 'crusher dust', or crushed tile or stone are all suitable as a sub-base for paving. Simply spread the material, then use a plate compactor to harden the surface. Small areas can be compacted by hand with a rammer, a heavy flat-based tool perfect for tight spots, such as corners.

Some conifers — the Mexican cypress (*Cupressus lusitanica*), Arizona cypress (*Cupressus arizonica*) and Mexican white pine (*Pinus ayacahuite*) — are also indigenous to this region. Corn, beans, avocado, vanilla, tomato, chokos, chillies, capsicums and cocoa are edible gifts from the Americas.

Maintenance

Weeding among sharp-spined plants is a dangerous business. It makes sense, therefore, to clear out all weeds and any seed sources before embarking on a Santa Fe garden. Be extremely cautious of any plant stock you bring into your garden, making sure it is weed-free before incorporating it into the scene. If weeds do crop up, use a wand applicator to apply a weedicide such as glyphosate.

Obviously, watering is low down on the list of things to do but make sure your site is well drained, as rot will be the enemy in poorly drained or high humidity areas.

Potting up a cactus garden

In many ways cacti make the perfect pot plants. They need little attention, will grow in a dry environment, only need watering occasionally and can cope with being pot bound forever. Late spring, straight after flowering, is the best time to repot. After potting, don't water for two weeks so that any damaged roots dry and drop off, rather than rot and allow disease to enter the plant. Good, deep, infrequent watering once a month is best. Feed with slow-release fertilizer no more than once a year. Too much food will prevent flowering.

The trick with spined plants, of course, is to avoid getting spiked. The spines can be very sharp and sometimes difficult to remove from your skin, so exercise extreme caution. Dress in long sleeves, glasses and gloves before handling them.

1 The easiest way to pot up or repot cactus is to get a polystyrene foam box, cut it up into pieces and use these as 'handles' for your cactus. Simply push the foam onto the spines and hold the outside of the foam pieces so the spines don't stab your fingers.

2 Alternatively, thick newspaper rolled around the cactus like a sling can work.

3 Repot the cacti into well drained potting mix with added grit, such as fine river pebbles. Place scoria or charcoal at the bottom to help keep the potting mix 'sweet' (that is, alkaline). Using a funnel of newspaper can help you direct the mix without getting your hands hurt. Top with a decorative gravel that not only looks good, but also helps keep your cactus free from soil if water splashes up onto the spines. Again, adding the gravel with a newspaper funnel works best.

Tip

• When you finally do water your cactus, only water the soil and not the plant itself. Any water on its growing point can lead to rot.

Mediterranean gardens

For many travellers, holidays to the Mediterranean provide a legacy of wonderful memories and imagery. Think of groves of citrus, fields of lavender, seas aquamarine and skies turquoise blue, hills studded with olives and cobbled streets with red geraniums on every window ledge. Scenes like these can be embedded forever in your mind, and it can be very tempting to re-create some of their special ambience in your own garden.

Below: Water rushes from the mouth of a medieval Italian font.

Opposite: A lavender field in the south of France. *Lavandula angustifolia* has been grown in France for the perfume industry since the seventeenth century.

A Mediterranean garden is all about ambience — outdoor eating areas, the sun dancing on water, clipped plants and fragrant herbs, shady pergolas draped in luscious grapevines and warm evenings filled with sensual perfume that caresses your senses into the night. It is also about cramped spaces, bustling activity, secret enclosures and the strong aroma of coffee. It is the outdoor arena, where the theatre of life plays and the garden is the stage setting and backdrop.

As the Mediterranean is regarded as the cradle of civilization, with cities dating back millennia, there should also be an intimation of age, whether it be the step tread worn by thousands of feet or the patina and wear on a wooden trestle.

Places suitable for a Mediterranean garden

The Mediterranean climate is typically hot and dry in summer, and receives most of its rainfall in winter during a very short cool spell. This area is normally buffeted by strong coastal breezes that wind-prune plants into tight shapes. It consists predominantly of limestone-based soils, which have a high pH and very low fertility.

This is a region where the population density is high, and medium density

dwellings such as townhouses and villas are commonplace. This has led to the evolution of 'town' gardens equipped with balconies, patios and internal courtyards, and to the popularity of the village piazza.

As a result, walled gardens, designed with some symmetry, formality and repetition, can often take on a Mediterranean look. It is a useful style where soils are poor and temperatures hot, or where space is at a premium.

Materials for a Mediterranean garden

Lime-washed walls, bleached terracotta tiles, subdued colours and the texture of cracked paint and worn stones are the essence of the Mediterranean look. The white-washed walls of Greece, the cobbled streets of Spain or the faded hues of terracotta from Italy are all easily replicated in your garden.

In fact, many products, especially paint-like treatments, can be used to give an authentic look without the high price tag. 'Liquid' terracotta, which contains real clay particles, can be applied to any outdoor (or indoor) surface, giving plastic pots and flooring (if sealed first) the look of terracotta (see how to transform plastic into terracotta on page 223).

Other products have a lime effect, and can be trowelled onto walls or floors. Some concrete manufacturers also supply a material that has ground limestone added to a cement base. This is poured like regular concrete, yet dries with a softness and patina similar to stone. It is also heat resistant, making it perfect for areas in full sun, such as pool surrounds, where you are likely to be barefoot.

Above: Geraniums and begonias on a baker's stand make an ideal garden for a Mediterranean-style courtyard. The red and pink flowers contrast well with the green foliage and the green-painted door, all beautifully complemented by the earthy tones of the stone wall.

Right: This old brass water font shows the patina of age. Resist adding shiny, new elements to your Mediterranean garden — just stick to secondhand, antique or worn items.

Mood board for a Mediterranean garden

Herbs (top) and olives (bottom) are synonymous with the Mediterranean. The terracotta jars (centre) were onced used to store oil, but make a handsome feature when grouped together.

If you have the budget, there is a superb range of stone tiles that make the perfect flooring for high traffic areas and entertaining zones. You will need to lay these on a concrete slab for strength. Look for travertine and marble tiles that are cut to reveal the wondrous qualities of these materials. Both marble and travertine are very porous, however, so you will need to seal them to stop moss from growing on them. Alternatively, you can scrub them down regularly with an algaecide. Terrazzo is a mixture of stone chips and cement, which is poured *in situ* and polished, or bought as slabs.

Protection from the sun should also be a priority. Lime-washed timber blinds or striped canvas awnings work well. Other details, such as small mosaic tiles for trim and tezzoras (small decorative tiles) in walls will also add authenticity. White lace table runners and napkins or temporary outdoor, curtain-like screens can also be charming.

Al fresco dining

All truly Mediterranean gardens focus on food and its production. You don't have to devote the entire garden to edibles, but planting potted herbs and a few specimen fruits or crops will add not only to your pleasure in the garden and provide some

Lime washing a wall

For a soft patina that makes any new brickwork look aged without making a permanent mark, try a lime wash. Lime has been used for centuries to freshen the walls of houses, especially in countries around the Mediterranean, and to help deflect sunlight from glasshouses in summer.

1 Mix up hydrated lime with water until the mixture is the consistency of a paintable slurry.

2 Paint on the wash, using a criss-cross stroke to highlight the texture. Allow the wall to dry. Wash up the brush and bucket in water, being careful not to empty any residue onto lime-sensitive plants.

handy cooking ingredients, it will also lend some genuine Mediterranean ambience.

Because food is an important part of the Mediterranean lifestyle, an area for al fresco dining is essential for completing the look. Use the table as a starting point, provide a grapevine for overhead shelter and a jasmine-covered trellis for privacy, and you have the beginnings of a Mediterranean garden.

The table should be made from a durable material that can withstand the weather and be wiped down easily. Stone is ideal, with marble, limestone, slate or sandstone all good alternatives. Although these surfaces may become stained with oil marks, fruit stains and wine spills, many people think this only adds to the patina.

If you don't like that look, sealing the more porous stones will help. Mosaics are also a good choice, as is weathered hardwood, which can be oiled to help repel marks and stains.

Above: Dining outdoors in the French provincial style.

Above left: With their glossy leaves, fragrant flowers and bright fruit, citrus are among the most ornamental of trees.

Tying it all together

Colour is an important consideration with this style of garden. Think sun bleached. Avoid bright tones on any hard surfaces. Choose muted and soft shades that have the patina of age. Sand, beige, chalky white, muted pinks, faded terracotta and denim blue that has faded and worn are typical. Use lime washes, wood washes and cement-based paints, and cut back new shiny surfaces with a coat of wax or some sandpaper. The desired effect is layers of texture, degrees of colour and signs of age and wear.

One of the easiest ways to replicate this look is to use pot plants grouped together to form a garden. This overcomes the need to adjust the soil pH, as potting mix with added lime can be prepared. Pots can easily be given a sympathetic paint treatment, or painted with a few applications of yoghurt or milk to hasten along the ageing process.

Don't just cram a whole lot of mismatched items together, however. A garden of this sort relies on symmetry and repetition to achieve its effect, so don't buy one window box —

Above: Many Mediterranean towns and cities still enjoy the security of their medieval stone walls. A secret garden, glimpsed through an open gate, tantalizes those who pass by.

Above right: A series of plants — bougainvillea, trailing geraniums and fragrant star jasmine — cascade from one level to another.

Opposite: A climbing rose with a single white flower and a clipped hedge against a stone wall are reminiscent of farmhouses in France and Italy.

how to...
Age a pot

A simple way to age a pot, or to disguise a chip on a pot, is to rub it with grass. It stains green at first but quickly fades to brown and works a treat!

buy several of the same sort and fill them with geraniums or espaliered olives, then add clipped topiary balls of rosemary and lavender in whitewashed tubs. If you do have a collection of mismatched items and want to reuse them, consider giving them all a uniform treatment to tie them together.

You have now started to replicate the ambience of the Mediterranean, but touches such as an Italianate statue or Grecian urn will finish the look.

Plants from the Mediterranean

The list of plants from this region is extensive, with many of the staples and herbs used in today's cuisines indigenous to the Mediterranean. Figs, dates, olives, pomegranates, grapes and globe artichokes are just a few common fruits of the area, and oregano, rosemary, marjoram, lavender, fennel and thyme are herbs that we find indispensable today.

Many of the flowers that grace our gardens are also from the ancient gardens of the Mediterranean. Plants such as

Fig trees

Fig trees have long been associated with the Mediterranean. The fresh fruit is a delicious delicacy on its own, but it can also be dried, made into jams and even frozen.

In ideal conditions, the fig tree can grow to 10 m (30 ft), but in many countries gardeners train fig trees as espaliers. Select varieties that are self-fertile, such as 'Brown Turkey', 'Black Genoa', 'Preston Prolific', 'White Adriatic' or 'Cape White'. As with many Mediterranean plants, add lime if the soil is too acid, as figs prefer a neutral pH.

Above: Luscious white figs, packed and ready to eat.

chamomile, *Muscari* sp., *Fritillaria* sp., hoop-petticoat daffodils (*Narcissus* sp.), snowdrops (*Galanthus* sp.), *Campanula* sp., *Nigella* sp., *Anemone* sp., *Cercis* sp., *Geum* sp., sweet pea (*Lathyrus* sp.), stock (*Matthiola* sp.), horned poppies (*Glaucium* sp.), *Dianthus* sp., *Silene* sp., *Sedum* sp., *Cistus* sp., *Lavatera* sp., rue (*Ruta* sp.), oleander (*Nerium* sp.), *Phlomis* sp. and *Linaria* sp. all belong there. Box (*Buxus* sp.) and evergreen oaks (*Quercus* sp.) are also native to the area.

Maintenance

Because the Mediterranean soils are basically chalk-derived, adding lime to most soils is a key factor in plant survival and vigour, especially to soils with a naturally low pH.

Mimicking the strong, buffeting winds of the Mediterranean by regularly pruning should also be on your to-do list. Use herbs constantly and trim them back hard annually to encourage a fresh spurt of healthy new shoots in spring. The shape of other stalwarts

Right: A popular delicacy in Mediterranean cuisine, artichokes are actually flower buds.

Far right: A spring display of cornflowers and poppies.

Transforming plastic into terracotta

You can make a plastic pot look as if it's made from terracotta with a paint-on product.

1 Make sure the surface of the plastic pot is clean and dry, free from dirt, algae or oil. Wipe over with mineral turpentine and then dry it with a clean cloth. Porous materials may need sealing first with a clear water seal, which can be used on concrete, brick, stone, canvas, leather, timber and terracotta.

2 Stir the terracotta product well before use, as it contains real clay solids that may settle and sink to the bottom. Then, using a paintbrush, apply your first coat. Wait until it's dry (1–2 hours) before applying a second coat, or third coat for a really rich colour. Wash up the brushes in water and seal the pot when dry if you wish. If you leave it unsealed, it will continue to age and develop. For a quick, aged look, add a final coat of lime wash by dabbing the surface with the end of the brush. This is called stippling.

3 Finally, wipe off any excess.

how to...
Rid a fig of pests

Painting the stems of your fig tree in winter with a mixture of lime, made into a paste, and copper oxychloride treated the same way, and then diluted together (50:50) in water, will help keep many pests and diseases at bay. Roses, citrus and stone fruit will also benefit from this treatment.

Above: One of the hundreds of fountains featured at Villa d'Este in Tivoli, near Rome. Created for Ippolito d'Este by Pirro Ligorio in 1559, this is one of the greatest gardens of the High Renaissance still in working order.

of the Mediterranean garden — including olives, figs and grapes — will also be improved by an annual hard prune.

Espalier

Espalier is a specialized technique of growing plants flat against a wall, fence or trellis, useful if you have only a small or narrow space. The technique is particularly helpful if you are growing fruit in other than a warm climate zone or in an area where frosts are likely, as the wall can protect plants from weather extremes.

To create a tiered espalier, which is one of the most attractive shapes, you will need a young sapling or cutting, which can be taken in late winter.

1 To create the first tier on your one-year-old plant, cut the central leader down to 5 cm (2 in) above a horizontal wire support. Rub off all but three shoots.

2 Once these buds have sprouted, gently tie or lever down the new growth of two of the shoots to the wire while they are still pliable and flex easily, some time in late spring. Allow the remaining shoot to be the central leader.

3 Repeat steps 1 and 2 each year to create more tiers.

Did you know? The 'grotto' is an essential component of the classical Italian garden. It is actually a cave or room, adorned with shells, coral and other natural materials and used as a cool, welcoming retreat on a hot summer's day. The word 'grotesque' is derived from the same root word, *grottesca*, which describes a style that is 'decorative with fantastic interweaving of human or animal forms with foliage'.

how to...
Train a bougainvillea

Like climbing roses, the branches of bougainvillea always flower better on horizontal branches, so tie them down and across a trellis so they don't grow skywards. And don't overwater or overfeed bougainvillea: too much water and too much fertilizer, especially high-nitrogen-based products, will only produce leaves.

Left: It's easy to have a display of geraniums like this in your garden. Strike as many as you need to enjoy masses of them, and don't water them too often.

Gardens of the Middle East

The gardens of the Middle East were, and still are, places to escape the harshness of the desert and block out the world. Houses present blank walls to the outside and have internal, protected courtyards, often with sunken gardens, where ceramic floors stay cool underfoot and palms overhead create shade.

Opposite: One of the many walled gardens within one of the great palaces of the world, the Alhambra, in Granada, Spain.

Below: This carving is known as an arabesque, a popular ornament in Muslim architecture. According to Islamic law, only flora and objects can be depicted.

They are also places that have a luxurious quality. Not only is it indulgent to have a shady moist place in the desert with water freely flowing, but the detail and craftsmanship in the architecture, including the mosaic work and plaster carving, is lavish.

Like the 'Arabian Nights', a Middle Eastern garden should conjure up images of warm, sultry nights, mysterious women and sultans, glimpses of forbidden sights and exotic, spicy smells. However, all this excitement lurks just below the surface of what may look barren and boring from outside the walls.

The concept of the Middle Eastern garden has been influenced by Islamic beliefs. For example, figured representations are discouraged, and so decoration usually consists of intricate geometric patterns. The distinctive design of Islamic gardens developed from the gardens of ancient Persia, and they, in turn, feature imagery from the culture of ancient Mesopotamia.

According to the Islamic concept, a walled space contains a symbolic Fountain of Life at its centre, surrounded by flowering plants and four rills of water, which represent rivers of sweet milk, honey, pure water and wine gushing back to the central fountain. The importance of water as a luxurious status symbol in a harsh environment is obvious.

One famous garden in this Islamic style is in the Alhambra, a palace built by the Moors when they ruled southern Spain. Around the rim of the basin in the Court of the Lions are words about water, describing it as 'pearls of translucent brightness' and 'liquid silver that runs among the jewels'. Here, it also acts as a soothing agent, preventing the lions (symbols of sovereignty and power) from venting their ferocity. Water flows from the twelve lions' mouths into the central pond and then into the four rills, a typical feature of the Islamic garden.

Other features of Middle Eastern gardens

Many built structures and architectural features are prominent in this design style. For example, the patio as we know it today had its origins in Middle Eastern garden design. It was part of the intermediate space that linked the garden with the interior. Other features, such as an *ivan* (also called *liwan* or *iwan*) were used. This is basically a garden pavilion or open hall with a high, vaulted ceiling, but it can sometimes be more cave-like, reminiscent of an Italian grotto.

Sunken gardens, designed like floral carpets, are thought to have originated in the Middle East. They were built deep into the ground to help access water and to stop them drying out too quickly. Courtyards built around these sunken flower beds are a feature of Moorish gardens, and were used in a similar way to the later French *mosaiculture* (see page 62).

In areas where water was more accessible, the *chaddar* (a Persian word for shawl or sheet) is used to describe the stepped or decorative water chutes that were common in Persian and Mughal Indian gardens (see pages 13 and 17).

Opposite: The star is one of the classic motifs of Islamic architecture. This courtyard is in the garden of the Casa de Pilatos in Spain.

Far left: Pink and red roses climb the wall in the Alhambra.

Left: An example of *atauriques*, or oriental work that is carved or painted with vegetable motifs.

Below: Rills are a feature of Arabic gardens. It is said that 'the Arabs who love water so much like it to flow like a whisper, almost silently and humbly, making the least noise'.

Above: The modern take on a Middle Eastern garden, designed for the Chelsea Flower Show.

Below: In Middle Eastern gardens, the star motif is used for many things, from timber screens to hedges.

Did you know? 'Lands flowing with milk and honey' is not just an Islamic concept. The Jewish and Christian faiths also use this description as a metaphor for all good things. Honey too has long been thought of as a divine gift: pots of honey, once considered an essential food for the afterlife, have been found next to the dead in many Egyptian tombs.

Places suitable for a Middle Eastern garden

Many skyscapers have rooftops that would be perfect for an interpretation of a Middle Eastern garden, as would any walled courtyard or balcony. Colourful tiles, gravels, shallow channels of water, palms, citrus trees and bedding plants all translate to a modern setting. Also, because this style of garden often features a pavilion, it could be the perfect entertainer's garden.

A Middle Eastern garden is fabulous, of course, for dry climates. It makes use of water not by keeping a myriad of dependent plants alive, but rather by using drought-tolerant species and elevating water to feature status. With climate change likely to affect many parts of the world in the future, it is no wonder that this style of gardening is gaining in popularity.

Mood board for a Middle Eastern garden

Above: Cobble paving is often used as flooring in this garden style. It stays cool in the shade and is often used in intricate inlaid patterns.

Materials for a Middle Eastern garden

To successfully create a sympathetic Middle Eastern style in your garden, use materials that lend an air of authenticity. Products such as geometrically patterned ceramic tiles make great hard-wearing surfaces for patios; tiled mosaic work is perfect for highlighting features, such as tabletops and water features; and precast concrete that has been coloured to off-white and slightly buff tones is ideal for main traffic areas.

The American designer Martha Schwartz created a modern take on the Islamic garden in Santa Fe, New Mexico. Here, four elevated brick squares containing water jets are linked by raised rills, lined with brightly coloured tiles, all in a sea of gravel, stone and specimen crabapples.

Solid walls with sturdy gates add to the sense of enclosure, so important to a walled garden. For details, traditional materials — such as beaten copper vessels, marble water features and plaster or timber fretwork — will add authenticity to your Middle Eastern garden. Decorate with gilt-edged tea glasses and shimmering fabric edged with amulets or

Did you know? The Taj Mahal in Agra, India, is a mausoleum in the Islamic style, built by Shah Jahan in the seventeenth century for his favourite wife. Leading up to the facade is an avenue of cypress trees, symbols of death, and each of these is surrounded by a star shape, one of the motifs of Middle Eastern gardens.

Above: Velvety, dark red roses (*Rosa gallica*) in a copper vessel.

Left: The pomegranate is one of the oldest fruit trees in cultivation. It is quite beautiful, with ornamental, usually orange flowers appearing in spring. The fruit ripens in autumn.

Above: The combination of square and circle is another motif found frequently in Islamic design.

Opposite: A circle formed by four hedged beds. Four is considered a holy number in Islam. There were said to be four rivers in the Garden of Eden.

shiny discs and beads to ward off evil spirits as they chink and glint in the sun. Silk tapestries and prayer rugs hung on a protected wall or brought out for special occasions also help create a feeling of extravagance.

East meets West

The strict replication of the Islamic Garden of Paradise is obviously not essential if you want to create a Middle Eastern paradise. As HRH the Prince of Wales found when he designed his award-winning garden 'Porcelanosa' for the 2001 Chelsea Flower Show in London, it is more about extracting the elements of design from the traditional gardens and making them work in your own space.

Prince Charles's garden was inspired by two small Turkish carpets in his room at Highgrove, his country estate. He set out to capture some of the intricacy, vibrancy and colour of the rugs he had been staring at for years. Like the traditional Islamic garden, 'Porcelanosa' was divided into four quadrants by four rills running from a central fountain as the feature.

Many interpretations are possible, however, and gardens are often designed to feature a central cross, much like the Christian monastic gardens, with a single rill, or a series of rills, or a rectangular pool.

Design your garden's water feature. This will be the main focus, as water is the principal design element of any Middle Eastern garden.

Shade is obviously paramount in a hot climate. Build some sort of protected vantage point, be it a patio or traditional *ivan* or pavilion, and line it with fretwork for privacy

Did you know? The most important thing in Islamic garden design is not to offend God (Allah) by representing any animals or humans. According to the Muslim belief, God created the real thing, so depicting a second-rate copy is an offence to God. All ornamentation, therefore, is often reduced to geometric patterns, such as stars, crosses, octagons, diamonds and pyramid shapes. The elaborate designs may be used in ceramic work, stucco decoration, latticework made of cedar, or carved plaster.

Adding a tile frieze to a pond

Tiles can be an attractive way to decorate a wall or water feature, or can even be used as an insert in traditional paving. They can also add a sense of the exotic to any location, especially if you choose the right style of tile. To make a wall or water feature frieze with tiles is a very easy matter, especially now that adhesives come in such superior strengths and are so versatile.

Before you start, ensure the surface is prepared well. It will need to be clean, dry and sound, with no flaking paint or oil that might render the bond useless. Draw a pencil line as a guide.

1 Apply a suitable high-strength construction adhesive to the back of each tile at five points, one on each corner and one in the centre, staying clear of the edges. For larger tiles, you may wish to add strips of adhesive.

2 Immediately press the tile onto your wall, before the adhesive 'skins' (that is, starts to dry), making sure it is positioned correctly and is level. Larger tiles may need supporting with tape while the glue cures. Repeat the process with the next tile, leaving a gap for the grout. Finish the line of tiles, then allow the adhesive to cure. This will take 72 hours, depending on the adhesive you use. Once the bond has cured, you can apply a ready mixed exterior grout. Press this into the joins with a spatula, removing the excess as you work.

3 Next, allow the grout to go off slightly (start to form a crust as it dries) before going over it with a damp sponge, smoothing the joints as you go.

4 Buff off any powdery residue with a dry cloth.

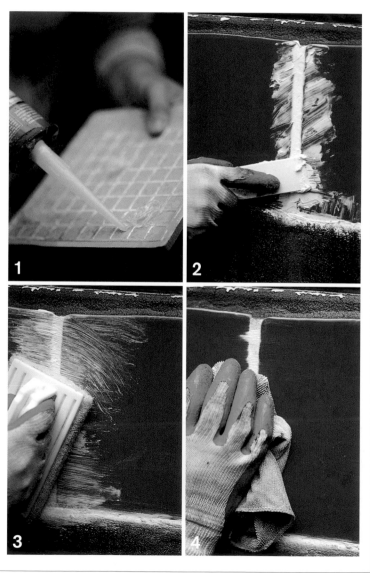

and shade. Or if your budget is modest, construct a timber framework or pergola that can be swathed with fabric.

Naturally, plants will feature in the fabric of your garden design. While traditionally palms, such as the date palm (*Phoenix dactylifera*) were used, any bold-leafed, drought-tolerant palm, such as the bismarck palm (*Bismarckia nobilis*) or the butia palm (*Butia* sp.) could be substituted. The dwarf date palm (*Phoenix roebelenii*) is also an option for smaller courtyard gardens, provided you are wary of the spines and give them some space.

For your main planting, choose species with plenty of rich perfume and intoxicating scent. Jasmine and red roses are ideal, while bedding out with plants like *Celosia* sp., delphiniums and tulips will add richness. Highlighting these blooms against ruby red leaves, such as *Berberis* sp. and *Prunus* sp., can also give an embellished, luxuriant look. Sunken gardens will not only display the blooms better, but will also retain their perfume. Hedging can also be used for this purpose.

Colour in this style of garden is deceiving. At first glance there is a predominance of ochres, bleached by the sun, set against a backdrop of never-ending blue skies. The details, however, are where bright colour comes into play — vibrant glassware, shimmering fabrics, sparkling jewels and tiles, and sun-spangled water.

Plants from the Middle East

Many cypresses and some willows are from this region, as are fruits such as dates, figs, pomegranates, sour cherries, apricots, almonds and mulberries. Rose of Sharon (*Hypericum* sp.), some true roses and flowers such as delphiniums, statice (*Limonium* sp.), cyclamen, *Verbascum* sp., *Borago* sp., *Salvia* sp., foxtail lilies (*Eremurus* sp.), tulips,

Above: The mulberry tree forms a dense canopy that in summer is laden with fruit.

Fritillaria sp., *Crocus* sp. and some irises are also native.

Beside the date palm, bismarck palm (*Bismarckia nobilis*), Mediterranean fan palm (*Chamaerops* sp.), latan palm (*Latania* sp.) and feather duster palm (*Ravenea* sp.) are also popular.

Maintenance

The maintenance level of this style of garden is really very low. Pruning hedging and perhaps indulging in an annual bedding tapestry would be the most significant drains on your time, apart from keeping your water features clean and working properly.

Did you know? One of the most famous gardens in the Alhambra is the Court of Arrayanes, which is the centre of the royal palace. *Arrayan* is the Arabic word for myrtle, and it is this sweet-smelling plant that lines the rectangular pool in two perfectly clipped straight rows. Myrtle is believed to be descended from *myrtos*, the Greek herb of love, which was planted around the temples of Venus.

Tropical Balinese-style gardens

The paradise garden is a popular image in various religions, and according to many who visit South-East Asia, it can be found in Bali. A haven of fabulous fruit and intoxicating fragrances, its breathtaking gardens and lushness fill the entire landscape, which is carved into terraces and rice paddies.

The predominant colour of the tropical garden is green, although vibrant touches of colour — shades of flamingo pink, mango yellow and Caribbean blue — can be carried off successfully in the white-hot light. Traditional backyards are communal affairs where herbs, vegetables and coconut palms dominate, but the more commercial landscapes include splashes of brash foliage plants such as acalypha and crotons (*Codiaeum* sp.), bromeliads and dracaenas, as well as flowering hibiscus, lotus (*Nelumbo* sp.), frangipani (*Plumeria* sp.) and bougainvillea adding touches of extravagance.

Stone, wood and bamboo are the dominant building materials, forming a rich textural background that contrasts well with the shiny green foliage of palm fronds and lotus leaves. Additional colour is provided as ephemeral touches during times of celebration, when lanterns and ornaments are festooned gaily, and fruit and floral tributes adorn temples.

A traditional Balinese garden follows a strict symbolic layout. Located in the north-east is the household's temple, likened to the head of the body, where the family meets to pray and meditate. Linked to this are the living quarters — the trunk of the body — and in the south-west are the kitchen, toilet, garbage and food storage areas — the bowels.

Below: The gorgeous striations of red, purple and orange on the leaves of the Indian shot plant called *Canna* 'Tropicana'.

Opposite: A water garden of lotus, water lily and papyrus.

Places suitable for a tropical Balinese-style garden

Rainfall and temperature are the two limiting factors when creating a lush, tropical-style garden. For true tropical and subtropical gardens you'll need a frost-free area or a heated glasshouse. As a useful litmus test, check whether oranges grow in your area, and if they do, chances are you'll be able to grow some other tropical-style beauties.

But it is possible to create a similar look in cooler areas by carefully selecting cold-tolerant species with similar characteristics. Cold-tolerant plants include lady palm (*Rhapis* sp.) (which will need protection from frost while young), the Chinese windmill palm (*Trachycarpus fortunei*), sago palm (*Cycas* sp.), New Zealand flax (*Phormium tenax*) and all the other grasses. Bromeliads are hardy down to 10°C (50°F); cordylines and philodendrons can be grown in frost-free warmer zones only.

If you really want this look but live in an area where the winters are too cold, consider planting your garden in pots and keeping them indoors until the chance of frost has gone. Alternatively, limit this style of garden to your sunroom or pool house, but make it a large enough space in which to create a tropical oasis.

Opposite, top: This small courtyard decked out in tropical foliage is the perfect urban oasis.

Opposite, bottom: Water lilies that hold their blooms up high are normally tropical varieties.

Right: Although native to South America, bromeliads grow happily in any tropical zone.

Right: Carving is a popular craft in Bali, and many statues and garden ornaments made there are available worldwide.

Below: Large, lush leaves of various shapes and sizes characterize the tropical garden style.

Materials for a tropical Balinese-style garden

Wood and bamboo are the most common building materials in a tropical garden and are often combined with thatch to create outdoor rooms or pavilions. These are decorated with brightly painted teak screens and elaborate latticework panels, highly carved or sometimes inlaid with other timbers, shell or stone. Interestingly, these panels are often stripped back or worn to reveal partial paintwork only for the world market, as the brightness of their true colours, although culturally authentic, doesn't have as much commercial value.

Garden beds should be mulched with wood chip or bark fines so that they can be self-mulching once the garden is established. This is also useful for meandering garden paths, although teak decking is better for high traffic areas. Paving for the main entertainment areas may take the form of elevated timber decks.

Stone, such as rumbled marble and pebbles, can look fantastic when used both as a feature wall or an insert in paved areas. Dark grey or inky black volcanic stone is common across this area. Soft enough for carving, the stone has been used to make all sorts of ornamentation, from statuary and figures of Buddha to bowls and lanterns. Other details, such as frog statues, show this culture's fascination with amphibious creatures. White limestone is also used for carving, and lotus flowers are a popular subject.

Bamboo and rattan, which comes from an Indian climbing palm, are woven into furniture. Lanterns, glazed pots, shade umbrellas and garlands add touches of colour and a feeling of festivity.

Mood board for a tropical Balinese-style garden

How to structure this style

Creating a Balinese garden is about attaining a careful balance between restful shade, cooling water and lush greens. Bright tropical blooms, the sparking quality of moving water and the intense heat and humidity of the tropics all contribute to the luxuriant atmosphere of this garden style. It is generally a curvaceous style, with meandering paths and quiet retreats.

The modern tropical-style garden doesn't follow the traditional layout of a communal garden, but uses a water feature or pool as a focus. This is normally flanked by a garden pavilion, which (in traditional Balinese style) has a thatched roof. Carved teak panels

Did you know? Any amphibious creature is treated with reverence in the Balinese culture. They are an allegory for being halfway between heaven and earth, or in reality, able to cope with water and land. Consequently, frogs regularly feature in statuary.

Shopping list

- brush panels for fencing
- carved teak panel for decoration and privacy
- decking squares
- statuary such as a Buddha or frog
- casual rattan or bamboo furniture
- water feature – either a bowl for still water or a sunken fibreglass moulded pond with sympathetic planting
- aquatics, such as water lilies and lotus plants and reeds
- lush plants like palms and Abyssinian bananas
- flowering plants such as frangipani, heliconias and hibiscus
- an extravagant touch such as a flowering bat plant or potted orchid
- candles, lanterns and colourful parasols for decoration

provide shade from the hot sun and gamelan (Balinese) music can almost be heard in the background.

The garden itself is best set up as a series of layers or storeys. Gargantuan figs, palms and flowering trees make up the upper storey while lush evergreens and exotic flowers can create a middle storey. The garden floor is best kept as flat planes of colourful ground covers or luscious ferns, while simple serpentine paths meandering through the jungle-like garden lead you on to new discoveries. Island beds can work well in this style of garden.

Clearings and curving ponds provide some respite from the lushness, which otherwise could become overbearing. The lotus flower often fills watery havens, as it has special spiritual significance to the Hindu culture as the symbol of life. Even small stone water dishes provide a cooling reprieve from the heat and humidity.

Plants from Indonesia and South-East Asia

Many perfumed plants originate in this region of the tropics. This is especially useful in design terms as they can be placed to advantage near pavilions and paths. *Hoya* sp., ylang-ylang (*Cananga odorata*) and *Michelia* sp. are particularly delicious, especially at night when their scent is strongest.

Opposite: The superb blooms of heliconia are like a living garland.

Below left: A tropical foliage effect can be achieved in cooler climates with lush leaves, such as the hosta and arum.

Below: The bearer of stunning flowers in summer and autumn, the crepe myrtle easily adapts to a wide range of climates.

Cleaning your water feature

There are basically two ways you can go here. One is to create a totally sterile environment with enough chlorine bleach or salt to prevent algae from growing. This may be ideal for a stone bowl that is supposed to stay pristine and clear, but is inappropriate for a pond that is home to fish and pond plants. In this situation, a better solution is to help nature to create its own balance: provide all the necessary ingredients — a mix of oxygenating plants, fish to eat up algae and snails to clean up decaying vegetable matter.

1 Clean out the pond by removing debris and leaf litter.

2 Scrub any accessible surfaces. Put in a selection of plants, both oxygenating and surface spreading. These work in harmony, keeping the water fresh and the sunlight out and this, in turn, stops algae from attaining a hold. Add fresh water slowly so as not to disturb the plant-growing medium. Add a water pH stabilizer or water conditioner, which will get the water just right for fish.

3 Add fish, but don't empty them straight into the pond. While they are still in their plastic bag of water, lower them into the pond and leave them there for an hour or so, then open the bag and let them swim out. Try and keep leaves and other debris clear of the pond so that they don't blow in and rot. If slight algal blooms occur, add some Condy's crystals to the water (see page 181).

Superb flowering trees are also useful plants in a tropical garden. The golden rain tree (*Cassia fistula*), poinciana (*Delonix* sp.) and crepe myrtle (*Lagerstroemia indica*) all have gorgeous blooms, right at summer time when you're outside using the garden most. Some ground covers, such as *Nepenthes* sp., *Lysimachia* sp. and goldfish plant (*Columnea gloriosa*) are also from this region, as are wonderful flowering *Thunbergia* sp., *Heliconia* sp., ginger (*Zingiber* sp.), bat plants (*Tacca integrifolia*), orchids (including *Vanda* sp. and *Dendrobium* sp.) and the insectivorous pitcher plants (*Sarracenia* sp.).

Filling your garden with exotic edibles is another part of the tropical fantasy. Edible plants may include lime, mango, jackfruit, corn, rice, cassava, taro, sweet potato, turmeric and ginger as well as many Asian greens and vegetables.

Maintenance

In the right climate, tropical and subtropical plants can easily romp away. Rapid growth, bordering on rapacious, is commonplace and can lead to garden escapees, which harm the environment, or to less vigorous species being overshadowed, which may play havoc with your garden design. Careful selection and maintenance is therefore needed to keep exuberant growth in check.

Underplanting the middle storey to continue effective screening or layering, removing dead palm fronds and keeping ground covers in check are just some of the tasks involved. Mulching in autumn will help to keep the soil warm, and liquid fertilizing with seaweed solution will help maintain lush foliage growth. Keep weeds out of ground covers by painting glyphosate directly onto offending foliage with either a paintbrush or sponge brush.

The ubiquitous lawn is another feature that needs a substitute in the tropical garden. Because of the continual growing season, lawns in these regions need constant mowing and they often succumb to fungal attack. A better option is to plant swathes of ground covers, some of which can even be mowed on a high setting or cut back with a brush cutter once a season to keep them in shape.

Top: The tropical blooms of frangipani have a heavenly scent. They range in colour from pure white and soft pink to brick orange and burgundy red.

Above: Hibiscus are native to China.

Above right: Coconut palms are easy to grow indoors if you can get your hands on a fresh seed.

Right: Perhaps one of the most beautiful trees in the world, the poinciana must be grown in a frost-free area or it won't flower.

Colour palette

Painted feelings. White, Antarctic fresh. Black,
shadow and darkness. The warmth of burnt
umber spiked with tangerine. The airy cool of
turquoise and sky. Mystical plum. Gleeful yellow.

Opposite: Bursts of ephemeral colour are provided by these
African corn lilies (*Ixia* sp.).

Above: *Rosa glauca*'s stunning pewter-coloured leaves tinged with pink team well with other plants, such as these stately foxgloves.

Right: *Rosa canina* is the common briar rose, with scented bluish pink single flowers and orangey red hips through winter. It was often used in Gertrude Jekyll's day as an understock for standard roses.

Centre: The rosy pink flowers of *R. glauca*.

Far right: Foxgloves are biennials, which means they take two years to complete their life cycle. They then go to seed, and have the most delightful way of popping up everywhere and anywhere in the garden.

Planting with colour

Although colour is normally just one element in a range of design tools, it can also be used as the essential ingredient and basis for a theme.

For the true plant enthusiast, this is not a bad technique or theme to follow. It is easy to become seduced by the range of species that you simply 'must have', but by linking plants together with colour you can create a united theme that has a place for many treasures.

Colours are so linked to our emotive response to the environment that they have the ability to inspire, calm, enrage and empower. Colour can be used in a wide range of styles, from the oriental garden to the minimalist garden and the entire range in between.

Pitfalls

It is easy to become so seduced by colour that the other elements can lie unused. Remember to think of the big picture — the way foliage changes colour from one season to another and also the fact that a flower's season is limited — and you'll want to appreciate your garden for more than one brief period a year. So, think about a plant's other features, such as foliage, form, stem and seed pods.

Colour theories

Colour is a dominating influence in our lives, and people have studied and theorized about it for many centuries. In 1666 Sir Isaac Newton first discovered that white reflects back all colours or wavelengths, while black absorbs all colours or wavelengths. Just over 100 years later, in 1770, the scientist and naturalist Moses Harris created the first colour wheel, based on the scientific colour theory. In the 1920s, Johannes Itten, an important player in the Bauhaus movement (see page 22), added the secondary and tertiary colours to the wheel. Itten was also responsible for the idea that colours can have a warm or cool base, dividing the colour spectrum into halves, one warm and one cool. The colour wheel today is a graphic representation that shows the relationships among colours and is helpful for choosing harmonious colour combinations. It consists of three primary (red, blue, yellow) and three secondary (purple, green, orange) colours, separated by six intermediate colours.

Colour is so strong an element of design that many designers are tempted to use it as the basis or theme for the whole design. This has been the case for much of the modern gardening era, especially since two French garden writers, Decaisne and Naudin, elaborated on the scientific colour theory and translated its effects into the garden in a book published in 1864. They stated in their *Manuel de l'Amateur de Jardin*: 'All primary

Made from flower colours, this simple colour wheel comprises the three primary colours of red, blue and yellow interspersed with the three secondary colours of purple, green and orange.

colours, when pure, contrast pleasantly with each other. In the same way complementary colours contrast with each other to great advantage.' Claude Monet and Gertrude Jekyll, two passionate gardeners and colourists, are thought to have been greatly influenced by this publication.

The Impressionists

The scientific colour theory underpinned the Impressionists' use of colour in their art works. As a group, the Impressionists were the first painters to translate contrasts of light and shade into colour on the canvas — for example, using purple as a shadow on a yellow hay field rather than black tints and tones. Like Monet, many of these painters were also keen gardeners, while others were astute observers of nature and the effects of colour. Cézanne observed that 'Monet is only an eye — but what an eye'. Vincent van Gogh once wrote to his brother Theo: 'Spring is the tender young shoots of wheat and pink apple blossom. Autumn is the contrast of yellow leaves with the shades of violet. Winter is white with black silhouettes. If summer is taken to be a contrast of blues with the orange of golden, bronze grain, it is possible to paint a picture in complementary colours for every one of the seasons.'

Did you know? If a plant's scientific name includes the following Latin epithets, then it is revealing something about its colouring – for example, *alba* = white, *carnea* = flesh-coloured, *flava* = pale yellow, *nigra* = black, *rubra* = red, *violacea* = violet.

The Arts and Crafts Movement

In 1888 the Arts and Crafts Movement began. It emphasized craftsmanship and quality as a reaction against the mass production values of the Industrial Revolution. Within this movement, the great plantswoman Gertrude Jekyll gained an audience for skillfully creating flower borders.

By the turn of the twentieth century Vita Sackville-West had popularized the idea of monochromatic planting with her most famous work, the White Garden at Sissinghurst in Kent. Here white flowers wash over a serene backdrop of green, the flowers performing month after month while still adhering to the strict code of colour.

Of course, it is not just flower colour that creates a scheme. Foliage, stems and bark are other natural elements that add to the overall

Above: The fresh combination of white and silver plants repeated in this border adds a sense of distance, depth and rhythm.

Left: A complementary colour scheme — the tiny, glittering yellow flowers of *Bulbinella floribunda*, a South African bulb, show up brightly against blue and purple flowers.

picture. The colours of materials and hard surfaces also have an impact on your design. When sourcing these, remember that you can use an array of manufactured and naturally occurring materials to add colour or tie in with an existing scheme.

Colour becomes modern

The burgeoning influence of the Modern Movement was naturally going to make a huge impact on the way gardeners used colour in the future. In what was probably one of the earliest reinterpretations of the classic parterre, French designers André and Paul Vera blended classicism with colour and brightness, as well as with modern materials such as concrete. The results, seen in public and private gardens throughout France in the 1920s, paid homage to the French gardening traditions of the parterre but used bold colours and native plants.

In the late twentieth century Martha Schwartz reinterpreted the colour wheel and classic French parterre (a garden of pattern and line; see page 349) using biscuits, called Necco wafers, and coloured tyres in her Transfiguration of the Commonplace, a garden at Killian Court, Massachusetts Institute of Technology. Schwartz also designed a contemporary private residence in Texas that she treated as an updated version of the traditional *hortus conclusus* or enclosed garden of the Renaissance, a twist on the colour gardens of the Edwardian period. It is a garden of walls, almost like a maze, with each wall painted in a dazzling colour. There is a gold garden; a changing room with pink walls, prickly cacti and mirrors; an orange room; and even a bathing room which is white with blue glass shards embedded in the tops of the walls.

Towards the end of the twentieth century designers were still experimenting with the effects of colour. In a show garden installation, the French landscape architect and designer Bernard Lassus created the most amazing garden based on the optical illusions that can be achieved through conceptual art. He interplanted bright sinuous lines of colour with pots of dazzling colour — gold and yellow marigolds, and red and purple petunias. The result is a reflection on what Lassus calls 'imaginary space' and 'real space'.

Colour and its many moods

Colour has always had symbolic significance, with bright, vivid colour suggesting happiness and vitality, and cool, subdued colours conveying reflection and contemplation. Even the English language has adopted colour to reflect emotion — think of 'feeling blue' or 'in a black mood'. For this reason, gardens are most effective when colour is teamed with the ambience you are trying to create. Use soft colours where you want to create a serene scene, and use bright colours in lively areas such as entertainment zones.

Using colour to vary mood is, of course, a common tool for interior designers. Another technique is to vary accessories according to the season to make you feel more comfortable. White linen and cooling greens and blues can be used to 'cool down' a summer space, and hot colours to warm up a winter room. Flowers and foliage can be used in the same way in the garden — for example, use the fiery blaze of autumn plantings to enliven a bleak day.

Colour has a place in the spiritual world too. Chakras, the energy points of the body

Opposite: The grey skies of autumn are lit up by the display of foliage fire.

Above: Silver is the best colour tool of all for gardeners. It can be used to enhance any colour scheme and it rarely offends, only reinforces.

according to yoga practitioners and others, are also colour based, with each energy centre supposedly being a colour. Some people believe in 'auras' — an envelope of light that surrounds you — and can read your personality according to the colour of your aura.

The effect of location and climate

When you choose a painting to hang in your home, you can enhance its beauty in various ways: you can paint the room in a colour that brings out the best in the art, choose a frame that highlights a particular colour, install lighting to manipulate the colours that your eyes see, or you can even select the painting that matches your existing décor.

In much the same way, creating a picture with plants relies heavily on the success of the colour scheme for that particular environment. Picking up not only on the colour of the sky, but also on the tones of the earth and the very strength of the sun itself will add to the coherence of your scheme. In this way, bright hot climates with strong-coloured earths can get away with brighter schemes, whereas soft schemes may become bleached out in harsh light. The reverse is true too, as bright colours appear garish in some grey lights yet soft pinks, for example, appear rosier under a strong light.

Many areas are known for the colour schemes of their natural environments. For instance, the greys found in the flora and chalky white soils of the Mediterranean coupled with the intense blue of the sea and sky create a colour scheme that looks great in the area. The dusty red soils of the desert look wonderful with equally bright wildflowers, while the emerald green hills of the United Kingdom are luminescent under a misty sky. In Australia, eucalypts, with their soft olive tonings and often black or white trunks and sandstone surrounds, emit an ethereal glow marked by purple shadows in the bright sunlight.

Light intensity

The intensity of light will also vary according to your garden's climate and aspect. In a warm climate in the southern hemisphere, those gardens facing east and receiving only the morning sun will have a different look to those that face west and cope with the full brunt of the afternoon sun.

So when you select plants for hardiness to a certain situation consider also the effect the light will have on the colour. A favourite time for you might be late afternoon, so a garden of sunset colours such as claret, muted pink, indigo and salmon shades, set off by soft golden foliage and burgundy leaves, may be the perfect marriage for a garden in which you intend to sit and relax during the twilight hours.

Behind the schemes

Experts estimate that humans can distinguish perhaps as many as ten million colours with the naked eye. With millions more combinations possible, it would take a vast tome to experiment with them all. However, it does help to understand the technical terms for grouping colours. In this section we also explore some schemes that have been popular in the past and some others that may be exciting to try in the future.

Above: The blue border is popular and works well under the light of many skies, although blue tends to be the first colour to disappear at night.

Simplistic colour combinations

Simplistic colour combinations are just that — simple, relatively easy to orchestrate schemes that create a high impact. Just choose one or two colours and stick to your scheme.

Monochromatic schemes

This colour scheme uses a single hue — for example, blue and its varying tints and shades. Always popular for indoor use, monochromatic schemes are an exercise in self-control, and allow the possibility of rich textural contrast and patterns of shadow to be highlighted.

This may be perfect for a seaside location where perhaps turquoise water meets a relaxed mass of blue plumbago and swathes of agapanthus. This, in turn, may become a

swimming pool, lined with glass tiles and reflecting a blue sky.

Flowers and foliage may even be schemed to earthy tones — such as brown, tan, copper, fawn and rust — allowing the tapestry of bark, leaves, pebbles and materials such as woven willow and salt-glazed terracotta to become the feature. Think of a swath of brown grass heads billowing and rustling alongside a drystone wall — all texture and movement creating visual contrast and interest.

Analogous schemes

These schemes use adjacent hues, such as red combined with red–orange, or purplish red. Again this scheme requires some restraint, but it does open up a huge range of plant choice. Groups of plantings can be smaller and repeated alongside similar, yet slightly different shades, creating almost a tapestry or brocade of one colour.

Contrasting schemes

Using one colour as a base but highlighting it using a complementary colour is a good way of drawing attention to both. The most common ways of achieving this are with complementary, split complementary and triadic schemes.

Complementary schemes

If two hues are opposite each other on the colour wheel they are considered to be complementary colours. When used together in a design they make each other seem brighter and more intense. Some examples are red and green, and purple and yellow.

In the words of Gertude Jekyll: 'Any experienced colourist knows that the blues will be more telling — more purely blue — by the juxtaposition of the rightly placed complementary colour.' This may be a simple

Below: The complementary colours of red and green appear opposite each other on the colour wheel. Here, the dominant colour, the red of the azaleas, is used to highlight the serene green in the rest of the garden.

Above: Lit by a bright summer sun, this warm temperate garden can carry off the flamboyant mix of colour provided by geraniums, verbena and gazanias against a hedge of *Photinia glabra* 'Reubens'.

flower pot of blue *Lobelia* sp., combined with the clear yellow of Bidens daisy (*Bidens pilosa*) or a long flower bed of blue *Delphinium* sp. and bright yellow *Ligularia* sp.

Split complementary schemes

This colour scheme uses three colours — any hue and the two adjacent to its complement. Red combined with yellow–green, or with blue–green, are two examples of split complementary schemes.

Triadic schemes

The triadic scheme also uses three colours — such as red, yellow and blue — that are evenly spaced from each other on the colour wheel. Imagine a meadow garden filled with yellowing wheat, blue cornflowers and red Flanders poppies — simply delightful, welcoming and unassuming.

Discordant schemes

A more complex way of blending colours that still follows a set pattern can lead to multiple colour schemes.

Double complement

This colour scheme uses two pairs of complements — for example, yellow and violet, and blue and orange.

Alternate complement scheme

This scheme uses four colours — a triad and a complement to one of the hues, such as red, yellow, blue and violet.

Tetrad scheme

This scheme uses four colours evenly spaced on the colour wheel — a primary (for example, red), a secondary (green) and two tertiary colours (yellow–orange and blue–violet). In warm temperate climates, this tetrad is often played out as a beautiful garden in the sky, when golden silky oaks, purple jacarandas and red Illawarra flame

Did you know? All the colours of the rainbow are visible whenever droplets of water catch the rays of the sun. You can never see the end of the rainbow because it bends into a complete circle behind the horizon.

trees (*Brachychiton acerifolius*) all burst into spontaneous bloom against the intense blue sky of late spring and summer.

Tints and shades

With the addition of white, a colour becomes tinted or lightened. Shading, on the other hand, is achieved by the addition of black. For example, red with white becomes pink, making pink a tint of red, while red with black is a red–brown, chestnut shade.

The cottage garden

The romance of the cottage garden has been capturing the hearts of gardeners for over a century, with swags of roses covering a cottage and, as Stewart Dick put it in his *Cottage Homes of England* (1909), 'tall hollyhocks reaching almost to the thatches' eaves, sweet-smelling wallflowers spreading their fragrance far out into the dusty road…'

Maybe it's due to generations of children fed from 'Bunnykins' bowls and reared on Beatrix Potter stories, filled with flowers and vegetables (beware of Mr MacGregor!) and delightful creatures playing among the foxgloves (all scenes from the Lakes District in England and Hill Top, where Potter lived). Whatever the reason, this style has its roots firmly planted in a bygone era, a time when growing flowers and vegetables together was due more to necessity and lack of space than design.

The cottage garden today is more often than not a result of a colour-schemed, less haphazard technique, in which perennials and annuals are planted out together with herbs and vegetables, often chosen deliberately for their colourings rather than as a food staple for the inhabitants. Plants such as the purple-leafed cabbages, golden marjoram and feverfew, scarlet runner beans and mignonette lettuces are all key ingredients in such a garden (see page 369).

The cottage garden has been particularly popular with those who actually own a cottage. The greater value that these dwellings now have in the marketplace has spurred on owners keen not only to have authentic accessories such as picket fences and painted trims but also plants that fit the scene.

This factor, along with the realization that the old garden varieties of many species have qualities such as disease resistance, superior taste and perfume, has catapulted them out of Granny's country backyard and into the gardens of suburbia.

Although the cottage garden style may have its roots in an idealized version of rural life in the United Kingdom, you don't have to religiously copy the plants in order to achieve the same effect. Wildflowers from native areas can just as easily be incorporated into a cottage scheme and mixed with indigenous flowering shrubs to create a relaxed style that is suited to the local environment.

The flower border

During the Edwardian period, garden designers like Gertrude Jekyll propelled the flower border, planted mainly with herbaceous perennials, into the forefront of gardening styles. Until this time, flowers had been languishing away in the cottage garden among the 'peasants', or were hiding in walled gardens on the estates of stately homes. Here they were grown in a place called the cutting garden, which supplied cut flowers for the house; they were not grown to ornament the garden.

By this time, gardeners recognized that these plants could be the 'living paint' they could use as brushstrokes on the landscape.

Opposite: The tall spires of lupins, bursting up from a froth of colour, typify the cottage garden ideal.

Did you know? The white markings inside the flowers of foxgloves were once believed to be the fingerprints of elves!

Opposite, from top to bottom:
Eupatorium megapotanicum,
Penstemon sp., *Rudbeckia*
'California', *Allium* sp., *Aquilegia* x
hybrida and *Solidago* sp.

For the most part, these old-fashioned varieties of herbaceous perennials flowered from midsummer and autumn, so the scene would be set for an orchestrated masterpiece of blossom that coincided with the weather being warm enough to enjoy the outdoors.

Of course, nowadays that simply will not do. The average landowner cannot afford the space to devote beds exclusively to a flower show for one season and then let them lie fallow for the rest of the year. Only a large estate can accommodate many different garden rooms for one season alone.

For this reason the flower border has evolved into what is also known as a mixed border. This usually contains bulbs, which start off in spring, annuals that may fill up a gap or lull in flowering, early summer perennials and even some shrubs for evergreen structure or seasonal colour.

Although the label may infer a mix, rarely does the flower border stray from what is almost always the key factor in its design: the border's appeal and beauty lie in its carefully orchestrated colour schemes, an ideal way to show off how colours can combine, and how plants en masse can create a beautiful scene.

Many herbaceous perennial borders are not just restricted in colour but are also specific to a particular season. An all-white border, for example, may be a summer scheme that changes to fiery tones with the beginning of autumn.

Above: Plant out the heavenly perfumed sweet pea by seed each autumn and enjoy its flowers in spring.

Sweet peas

In recent years many old-fashioned plants, known as heirloom plants, have been rediscovered. Renowned varieties include vegetables, sweet peas and roses, and although they might not store well, they tend to have superior flavour or perfume.

Annuals are very useful for the colour garden, as planting schemes can easily be altered with a fresh batch of seedlings. Sweet pea (*Lathyrus odoratus*) is an old-fashioned plant that offers not just a delicious perfume but also a dizzying range of colours. Its beauty as a fast climber is highly valued, especially in the cottage garden where temporary vertical accents and rustic screening, like trellises, work so well.

In Victorian times sweet peas were bred in huge quantities, principally as cut flowers, but they actually predate this period.

John Ray recorded sweet peas in 1686 in his *Historia Plantarum*. They were first domesticated by a monk named Father Cupani, who found them growing wild in Sicily. It is said he sent some seeds to an English schoolmaster in 1699. The variety known as 'Cupani', which has intensely fragrant, compact maroon and purple flowers, is apparently descended from the same wild seeds.

Other heirloom types include 'Painted Lady', which is a deep cherry and palest pink, striped bicolour, thought to have been found growing in the Chelsea Physic Garden in London in 1737. The comparatively small flowers with a spicy scent are sometimes sold as one part of a mix known as 'Old Spice', which includes very fragrant flowers. Other mixes include 'Antique Fantasy', which includes a selection of old-style, non-frilled but well scented varieties. Varieties such as 'America', 'Miss Wilmott' and 'Mrs Collier' were all bred around the turn of the twentieth century.

These gardens require great skill and knowledge of flowering times, which may vary considerably from place to place. For example, many southern hemisphere gardeners are shocked to discover that what may bloom in one intense month of spring in, say, Australia, may bloom for over three months in the United Kingdom. So if you are creating colour schemes inspired by books, you'll need to use careful observation and local knowledge to adapt it to the climate and conditions of your garden.

The 'new' perennial garden

The 'new' perennial garden is a term used to describe a perennial garden composed of plants that grow happily and easily in their selected environment. Popularized by the likes of Dutchman Piet Oudolf, but forged by greatly skilled horticulturalists and nursery people such as Beth Chatto, this garden style has enjoyed a recent resurgence in popularity.

The advantage of this model is that it is less dependent on herbaceous perennials and also blends with other permanent plantings and grasses. This greatly extends the time such a garden looks good, making it more suitable for smaller yards. The addition of ornamental grasses and foliage plants has also given this type of garden a greater sense of movement and texture, qualities that make it compatible with both modern and traditional styles of architecture.

It also stands as a warning to those who slavishly copy the classic 'English' border, or other gardens lavishly illustrated in books and magazines that may be inappropriate for their climate and soil. The key to designing this type of garden is how you mix plants together, carefully considering how the colour, leaf type and flower form of each flower will combine before you plant in drifts of each type.

Flowers with **different shapes**

The outline of a cluster of flowers also creates a form worth contrasting in the garden.

Umbel
Achillea sp., *Angelica* sp., *Astrantia* sp., *Eupatorium* sp., *Foeniculum* sp., *Fatsia* sp., *Hedera* sp., lacecap hydrangeas, *Sambucus* sp., *Sedum* sp.

Spire
Acanthus sp., *Delphinium* sp., *Digitalis* sp., *Echium* sp., *Lupinus* sp., *Lythrum* sp., *Penstemon* sp., *Rehmannia* sp., *Salvia* sp., *Verbascum* sp., *Veronica* sp.

Daisy
Aster sp., *Chamaemelum nobile*, *Echinacea* sp., *Euryops*, *Felicia* sp., *Gazania* sp., *Heliopsis* sp., *Osteospermum* sp., *Rudbeckia* sp., *Stokesia* sp.

Globose
Agapanthus sp., *Allium* sp., *Armeria* sp., artichoke, *Centaurea* sp., *Echinopsis* sp., *Hydrangea* sp., *Ixora* sp., *Knautia* sp., *Viburnum* sp.

Dainty and delicate
Abutilon sp., *Aquilegia* sp., *Convallaria* sp., *Dicentra* sp., *Fuchsia* sp., *Polygonatum* sp., *Silene* sp.

Plumes and panicles
Astilbe sp., *Filipendula rubra* 'Venusta Magnifica', *Miscanthus* sp., *Persicaria* sp., *Rodgersia* sp., *Solidago*, *Stipa* sp., *Thalictrum* sp.

Did you know? There is a majestic 330 m (1000 ft) herbaceous border, called the Broad Walk, at Hampton Court on the Thames, near London.

Black and white gardens

In garden terms, a black and white garden, or non-coloured garden, may sound boring and sterile. But it need not be so. By removing colour from the tools at your disposal, you make the other elements of the design — the textural qualities of bark, the tonal variations of light and shade, and the range of foliage shades and leaf shapes — become much more important; in fact, they are intensified.

Below: The sweet-smelling, creamy white blooms of gardenia.

Opposite: Standard white roses are underplanted with white sweet Alice and dianthus, like a lace tablecloth spread delicately for a grand function. A shepherdess stands guard at the end of the pond, which is enclosed by dark green Bhutan cypress hedges.

Combining black and white together in one garden can be startling and effective. Imagine a grove of silver birch (*Betula pendula*), the white papery bark of their trunks offset by a smooth floor of black granite. Or for a restrained yet impressive scene, think of pavers in a black and white chequerboard pattern, surrounded by a formal clipped hedge featuring the same toning, such as the white-edged leaf and black-stemmed *Pittosporum tenuifolium* 'Stirling Mist'.

Even van Gogh was impressed by the combination of black and white in the garden. He painted still lifes of the silvery white seed pods of honesty combined with dark maroon peonies and black hollyhocks. Water too can be used to create black pools of darkness that are remarkable because they still reflect light.

White

The pure, crisp, clean effect of white is often used in interior design, especially contemporary décor, as a foil to highlight rich textural fabric and floor coverings. This technique can also be used in the garden.

But white is not that simple. There are, in fact, many shades of white, each with its own nuance. Some, such as the creamy whites of gardenia and magnolia, are more luxuriant, while others, like a lime wash or antique

Above: A formal garden using white and green, form and structure as the basis for its design.

Below: A standard wisteria adds a touch of height without bulk to a garden.

white — found in rock roses (*Cistus* sp.), hydrangeas and tree poppy (*Romneya* sp.) — add a sense of age. Then there are the white whites, which have a stark brightness, such as the perennially popular rose 'Iceberg'.

No colour instils the same sense of peace, tranquillity and wellbeing as white. It symbolizes truth, purity, virginity and simplicity. The fact that white is without a dominant wavelength of its own and actually reflects all the other rays in the spectrum means that, in a design sense, it makes spaces feel larger than they really are.

In fact, white is not truly a colour at all, which makes it achromatic. Being devoid of colour means that white doesn't have a complement or contrasting colour. Black is the only other 'colour' that has quite such a peculiar place.

The association of black with death can make it a morbid colour to use, and too much will leave a garden feeling gloomy, but it is useful for punctuating strong contrasting colours in the garden, such as breaking up swathes of red or yellow.

Opposite: Cobbles, or small round pebbles, form a textural chequerboard pattern.

project

Planting a black and white pot

Black and white plants make a striking combination. Use
various textures and different shaped leaves to create visual
interest. We've mixed the succulent *Echeveria* 'Black Prince',
the black mondo grass (*Ophiopogon planiscapus*
'Nigrescens') with the white-edged form of mondo called
'Variegata', a dark plum, almost black-leafed form of *Cordyline
fruticosa* called 'Cobra' and the white-edged form of
Euonymus fortunei called 'Silver Pillar'. The stunning
centrepiece is a black pineapple lily (a *Eucomis* hybrid).

For a black and white pot to work really well, it should be
carefully constructed so that the black plants highlight the
white and don't disappear into a general gloomy mass. It
should also be placed in a bright position. This white verandah
is ideal because it will highlight the tonal contrasts and bring
out the silhouette of the silvery grey pot to perfection.

Position your planter before you start planting. This is
always a good idea, as pots can get quite heavy once they're
filled with potting mix and plants, particularly after they have
been watered in.

1 Fill your planter with a good quality potting mix. If your plants don't thrive, the
display will look dreary.

2 Position the largest plants first, including the featured pineapple lily.

3 Remove excess potting mix from around the roots of the smaller 'filler' plants,
such as the various mondo grasses. Plant the remaining miniature 'hedge' of
Euonymus fortunei.

4 Position the black pineapple lily in the foreground where it can be seen easily.
Finally, water in, then mulch with white quartz gravel to highlight the black
leaves and provide contrast with the pot.

Did you know? Queen Victoria wore a white silk gown when she married Albert in 1840, and from then on it became fashionable to wear bridal white.

White, on the other hand, exudes a sense of cleanliness and healing. It can look too much so, to the point of being clinical, so pure whites are often avoided in favour of flowers that are slightly off white, such as gardenias. Solid blooms such as roses and the voluptuous bull bay magnolia (*Magnolia grandiflora*) even have a carved sculptural quality about them, with each waved petal creating a shadow. The opposite could be said of the papery thin blooms of poppies (*Papaver* sp.) and sweet peas (*Lathyrus* sp.), whose flowers are so tissue-paper thin that light actually passes right through each petal, giving them a soft translucency.

The white garden

From its beginnings, the famous white garden at Sissinghurst, created by Vita Sackville-West and her husband Harold Nicolson, has inspired a number of replicas. But the white garden of this era has evolved too, and finds a place in the minimalist schemes of modern, cutting-edge garden designers as well as die-hard traditionalists.

Traditional white flowers from the Arts and Crafts 'flower border' period include *Achillea ptarmica* 'The Pearl' or *Rosa* 'Boule de Neige', broom (*Cytisus albus*), tree lupin (*Lupinus arboreus*), *Lilium candidum*, *L. longiflorum* and *L. regale*, baby's breath (*Gypsophila paniculata*), sweet pea (*Lathyrus grandiflorus*) and the shasta daisy (*Leucanthemum* x *superbum*).

Modern, minimalist schemes call for bolder forms, such as *Yucca* sp., which have

Opposite, clockwise from top left: The tissue-thin flowers of white poppies decorated with golden stamens; the bizarre black and white flower of the bat plant; and the flowers of *Michelia doltsopa*, like carved ivory.

Black and near black plants

Above: *Aeonium arboreum* 'Zwartkop' tolerates salt spray and sandy soils.

Black flowers may be morbid to some, and extremely unpopular for some cut flower markets such as the Japanese trade, where they are considered unlucky, but there are strange and unique black flowers that are truly fascinating – for example, the bizarrely beautiful bat plant (*Tacca integrifolia*), cobra lily (*Arisaema triphyllum*), Titan arum (*Amorphophallus titanum*) and black arum or stink lily (*Dracunculus vulgaris*).

Other black flowers have no sinister presence, and are simply a charming addition to the flower garden. The black hollyhock (*Alcea rosea* 'Nigra'), *Scabiosa* 'Midnight', *Aquilegia vulgaris* 'Blackbird', *Dianthus barbatus* 'Nigrescens', cranesbill (*Geranium phaeum*), *Paeonia* 'Poppy Black', *Delphinium* 'Black Knight' and near-black, sweetly smelly chocolate cosmos (*Cosmos atrosanguineus*) are all fine examples.

For a seasonal burst of black, try a clump or two of black *Ranunculus* 'Nearly Black', or any of the many black tulips such as *Tulipa* 'Queen of Night', *T.* 'Negrita' and *T.* 'Black Parrot'. Mass plant the base with some annual black pansies (*Viola* 'Blackjack', 'Black Devil', 'Bowles' Black' and 'Molly Sanderson' are good cultivars), and the result is anything but disheartening.

The edible garden need not miss out on a touch of delectable misery either. Black aubergine, 'Black Russian' tomatoes, black artichoke ('Violetto di Chioggia'), chocolate capsicum and blue/purple sweet popping corns are all worth a go, as are black zucchini, black figs and sweet black passion fruit or grapes.

Damp beds can be massed with black iris (*Iris chrysographes* 'Black Knight' or 'Black Velvet') and black hellebores (*Helleborus* 'Queen of the Night'). Other useful black plants include black-stemmed bamboo (*Phyllostachys nigra*) and black mondo grass. For lovers of Australian natives, look no further than the exceptionally beautiful black kangaroo paw (*Macropidia fulginosa*) or the outstanding black trunks of the grass tree (*Xanthorrhoea* sp.).

For those with a penchant for succulents, the drop-dead gorgeous succulent *Aeonium arboreum* 'Zwartkop' is hard to go past, as is the stunning *Echeveria* 'Black Prince'.

Above: The meadowfoam, or poached egg flower (*Limnanthes* sp.), lining this path are free flowering and perfumed throughout the spring. They like it moist and will naturalize if happy, much to the delight of bees who drink their nectar.

Opposite: White reflects beautifully in water, especially in still, dark ponds.

Did you know? The green part of a leaf contains the chlorophyll, which is responsible for producing sugars and food so the plant can survive away from sunlight. If a plant had all white leaves, it would eventually die.

tall spikes of cup-shaped white or cream flowers, *Crinum* sp., with bold, strap leaves and spider-like white blooms, and even iris and agapanthus in their white forms.

Using white in the garden

Whether it be foliage with white markings, white for night effects or white flowers for a border, each has its own place in the garden. As Decaisne and Naudin wrote in *Manuel de l'Amateur de Jardin*: 'All colours, whether primary or compound, are enlivened by the proximity of white.' Bright during the day, yet luminous at night, white is especially beautiful against a moonlit night, dark storm clouds and even a heavy grey fog, where it stands out like a beacon. This makes it a great choice for shade and part shade.

The simple, striking quality of white also makes it suitable for restrained formal gardens (see page 266).

White variegations

White variegations are particularly attractive and useful in garden design. For a simple yet effective remedy for an overly shaded glen, add white-edged plants to help lift the whole garden and give it the impression of light.

Some examples include *Hibiscus rosa-sinensis* 'Cooperi', which is stunning for warm climates and semi-shaded areas. Its blood red flower jumps out at you from its snowy backdrop. Also delightful for light shade is the sweetly perfumed, variegated *Bouvardia humboldii* 'White Star'. The spring-flowering, white-edged *Weigela florida* 'Variegata' is also back as an attractive contrasting shrub.

Ground covers such as the bugle flower (*Ajuga reptans* 'Glacier') are very useful for the shade, as is the deliciously fragrant variegated applemint, *Mentha suaveolens* 'Variegata', whereas the white-edged strawberry and white-edged nasturtium (*Tropaeolum majus*

Above: Murraya is used in many gardens where temperatures do not drop below –1°C (32°F). Its common name of orange jessamine relates to the sweetly perfumed flowers. It makes a good privacy screen or formal hedge.

Did you know? The greyness of most plants is caused by a layer of white hairs on the leaves, as on lamb's tongues, allowing plants to create an environment of humidity and hence cope better with dry situations. Some, like purple cabbages, also have a glaucous waxy coating, and others actually have a metallic-like sheen, which reflects the strength of the sun's rays and helps reduce water loss. A few — such as cyclamens, deadnettle (*Lamium* sp.) and lungwort (*Pulmonaria* sp.) — are truly silver.

Alaska Hybrids), best in sunnier spots, look charming in a potager.

For strong vertical contrast, try the striking *Iris pallida* 'Variegata' or rapacious gardener's garters (*Phalaris arundinacea* var. *picta*), both with terrific strap leaves, or the upright pannicles of the flowering *Phlox paniculata* 'Norah Leigh', delightful snow-on-the-mountain (*Euphorbia marginata*) or dainty white honesty (*Lunaria annua* 'Variegata').

White flowers

White flowers are useful for breaking up strong jarring colour combinations, and also for helping each colour stay true to itself without taking on the hue of its neighbour. Mixed with grey foliage, the effect is less startling than with green leaves alone as a backdrop.

A similar effect is achieved when the white cup blooms of the Yulan tree (*Magnolia denudata*) are held aloft by bare branches against a grey winter sky. The effect is simple, austere and dignified, almost as though each

White flowers for the **night garden**

Under a dark sky, white flowers lit by moonlight have an ethereal quality that can be quite magical. Many white flowers have exquisite perfumes, as they rely on scent, rather than colour, to attract pollinating insects. Couple this with the fact that many plants release their perfumes at night, and the effect can be breathtaking and enchanting.

Notable shrubs for the night garden include orange jessamine (*Murraya paniculata*), gardenia and sweet olive (*Osmanthus fragrans*), night cestrum (*Cestrum nocturnum*) and angel's trumpet (*Brugmansia* sp.), while outstanding trees include the white lilac (*Syringa* 'Vestale'), Yulan tree (*Magnolia denudata*), frangipani (*Plumeria* sp.) and bull bay magnolia (*Magnolia grandiflora*).

For stunning bulbs, try lily-of-the-valley (*Convallaria* sp.), paper whites (*Narcissus papyraceus*), tuberose (*Polianthes* sp.), Amazon lily (*Eucharis amazonica*) or the flowers of the succulent queen of the night (*Epiphyllum oxypetalum*). Many perfumed white climbers can also be used to festoon walls and pergolas. Try star jasmine (*Trachelospermum jasminoides*), *Mandevilla laxa*, *Petrea volubilis* 'Albiflora' and various jasmines such as *Jasminum sambac*, *J. grandiflorum* and *J. nitidum*.

Left: *Mandevilla laxa*.

The Yulan tree (*Magnolia denudata*) is so precious it is often planted outside Buddhist temples (above left). This spurge (*Euphorbia marginata*, above right) is known as snow-on-the-mountain due to its dainty white edge. It will grow to 60 cm (2 ft) and makes a lovely cut flower and foliage.

Below: Each plant's unique leaf shape and texture break up the soft and silvery tones of this grey garden.

Grey plants

Ground covers
Arabis caucasica, Cerastium tomentosum, Dianthus 'Mrs Sinkins', *Festuca glauca, Gazania tomentosa, Helichrysum petiolare, Lamium* 'White Nancy', *Lotus berthelotti, Stachys byzantina*

Succulents
Cotyledon orbiculata, Euphorbia myrsinites, Kalanchoe 'Quicksilver', *Pachyphytum overiferum, Senecio serpens*

Perennials
Achillea sp., *Artemisia* sp., *Astelia* sp., *Echium* 'Silver Pink', *Eryngium giganteum* 'Miss Willmott's Ghost', *Iris pallida, Plectranthus argentatus, Romneya* sp., *Senecio cineraria, Verbascum* sp.

Shrubs
Buddleja sp., *Correa alba, Cupressus macrocarpa* 'Greenstead Magnificent', *Elaeagnus* sp., *Eremophila, Melianthus* sp., *Rosa glauca*

Trees
Acacia baileyana, A. podalyriifolia, Bismarckia nobilis, Butia capitata, Cupressus cashmeriana, Eucalyptus cinerea, Picea glauca, Pyrus salicifolia

Above, from top to bottom: Cerastium tomentosum, Senecio serpens, Artemisia aborescens, Melianthus major and Acacia baileyana.

flower knows it has inspired its audience without being a show-off.

Grey and silver
Grey is sometimes used to blend with other pastel colours (such as mauve, pink and purple) to create an ethereal haze. This was a practice perfected by Jekyll. Grey also works beautifully as a foil for white.

Landscaping materials
The range of stone products in grey, black and white is enormous, so whether you prefer a simple slab of white marble, bluestone, white sandstone or black granite setts, there is bound to be something appropriate for your garden scheme.

Many metals come in these tones, and you can choose from the modern, sleek look of stainless steel or polished aluminum, or go for the more rustic with cast iron, lead, tin, woven wire or galvanized chain link.

Hardwood can easily be treated with creosote to achieve a weather-resistant, near-black finish. It can also be white washed or painted grey or white. Some timber poles, like paperbark and silver birch, are white naturally.

Black as tar, asphalt is a durable poured product that, if laid with interesting borders or trim, can be quite a decorative and hard-wearing alternative to concrete, and ideal for high traffic areas. Concrete blocks and pavers are some of the cheapest and easiest to use landscaping materials.

Blue metal, charcoal, lava chips, black and white stones, quartz white and sand can all be used as decorative toppings, while frosted glass and perspex panels are useful vertical elements in a black and white garden.

Mood board for a black and white garden

Pastel gardens

When a little colour is added to white, a pastel colour is the result. This delicate colour, or tint, contains not much more than a suggestion of the colour, like cream (which contains a tinge of yellow) and apricot (which has a soft orange hue).

Below: Columbines (*Aquilegia* sp.), or granny's bonnets as they are affectionately known, are a delightful flower for the pastel garden. The poet John Clare once described them as 'each cottage garden's fond adopted child'.

Opposite: Every colour of the rainbow is shown here, but only in its softest tint.

Pastel colours are sometimes used for morning gardens, when the light is softer and flower colours won't look faded so quickly. The colour master Monet did this in what was called the Sunrise garden at Giverny in France. There, the pink stucco house with its turquoise-coloured shutters was the backdrop to a garden filled with pastels — pink and blue aquilegias, mauve and pink tulips, soft pink lupins, and the white and pink bicolour cleomes, or spider flowers, mingled with forget-me-nots, pink peonies and lavender delphiniums, perfect for the early morning mists and soft sunrise light.

There are many pastel-coloured plants to choose from, of course. Some wonderful creams occur in the simple blooms of the Californian poppy (*Eschscholzia* sp.), foxglove (*Digitalis grandiflora*), the palest of marigolds (*Calendula* sp.), some sand-coloured petunias and the old zinnia species, some of which almost have a tinge of green. Many of the *Achillea* cultivars, such as 'Moonshine' and 'Terracotta', are also useful here.

For soft pinks it is hard to go past the windflower (*Anemone* x *hybrida*), with its flowers teetering on thin stems, varieties of bergamot (*Monarda* sp.) and Californian poppy, clary sage (*Salvia sclarea*), cosmos, everlasting daisy (*Bracteantha* sp.), foxglove, *Gypsophila* 'Rosy Veil', peony poppies, penstemons like 'Pink Cloud', *Nicotiana* sp. and meadow rue (*Thalictrum* sp.). Pale pink blossom — in trees (such as *Prunus* sp.),

shrubs (like *Syringa vulgaris* 'Madame Lemoine') and sweet peas — are all superb ways of introducing height.

Powder blues occur in some cornflowers (*Centaurea* sp.), *Aster* x *frikartii*, the annual baby blue eyes (*Nemophila menziesii*), Russian sage (*Petrovskia atriplicifolia*), and the true salvias (*Salvia azurea* and *S. patens*), the pincushion flower (*Scabiosa* sp.) and, of course, the quintessential blue flower, the delphinium. Shrubs and trees with powder blue flowers include lilac (*Syringa* sp.), buddleja and chaste tree (*Vitex agnus-castus*).

Misty-coloured themes are ideal for climates where the light is soft, or for creating a quiet, meditative mood. Delicate and dainty pastels in the garden help create a relaxed and peaceful scene that is easy on the eye. The light shades work particularly well in

Many annuals are fond of self-seeding. Year after year, cosmos and cleomes (opposite), columbines (above) and linaria (below) all manage to find a new home for themselves once they have been planted.

spaces that get used at night and at dusk; the palest colours remain visible the longest and are therefore useful for flanking outdoor entertaining areas.

For those gardeners just beginning to experiment with colour, pastel schemes are a safe starting point, providing less scope for technicolour blunders, such as those municipal council gardens with bright red salvia and golden marigolds!

Gertrude Jekyll loved using grey and silver leaves with pastels as she felt they brought out the mild tints of pastels and made them more effective. This was a technique that the English painter Turner used so brilliantly when he depicted scenes featuring smoke, ice, mist, snow and fog; Jekyll adapted this technique to the garden.

Landscaping materials

Pale crushed stone and pea gravel works well beside flower borders, gently reflecting light back to the beds. If you prefer a hard surface, consider ceramic and glazed tiles as well as the many soft shades of terracotta tiles; some have an almost pinkish white hue. Many mosaic tiles have soft gelato colours that have a soft, shimmering effect, again perfect for

Top: The wall protects this garden from the wind and forms a backdrop to the pretty pink and white flowers.

Above: Yellow *Solidago*, silver *Artemisia* and purple delphiniums form this classic tricolour scheme.

Painting pastel pots

Pastel needn't be 'prissy'. Reworking the pastel theme in a modern way can provide an exciting contrast. These empty tin cans, painted in pastel colours and teamed with succulents, have a retro chic about them, interpreting 1950s colours in a very contemporary way. First, remove the labels from some empty tin cans and wash them in the dishwasher for a thorough clean. Allow them to dry completely.

1 Select your colour range of acrylic paints. Some sample pots or leftovers from bigger jobs are ideal.

2 Paint on two coats of acrylic in your chosen colours. Leave the tins to dry between coats. Thoroughly wash the brush out in water each time you finish a coat.

3 Plant up your pots with hardy succulents in harmonizing pastel tones, such as the *Graptoveria* 'Debbie' we've used here.

Plants with **pastel-coloured leaves**

Grey foliage has been traditionally used to marry a soft pastel scheme. However, today many cultivars of plants have pastel-coloured leaves, which are beautiful in their own right and look stunning when combined with flowers.

Choose from the pink-spotted bugle (*Ajuga reptans* 'Multicolor'), *Fuchsia magellanica* 'Versicolor' and the warm temperate and subtropical selections of polka-dot plant (*Hypoestes phyllostachya*).

Many succulents have pastel colourings – for example, the frilled rosettes of *Echeveria* 'Blue Curls' or the simpler flower-like clusters of *E.* 'Violet Queen' and *Graptoveria* 'Debbie'. Even the retro plant chain of hearts (*Ceropegia linearis* subsp. *woodii*) can work beautifully in urns or baskets where its trailing habit can be shown to advantage.

For vertical coverage, try the climbers *Actinidia kolomikta* and *Ampelopsis* sp., or the wonderful clotted cream and gelato pink variety of star jasmine (*Trachelospermum jasminoides* 'Tricolor').

Above: The glaucous rosettes of *Echeveria elegans* are tinged with pink as the weather cools.

Above: It's hard to believe that something as pretty as this *Lavatera* 'Barnsley' could be native to the wind-swept wilds and wasteland areas of the Mediterranean coast.

night-time areas. Vitrified glass tiles are another option.

Some marble is less formal and more cottagey than others, and may be worth considering for outdoor tabletops. Sandstone also works really well, as pieces often have a soft pink grain through them. Compounds made up of quartzite are also in keeping with a pastel garden.

Use paint in pastel colours for wood surfaces, such as cottage pickets and latticework, and even on woven wire for gates and boundary fences.

For details such as pots, keep them soft with lime-based paints, matt acrylics and stone washes. Fabrics should be light and airy — think lace, sheers and delicate embroidered patterns.

Mood board for a pastel garden

Green gardens

For the formal gardens of the Renaissance and the park-like gardens of the eighteenth century landscape garden, green was the colour of choice. These gardens didn't need other colours to create interest or excitement; they were deliberately calm, reassuring, sombre and well proportioned.

Below: Hostas are renowned for their leaf variegations, and also for being devoured by snails. Mulching with stones and leaving out beer traps should help keep these pests at bay.

Opposite: In hot climates, nothing is more cooling and reassuring than a carpet of green, a canopy of green and even walls of green.

For many people, green suggests security, love and harmony. For the gardener, green is the background colour of all flowers, the canvas upon which 'paint' is applied. But playing with the idea of turning the canvas into the feature can also be an exciting prospect. The infinite possibility of leaf colours and the myriad shades of green can be a work of art in themselves.

The monochromatic nature of such a garden places the spotlight on the other elements of design. While there is more effort involved in choosing plants that may contrast in form, shape and structure with each other to create an interesting garden, there is also less scope for making wild mistakes.

For a clear picture of how this single colour scheme can be enormously moving and effective, think of the hypnotic effect of a field of long grass, and how compelling it is to watch wind ripple over it and create waves of light and dark. Or imagine a mossed clearing, with randomly scattered rocks, covered with lichen, the dancing canopy of a tree, or a park-like lawn stretching out from the door.

The complement of green is red, so striking landscapes can be achieved by using touches of red to highlight the all-green garden. The same field of grass can be exciting when some red field poppies invade a patch, for example. Another classic combination is the potted red geranium —

Above: With a sweeping view like this, it's best to keep the garden as low key as possible.

Opposite: This gorgeous-leafed herbaceous perennial, *Darmera peltata*, is the only member of its genus and grows wild along streams and in damp woods. For foliage contrast, it is stunning in any bog garden.

the apple green mass of the leaves is set on fire by the splashes of intense red blooms, and the whole effect is complemented by the baked earth tones of a terracotta pot.

Of course, interesting effects can be created with shrubs too. For a pleasing contrast in spring, juxtapose the apple green new growth of large, pointed *Fatsia* sp. leaves and the subdued green of yew (*Taxus* sp.), with its fine, linear foliage and upright habit. If shrub borders are composed well, they can

be a year-round pleasure, whether they are in flower or not. They are also a fairly low maintenance alternative to the flower border.

Green leaves

It may sound like stating the obvious, but many plants have gorgeous green leaves. You can create an elegant garden simply by combining foliage in certain ways. To achieve this, you need to choose foliage for its shape as well as plants for their form.

The graceful arching canes of Solomon's seal (*Polygonatum* sp.), the gargantuan foliage of *Gunnera* sp. and the delicate leaves of the wake robin (*Trillium* sp.) have long been admired and coveted by gardeners from climates where these plants cannot be grown. Of all the leaf plants, however, one of the

Did you know? The 1933 book *The Complete Gardener* describes *Cannabis* as 'ornamental foliage, suitable for the border'. It is now an illegal substance due to its narcotic component.

most outstanding would have to be the hosta (*Hosta* sp.), revered because of the many varieties with variegated leaves. (For more information on hostas, see page 290.)

Green flowers

Although there is nothing the matter with the everyday or commonplace, sometimes the unusual creates an exciting distraction. The same can be said for a garden of green flowers. While they may not have the biggest or the best blooms, they can have a certain simple charm.

A bunch of green moss roses (*Rosa chinensis viridifolia*) and cow parsley (*Anthriscus sylvestris*) makes a different summer posy. Bells of Ireland (*Moluccella laevis*) and the lime green *Chrysanthemum*

Hostas

Above: *Hosta plantaginea* is grown as much for its flowers and perfume as for its leaves.

Also known as plantain lily, the hosta offers a wide range of foliage that is irresistible. Some have ribbed leaves or striking variegations, others have perfumed flowers and still others look like lights of translucent gold.

Although they are grown primarily for their heart-shaped leaves, the white, mauve or purple flowers in midsummer are an added bonus, and are sometimes deliciously scented. The *Hosta plantaginea* hybrids from China and Japan are best grown for their flowers and perfume.

Hosta fortunei is thought to have originated in Japan, but it has been heavily bred in Europe. It has more fine-pointed, lance-shaped leaves, and includes popular cultivars such as 'Albomarginata', with white-edged leaves, 'Aurea', an all-over gold that fades to green with age, and 'Albopicta', which has light green and cream leaves.

H. sieboldiana is another Japanese species. It tends to be more rounded in shape, and the puckered foliage often has a blue–grey tone. A variety known as *H. sieboldiana* var. *elegans*, and the cultivars 'Big Daddy' and 'Blue Angel' are best known.

Hostas are known as *giboshi* in Japan, and they used to be called funkia in the United Kingdom. They are actually related to one of the other great foliage plants, *Agave* sp., which unlike the shade- and moisture-loving hostas revels in the hot sun and tolerates drought.

Did you know? Green Park, near Buckingham Palace in London, is one of Britain's Royal Parks. It was originally named Upper St James Park but was renamed Green Park after George II's wife Caroline caught her husband picking flowers there for his mistress and ordered the flowers to be removed.

viridis are also fabulous together in a vase, while both *Tulipa* 'Spring Green' and green *Cymbidium* orchids are wonderful as potted bunches of flowers. For the garden, try the green stalwarts *Helleborus argutifolius* and *Zantedeschia aethiopica* 'Green Goddess' for shaded areas, and spurge (*Euphorbia* sp.) for drier, sunnier spots. Lady's mantle (*Alchemilla mollis*) makes a charming ground cover and will cross over both positions nicely.

Grasses

Grasses and their relations are a huge part of almost any natural environment, whether as an understorey component of a forest or the dominant feature of grasslands, prairies and savanna. They are also a feature of the built environment, as lawns tend to dominate parks and suburban gardens.

Lawn — the ultimate green cover

For ruggedness and determination, grass deserves the award as greatest ground cover plant. While it is regarded as a major consumer of that precious resource, water — a problem in drought-stricken areas — and it does need a regimen of regular watering, fertilizing and weeding in order to look its best, grass also stands up to a fair bit of neglect and mistreatment and still manages to stay alive, ready for the next good season.

Choosing a suitable grass is half the battle. Many people persist in growing sun-dependent species in heavy shade, or cool season grasses

Opposite, top: The lime green flowers of spurge (*Euphorbia* sp.) provide some relief from the otherwise blue-toned greens of the rosemary and cotton lavender.

Opposite, bottom right: *Amaranthus hypochondriacus* 'Green Thumb' is grown for its spikes of green flowers, which are actually the edible cereal grain amaranth.

Opposite, bottom left: A *Cymbidium* orchid.

Above, from left to right: Green in various forms — the thin leaves of glossy mondo grass, the soft texture of maidenhair fern and the fresh apple green of lush Boston ferns.

in warm climates, then find themselves engaged in an uphill battle with weak grass that easily succumbs to weeds and disease.

For the best grass for your area, consult your local turf supplier. Ask them about slower-growing varieties, if mowing is not your favourite weekend occupation, or drought-tolerant species if your area is prone to dry periods. That way, you'll be able to enjoy your garden on the weekends instead of slavishly attending to your lawn.

Gardens of turf

Moulding and sculpting the earth into mounds, sinuous ribbons and curvaceous crevices may not seem like gardening, but for the creators of The Garden of Cosmic Speculation in Scotland, architect and designer Charles Jencks and his late wife Maggie Keswick, it clearly was. Using earth-moving equipment, the two moulded the land into various shapes to express complex themes, such as the Taoist theories

of geomancy (the invisible energies of the land) and cosmology (see pages 67 and 378).

Cutting grass into shapes and patterns is another way of carving an impression on the landscape: a wonderful picture can be created with nothing but green grass and the effect of light and tone, texture and pattern.

Ornamental grass

A swath of ornamental grasses is one of the most popular new plantings in the twenty-first century. Not only do grass gardens save water and require little maintenance, but with their billowing ripples, waving seed heads and rustling foliage they can also create a dynamic effect.

Look for the silky plumes of squirrel tail grass (*Hordeum jubatum*) for seasonal effect or golden oats (*Stipa gigantea*) for an evergreen effect. For a stunning red, go for Japanese blood grass (*Imperata cylindrica* 'Rubra'). In spring it shoots red-tinged leaves that gradually deepen, until by late summer and autumn they are completely saturated with red. It does best in a moist soil. For other grasses, like rushes and sedges, that don't mind the damp, see page 179.

Even grass-like lilies, such as giant liriope (*Liriope gigantea*), and ever-popular mondo

Did you know? Edwin Budding invented the first lawn mower in 1830. Until then, grass was either cut by hand with a scythe or controlled by grazing animals.

Greenhouses

Greenhouses and their glassed counterparts, glasshouses, were essential components of the Victorian garden, and popular again after World War II. Although today it might seem outdated, a well designed shaded structure outdoors can accommodate not just shade-loving plants like ferns, orchids and begonias, but also furniture, making it another garden 'room' to be enjoyed all year round.

Above: The muted grey of the columns is an excellent foil for this simple arrangement of single white rose blooms and green euphorbias amid a bed of sweet Alice.

Cutting a turf pattern

For this pattern we've chosen a spiral, which is particularly fun for young children to follow. (See also the cut spiral pattern pictured on page 374.)

1 Using a landscape marking spray, which works while it is upside down, mark out the pattern.

2 Cut the pattern out cleanly with a sharp spade.

3 The area you have cut out can be kept free of grass in various ways. Decorative pebbles, crushed rocks, road base and even a simple brick path will all look good. In this case a stunning quarried green stone, rumbled until smooth, was used.

Tips

- To stop weeds growing up through the rocks, line the cut-out with black plastic.
- Use flexible garden edging as a mowing strip, or keep the grass cut with a brush cutter.

Left: This garden of turf and trees at Biddulph Grange, England, is extremely easy to maintain. A winding path gives direction and focus to what could be described as an arboretum, or tree garden.

(either green, dwarf, black or white) look great en masse. The Australian native members of the lily family, called flax lily (*Dianella* sp.), have recently been released with a range of exciting colour variegations. 'Border Silver' has white and silvery stripes, and 'Border Gold' has, naturally, gold and green stripes. Both are hardy indoors as well as outside in the shade or sun, and have star-shaped purple flowers followed by iridescent blue berries. Given their great adaptability and tolerance of drought, these plants are bound to become more popular in warm climates.

Fern gardens

For shaded moist areas, there is no better greenery than ferns. The range is extraordinary: some ferns are tree-like, others vigorous ground covers, and some, such as bird's nest fern (*Asplenium nidus*), are striking accent plants. Many have beautiful markings, such as the brake ferns (*Pteris* sp.).

Ferns belong to one of the most ancient groups of plant families on earth. Club mosses (*Lycopodium* sp.), horsetails (*Equisetum* sp.) and true ferns like maidenhair (*Asplenium trichomanes*) were a major vegetation type in the Carboniferous period, about 350 million years ago. Let's face it — if they can survive for 350 million years, they're worth a try in our wall garden (see page 298).

Landscaping materials

Hard landscaping materials can be green too, or tinged with green. With age, copper becomes marvellous with verdigris, although

Above: The paint effect on this fence has been achieved with an undercoat of black wood stain followed by a coat of acid green paint applied with a dry brush.

Mood board for a green garden

project

Creating a fern wall

Creating a fern wall is really like a hip take on the fern house of old. Instead of growing ferns in their own shelter, you can grow them on an existing wall by simply hanging them up. You'll need:

- A screen of sorts that can be cut where necessary. Brush fence panels work really well.

- Fabric to hold the plants in place at the back, almost like a nappy or diaper for their roots and the soil. It needs to be a fabric that will drain, so choose shade cloth, geotextile material or weed mat. We used shade cloth.

- The plant-growing medium. You can't use soil because it is too heavy and doesn't drain properly on the vertical. Look for a plant-growing medium like sphagnum moss, peat or copra peat, which is coconut fibre in the form of a dehydrated brick. You rehydrate it (by adding water) and use it as a peat substitute.

- Your plants. They should be as small as possible because they'll fill the gaps in the brush fence better. Spreading ferns such as rhizomes are good because they'll knit together well.

1 Using a needle and synthetic garden twine, attach shade cloth to the back of the brush fence. Sew down three sides with a simple running stitch so that the twine is only visible on the reverse side.

2 Position some of the larger, feature plants first, cutting slits in the brush as you go so that you can push the roots through.

3 Working from the bottom up, plant the larger plants.

4 Again, working from the bottom up, make gaps for the smaller plants.

5 Plant the small plants, such as maidenhair ferns. When all the plants are in position, add the soil substitute to the shade cloth bag behind the screen. Sew up the last side of the bag and attach hooks to the top of the screen.

6 Hang up the fern wall, and water it back and front. An atomizer is perfect for keeping the ferns moist.

Did you know? A 'green room' — that is, a room in a theatre set aside for actors relaxing between scenes or at the end of a performance — is painted green because the colour is thought to have a calming effect.

this patina of mostly copper sulfate takes time to build up. Paint finishes containing copper powder treated with a reactant can also turn most surfaces — including wood, iron, steel and plastic — into a faux copper finish, perfect for those with champagne taste and a beer budget.

Pine that has been treated with copper, chrome and arsenate (known as C-C-A treated pine) has a greenish tinge, but its use in the manufacture of playgrounds and picnic tables has been banned in some countries. To be on the safe side, use it for retaining walls and the like — in fact, wherever children are *not* likely to play or eat. There are also other wood treatments and stains that can be painted onto timber to give a green effect. Green bamboo poles that have been cut will retain their colour.

Many naturally occurring stones are green too. Some slate, marble and soapstone can be used for paving, and green pebbles and rock chips are also nice alternatives. For details, try coloured glass beads and dyed stones.

For really hardworking surfaces, polished concrete and terrazzo are both beautiful and durable. Coloured concrete renders are also useful. Fake grass is practical, not only as a playing surface for sports but also as a hard-wearing treatment for children's play areas. It can be cut longer to give it a more natural look. Green rubberized underlays are useful here too, especially under play equipment where a soft fall is needed.

Laminated and sandblasted glass is worth considering for screens and light-transmitting panels, while mosaic tiles and vitrified glass can also give the illusion of more light.

Right: This courtyard is a twist on the Middle Eastern garden style. The narrow terracotta-lined rills form a grid of squares, each filled in simply with a potted silver birch and pad of turf. The grey-green of the foliage and wall colour is highlighted beautifully with touches of purple to keep the scene muted and soft.

Opposite: The fresh lemon yellow of this climbing rose adds some zest to an otherwise dark green colour scheme.

Purple gardens

The colour purple was much sought after during the Renaissance period, when it was an impossibly expensive dye to procure: it was made from a crustacean that could only be found in the deep seas of the eastern Mediterranean, making it extremely dangerous to collect. Purple is regarded as a 'royal' colour because several hundred years ago only monarchs and popes could afford to buy the dye.

Below: The four-petalled blooms of *Clematis integrifolia*.

Opposite: A charming composition. Delphiniums rocket up from a frothy sea of bellflowers, rose campion, seaside daisy and English lavender.

Today this majestic colour still maintains its regal and dignified image, even though it is no longer difficult to obtain. Made by mixing red and blue together, purple can vary from violet to lavender, mauve and jacaranda hues. The more blue there is in purple, the more sedate it seems, whereas the more red is used, the more vital purple becomes.

The cool shades of mauve and lilac go beautifully with grey skies and misty weather (even dew drops give them a magical tone), while the warmer burgundy, reds and violets add a touch of royalty and gala to any garden.

The tones of blues and violets are known as receding colours — that is, to the observer they seem further away than they actually are. These colours can be used to enhance a feeling of distance and space in the garden. Lavender walks and paths lined with catmint seem longer than they in fact are.

Most hues of purple work well with silver foliage. Purple with white flowers, and with those of purple's complement, yellow, are also classic combinations. Acid yellow leaves look splendid when contrasted with an aubergine background, as do purple flowers, such as iris, and yellow highlights, such as daylilies (*Hemerocallis* sp.).

The more red in the purple, the faster the colour will disappear at night, but the rosier it will appear in the late afternoon.

Below: This lavender walk appears elongated by the use of mauve, silver and purple as well as the repetition of the same handful of plants along the way.

Below right: Against a backdrop of golden leaves and lime green foliage, the blue and mauve flowers, such as the iris and Chinese forget-me-nots, are punctuated by splashes of yellow hot pokers.

Purple flowers

Many flowers are mistakenly called blue when they are actually purple. In fact, the number of truly blue flowers is very small, with blue gromwell (*Lithodora diffusa*), blue Tibetan poppy (*Meconopsis betonicifolia*), *Tweedia caerulea*, cape forget-me-not (*Anchusa capensis*), *Evolvulus* sp., *Plumbago* sp., *Ceratostigma* sp., forget-me-not (*Myosotis* sp.), cornflowers (*Centaurea cyanus*) and gentians (*Gentiana acaulis*) being some of the stand-out favourites. Then there is the

delphinium, the quintessential purple and blue flower.

Strangely, many names of colours, such as jacaranda and lavender blue, are not actually blues but really contain enough red in them to be classed as shades and tints of purple.

Popular plants with lavender and lilac shades include agapanthus, Jacob's ladder (*Polemonium* sp.), potato vine (*Solanum jasminoides*), catmint (*Nepeta cataria*), iris, cranesbill, chaste tree (*Vitus agnus-castus*), veronica, lilac, lupins and bluebells. The

more unusual dark plum flowers include *Achillea* 'Summer Wine', agastache, coneflower, *Penstemon* 'Sour Grapes' and 'Midnight', *Salvia* 'Indigo Spires' and 'Purple Rain', *Sedum* 'Autumn Joy', sea lavender (*Limonium* sp.) and *Trachelium* sp.

Made for the shade

Purple not only adds depth to views, it can also add an ethereal glow, making it perfect for shaded woodland areas where it can add a soft, haze-like, flowery mist. Many lavender,

Left: The butterfly bush (*Buddleja* sp.) uses its darker eye like a target to help direct a butterfly's proboscis for feeding.

Below: *Clematis* is a huge genus of over 250 species, although most people are only aware of the climbing species. Best known of all these are the Florida hybrids, like this one.

Did you know? Purple is the colour many feminists wear as a reminder of the British suffragettes and their struggle for equal political rights in the early twentieth century. Their colours of purple, white and green were devised by Mrs Pethick-Lawrence. Some people suggest that it was code for Give (green) Women (white) the Vote (violet).

violet and blue flowers seem to relish this position; however, you don't need a forest to grow these pretties as any shaded spot will suit.

The most renowned plant for growing under trees is the bluebell (*Scilla* sp.). The bell-covered spikes are carried through spring, although the bulbs themselves should be planted in autumn. It is well suited to garden situations, growing easily in a broad range of climates. For other bulbs with a similar effect, try the grape hyacinth (*Muscari* sp.), which is a more cobalt version of blue, or the delightful *Ipheion* sp., which has lilac blue flowers like tiny stars.

Of course, there are many charming ground covers that will also provide a carpet of lavender in the shade. The *Campanula* genus has many species perfectly suited to this situation. *Campanula poscharskyana* will continue the display from late spring onwards. Less vigorous and ideal for small gardens is *C. carpatica*, which has violet saucer-shaped flowers held aloft on wiry stems. It really is a sweet flower. Cranesbills, or true geraniums, are also suited to semishade and will flower from spring.

For interesting foliage contrast as well as blue flowers, look no further than the Chatham Island forget-me-not (*Myosotidium* sp.). Native to New Zealand, it has deep green, glossy leaves not unlike a rhubarb, coupled with stout flower heads of bright blue and white flowers. Although not tolerant

Opposite: The spires of lupins and delphiniums are great for adding vertical interest.

Below: A hazy garden scene in miniature. This border contains easy to grow favourites, such as felicia, petunia and lobelia.

Living in the shade and loving it...the forget-me-not (at right and in the border above) is a charming annual for under trees. Once planted, it will reseed each year and pop up with no intervention. The perfect plant for the lazy gardener.

of frost, it is very useful in temperate areas and will self-seed happily once it finds a comfortable spot.

There are other forget-me-nots that one should obviously not forget! The annual, *Myosotis sylvatica*, is native to most of Europe and has small dainty flowers in spring. Then there is the Chinese forget-me-not, *Cynoglossum amabile*, which is actually a biennial that grows naturally on the banks between paddy fields. Lastly, there is the African forget-me-not, or *Anchusa* genus. Although these striking plants are useful in the cutting garden, they won't grow well at all unless given sunshine.

Violets

A plant with a name like 'violet' implies a purple flower, and indeed, violets are this and more. The colour violet itself is seen at the end of the spectrum opposite red, and it is produced by the slight mixture of red with blue.

The most common violet is *Viola odorata* or sweet violet. There are many forms of this, including white, pink and lavender shades, although always test the fragrance before you buy this plant as some forms seem to have only a slight fragrance. Then there are the superb wood violets (*V. labradorica*), which have not only purple flowers but also leaves with purple undersides. These are both moisture-loving perennial violets, and grow best in the shade.

The annual violets, or violas as they are often called, are normally F1 hybrids of *V. x wittrockiana*. They cover a range of colours, from orange and yellows, through all the pink shades, whites and, of course, purples and blues. Some are distinguished by having 'faces', others are simply single colours. All relish the sun.

Annual types of violets, such as these, come in a wide range of colours, including an orange and purple variety called 'The Joker' (far left) and the moody blue flower, 'Universal Light Blue' (left).

Below: The perennial sweet violet has a lovely perfume.

Below left: Here grape hyacinths jostle for space with fragrant hyacinths in lavender and purple.

Purple foliage

Ground covers and annuals
Ajuga 'Catlins Giant', *Atriplex hortensis* var. *rubra*, cabbages and kale, *Iresine* sp., *Solenostemon* sp.

Perennials
Canna sp. (bronze-leafed forms like 'Purpurea'), *Dahlia* 'Bishop of Llandaff' and 'Yellow Hammer', *Eucomis comosa* 'Purple', *Heuchera* sp., *Phormium tenax* 'Purpureum', *Ranunculus ficaria* 'Brazen Hussy'

Shrubs
Acalypha wilkesiana, *Azalea* 'Plumtastic', *Berberis atropurpurea*, *Clerodendrum bungei*, *Fuchsia triphylla*, *Lophomyrtus* 'Black Stallion', *Strobilanthes* sp.

Trees
Acer palmatum 'Atropurpureum', *Cercis canadensis* 'Forest Pansy', *Dodonaea viscosa* 'Purpurea', *Fagus sylvatica* f. *purpurea*, *Gleditsia triacanthos* 'Ruby Lace', *Malus* x *purpurea*, *Prunus cerasifera* 'Nigra'

Above, from top to bottom: Purple cabbage, *Canna* x *generalis* cv., *Acalypha* cv. and *Acer saccharum*.

Did you know? Napoleon Bonaparte and his wife, the Empress Josephine, exchanged violets as symbols of their love.

Plants with purple foliage

Purple foliage, as it is known, can range in colour from really reddish brown tones to inky black shades. It is an excellent foil for red, purple and pink flowers, and also provides a good contrast with golden tones. However, many of these require sun in order to retain their rich colouring.

Imagine the fresh new growth in spring of the purple-leafed maples, and how good that would look contrasted with a golden form. A combination that has been used successfully for many years is that of the black-leafed plum (*Prunus cerasifera* 'Nigra') planted in the foreground with a golden elm (*Ulmus* sp.) in the distance. Alternate plantings of gold and

Far left: Fennel and cotinus.

Left: *Berberis* sp.

Below: For many, this is the garden ideal — sweeping lawns that flow onto beds of graduated height. The white *Zantedeschia* and the soft blue forget-me-nots and *Hyacinthoides* are all self-sufficient, so there's not much work involved in maintaining this garden.

purple beech (*Fagus sylvatica*) are also used together for contrast, even in the same hedge, as a living tapestry.

Lower down, the deciduous shrub Japanese barberry (*Berberis thunbergii*) comes in a range of cultivars that include rich purples, golden-edged forms and even speckled pink types. They all look fabulous when planted together, and have the added bonus of providing a fiery autumn display.

For evergreen contrast, the mirror bush (*Coprosma repens*) now has a range of stunning leaf variegations, from the purple–black 'Taro' to the rich chocolate-leafed form known as 'Cappuccino'. These look beautiful when set off against splashes of gold. For perennials with a dash of colour, try the stunning range of cannas. 'Black Knight' looks terrific against forms such as 'Striata' or 'Tropicana'.

Closer to the ground, the garden floor can also be used to show off purple foliage. For shady areas, try planting *Tradescantia pallida*

Left: Purple bluebells in the shade add a mystical haze to the forest floor.

Above: Lupins are native to California in the United States.

Adding purple power

Small backyards, such as the rear garden of this semidetached home, can feel closed in and cramped. The colour purple, and the illusion of depth that it provides, can be used in a tight spot to create the illusion of space. The old paling fence had weathered to a dark grey, only adding to the gloomy atmosphere.

1 Painting the fence with a wash of acrylic paint and water in a pale shade of lavender will help add a sense of depth and light. This wash (about 2:1 acrylic and water) allows the texture and grain of the timber to show, but gives it an instant lift.

2 *Plectranthus ciliatus*, a wonderful plant for the shade or sun, tends to be under-utilized in gardens. The leaves have a great textural quality about them, and the foliage colour is another highlight. The sprays of mauve flowers add to the haze effect.

3 Creating a stepped or staggered garden in this narrow bed will add to the feeling of depth and spaciousness. The woven willow boundary helps separate the two layers of planting, saving the smaller plants from being overwhelmed by the larger one. Here, the colour is picked up again by moses-in-a-cradle (*Tradescantia spathacea* syn. *Rhoeo discolor*), which has a purple underside and a pink-striped reverse.

4 Painting a contrasting trellis fan with a brighter shade of purple not only acts as a support for the bougainvillea, but also creates a focal point that helps hold the scene together. As it grows, the climber will also disguise the boundary.

Above: This garden has real vertical impact, using the spires of penstemon, salvia, lavatera and lupins to reach heady heights.

'Purpurea' together with either golden moneywort (*Lysimachia nummularia* 'Aurea') or the silver *Lamium* 'White Nancy'. Drier areas can look good too. The succulents *Aeonium arboreum* 'Zwartkop' and *Sedum mexicanus* 'Gold Mound' look great when planted together.

Landscaping materials

Purple is such an 'out there' colour that its effect can be really dramatic. For this reason, stick to dark inky purple for floor treatments, and use the brighter and lighter lavenders for walls. Not only is this more practical from a maintenance point of view, as dark colours won't show the dirt as much, but it will also make your space feel lighter and airier.

Dark-coloured pebbles, siltstones and slates (even York stone, with its dark grey shades) will work well for the garden floor. Ceramic tiles, both matt-finished and gloss, and glass mosaic tiles with an opalescent sheen are great for beautiful detail, be it in borders on paving and walls or as splashbacks for water features.

Metallic paint has also come a long way with technological advances. The micaceous iron oxides that can now be added to acrylic bases are sometimes shaded in deep purple or softer lavender tones, and can be applied to any paintable surface. Wood stains too come in purple and lavender stains, and can be used to treat timber.

Even plastic (perspex) screens can add a touch of whimsy and fun to a garden, and many shells have stunning colours that tie in with this theme.

Mood board for a purple garden

Hot gardens

Red, yellow and orange are known as hot colours. Red symbolizes power, strength and assertion while orange is a dynamic and cheerful blend of yellow and red. Yellow, in turn, is an optimistic and radiant colour, like a sunshiny day.

Below: Use the blooms of pot marigolds to brighten up the garden, and the edible petals to liven up a green salad.

Opposite: A superb range of flowering perennials. The taller reds at the back are cannas, red hot pokers and bottlebrush. Golden tones are provided by golden-leafed conifers, kangaroo paws, daylilies and *Bulbinella* sp.

Hot colours are known as advancing colours, because they appear closer than they in fact are. They can shorten backgrounds, almost jumping out at you in fact. Hot colours can also add a sense of mystery, especially those inky-scarlet shades that evoke an atmosphere of secrecy and intrigue.

Yellows make a garden feel light and airy, especially when they are mixed with golden leaves. When mixed with purple leaves, hot colours become darker, heavier, richer and more luxuriant.

Some people might say that hot colours are too jarring. But if you like anything but the conventional, hot colours can jazz things up and give others a bit of a thought-provoking jolt. The red borders at Christopher Lloyd's garden, Great Dixter, in Sussex, England, created a sensation when he first planted them with cannas, dahlias and verbena, but now they have an almost cult following around the world.

Great plants for autumn

It is curious that many gardeners regard the bright colours of some summer-flowering herbaceous perennials as being in 'bad taste', or too intense, but these same people may freely plant trees and shrubs that are ablaze with intense colour during autumn. Perhaps they feel the cooler months need brightening, or that the ephemeral autumn display is so fleeting that its vulgarity can be forgiven.

Above: Amaranthus are mostly native to South America, Mexico and the United States, where they are grown as a grain crop. They make a stunning bedding annual. This red-leafed form, called 'Pygmy Torch', grows to about 1 m (3 ft) and looks *hot* in the garden.

Right: A rich tapestry of evergreen and deciduous plants comprises this autumn scene. Featured here are coloured maples, heaths and conifers.

Whatever the reason, brilliantly toned autumn foliage plants are loved by gardeners all over the world. Those who live in subtropical and warm areas can only dream about growing them.

For the most stunning selection of autumn-toned plants, see page 322.

Hot flowers for the border

Gardeners will always gather inspiration from past designers, but they should remodel the ideas to suit their location and its demands. The famous plantswoman Gertrude Jekyll pioneered what is now known as the hot border. At Munstead Wood in Surrey she planted a huge mid-section of reds and yellows in her famous Long Border, which was 60 m (200 ft) long and 4.3 m (11 ft) deep. Jekyll wanted 'the cool colourings at the ends enhancing the brilliant warmth of the middle'. The garden was designed to peak in late summer, and so it is filled with dahlias, chiefly the dark purple-leafed forms, and *Celosia* sp., marigolds, cannas and *Helianthus* sp. The Long Border has been replanted at the Botanic Garden in Reading University, England, so admirers can still appreciate an example of her work.

Other hot borders Jekyll designed included masses of golden margeurite, spiky crocosmia, purple heliotrope and copper-leafed beet, red nicotianas and yellow *Achillea*

Below: This garden definitely has the 'wow' factor, with black (*Aeonium arboreum* 'Zwartkop') and red tones (cannas and *Alstroemeria* sp.) in stark contrast to the acid greens and yellows of red hot pokers, kangaroo paws, daylilies and verbascum.

Above: The colours in this hot bed graduate from pale pinks and creams through to the stark brightness of reds and oranges, creating a visual crescendo.

Right: The base of an immature golden cane palm, just as it is starting to develop a network of yellow trunks that will make it so beautiful in maturity.

sp. The key factor was that to add stability and permanence to these schemes, Jekyll mixed hot colours with other elements such as leaf shapes, flower shapes and even some shrubs, such as the purple smoke bush (*Cotinus coggygria*) or golden-edged box (*Buxus sempervirens* 'Aureovariegata').

Hot stuff

It's not just flowers that can be beautiful: often fruit, seeds, stems and cones can also provide a dash of dazzle. For the tropics, the stunning sealing wax palm is hard to surpass. Also known as lipstick palm (*Cyrtostachys renda*), it has red crownshafts and leaf stalks. Slightly more cold tolerant are two other extraordinary palms — *Chambeyronia macrocarpa*, which gets bright red new leaves, and the golden cane palm (*Chrysalidocarpus lutescens*), a better known palm that is popular for indoor conservatories and sunrooms. It has lime yellow trunks and mid-ribs, and grows with multiple canes.

Planting up a hot foliage border

For this border we drew on the existing planting in the garden. Lilly pillies (*Syzygium* sp.), with their flush of pink new growth, form an evergreen screen (not shown). The striking form of red cabbage palms (*Cordyline australis* 'Purpurea') will act as living punctuation marks, breaking up the length of the bed and adding height.

In the middle ground, *Canna* 'Tropicana' will give an intense splash of vibrant orange and red, and will be played off against the cool tones of white variegated plants like white mondo and *Dianella* 'Silver Streak'. Clumps of *Salvia* 'Raspberry Royal' will add seasonal flower colour into late autumn. The foreground is planted with a double border of coleus (*Solenostemon* sp.) — the annual citrus shades (sold simply as hybrids) as well as the perennial frogs' feet forms with their dark burgundy, deeply lobed leaves. This one is called 'Midnight'.

1 Clear any turf away, making sure to remove all runners that may reshoot and cause a weed problem in the bed. Position the plants first and make sure you've spaced them out correctly, then plant.

2 Add mulch.

3 Water in well.

If you live in a cold area, try experimenting with some of the colour-stemmed bamboos, such as golden bamboo (*Schizostachyum brachycladum*), which is sacred in Bali and probably the most decorative in the world. More common is the other yellow-stemmed bamboo known as *Phyllostachys aureosulcata* 'Aureocaulis' or 'Spectabilis' — a mouthful and eyeful in one!

Plants with show-off bark include the coral-stemmed maple, whose Japanese cultivar name 'Sangokaku' translates to 'coral tower'. The trunk and stems of this *Acer palmatum* cultivar glow red in winter to spectacular effect.

Another maple, *Acer pseudoplatanus* 'Erythrocarpum', not only has purple–red on the underside of its leaves, but also claret-coloured samaras (winged seeds) and red petioles. An interesting seed occurs on the golden rain tree (*Koelreuteria paniculata*). After its laburnum-like blooms flower, it displays a second burst of colour, this time with salmon red, papery, bladder-like pods that are a joy in themselves.

Trees to light up the sky

Some trees are literally like a beacon in the sky. So flamboyant is their display of foliage or flower that their beauty can be overwhelming. Normally such a display is the exclusive reserve of deciduous trees in autumn; however, many warm climate plants make their mark in late spring and summer.

The poinciana or flamboyant (*Delonix regia*) is one of the showiest flowering trees in the world. Bright red, pea-shaped flowers mass at the top of this flat, broad-domed tree. Alas, it will only do well in the tropics.

For gardeners in slightly cooler areas, there are other berried treats, such as *Cornus* sp. and *Sorbus* sp. Native to Australia are two spectacular trees — the Illawarra flame tree

(*Brachychiton acerifolius*) and the firewheel tree (*Stenocarpus sinuatus*). Both are reasonably tolerant of the odd frost, but still prefer to be warm during winter.

Also for warm coastal gardens, the flame of the forest (*Butea frondosa*) from Bangladesh is worth growing for its orange–red pea flowers. From the warm temperate zones of Africa and Central America come the coral trees (*Erythrina* sp.), which Los Angeles appears to have adopted as natives! Their red blooms are truly stunning, but the brittle branches, although easy to strike, fall in the slightest wind.

Faking it

Some plants have a display that is commonly referred to as flowers, but which are in fact showy bracts, or modified leaves. These include *Bougainvillea* sp., *Mussaenda* sp. and poinsettia (*Euphorbia pulcherrima*).

Centre: The breathtaking poinciana. Its flowers light the sky in summer and its canopy provides protection from the tropical heat.

Above left: The yellow blooms of the golden rain tree are surpassed by the seed heads, which turn salmon pink in autumn.

Above: Golden yellow flowers (gaillardia, abutilon and *Rosa* 'Graham Thomas') look great paired with the bright mid-green of these daylilies and the large glossy leaves of oyster plants.

Other plants have glorious crops of fruit. There are, of course, the well known crabapple, apple, apricot and the like, but also consider the Irish strawberry tree (*Arbutus unedo*), persimmons, tamarillos and the hot pink berries of lilly pillies. Beside the obvious shrubs like *Pyracantha* sp. and *Cotoneaster* sp., there are other shrubs worth discovering, such as the lesser known roses that have showy red, yellow or orange hips. Try *Skimmia* sp., with its red berries, or the Chinese lantern plant (*Physalis* sp.), a perennial with bright orange berries hidden inside a red papery pouch.

Gold and yellow flowers

Of the entire hot spectrum, yellow is the easiest to experiment with if you are feeling a little unsure about being brave with colour. It looks cheery when planted out with white and touches of blue — a popular scheme all over the world. When combined with golden foliage, yellow flowers can look like a bright, cheerful day.

Of course, yellow itself has many shades. The soft, buttery tones that you might find on the *Achillea* named 'Moonshine' are totally different to the clear yellow of a daffodil or the orange-tinged golden yellow of a sunflower. The more orange–red contained in the yellow, the more brazen your garden will feel, and the more you can combine it with

Opposite: Illawarra flame tree makes a fine street tree due to its compact size and adaptability.

Above left: Poinsettias are popular worldwide for their flame-coloured flowers at Christmas time.

Above: Daylilies are wonderful border plants in gardens. Their flowers range in colour from lemon yellow through to this luscious red to near black and brown tones.

Did you know? In 1986 the famous textile designer Jack Larson painted two bright red rows of rough cedar trunks as a feature in 'The Red Garden at the Longhouse', at Long Island, New York. These were underplanted with scarlet 'Christmas Cheer' Kurume azaleas for the ultimate twist on an avenue and Japanese Shinto look. He later set up a foundation that aims to show how landscapes can be a living art form.

other bright colours, such as lime greens and navy blue. The softer the yellow, the better it will combine with gentle shades such as lavender or cream, especially against a dark green background. This makes them radiate all the more.

Foliage for the hot garden

Plants whose leaves fall within this colour spectrum will go beautifully with matching flowers. For example, dark purple and plum-coloured foliage (see page 310) teams especially well with red blooms, and golden leaves work really well with other white flowers and yellow blooms.

Gold for opulence

The whole 'get rich quick thing' is so contagious that even the humble gardener can be enticed by plants with gold foliage. Refer to 'Gold foliage' in the box at right, and use gold to give your garden an opulent look.

Tropical heat

While it is true that, if you live in a dreary climate, hot and warm colours can cheer you, when the same combinations of colour are used in the heat, the effect can be sizzling. For many, this is an evocative scheme, reminiscent of the tropics, and one that can be used in conjunction with an exotic, tropical garden (see page 238).

Many tropical flowers are insanely good show-offs, strutting their stuff like dancers from Rio during Carnivale. Imagine the exotic ginger lily with its heady scent, gold flowers and striking red stamens, calla lilies with their rich mango shades and *Ixora* sp. with their red–orange, voluptuous, erotic blooms in your hot garden. Even the long-legged lipstick palm and dangling flowers of *Heliconia* sp. are enough to get your blood pumping.

Gold foliage

Ground covers
Carex elata 'Aurea', *Helipterum petiolare* 'Limelight', *Mentha* x *gracilis*, *Origanum vulgare* 'Aureum', *Sedum adolphi*, *Thymus vulgaris aureus*

Perennials
Canna 'Striata', *Heliotropium* x *aureum*, *Pelargonium* x *hortorum* cultivars, *Phormium tenax* 'Variegatum', *Sambucus racemosa* 'Plumosa Aurea', *Tanacetum parthenium* 'Aureum'

Shrubs
Aucuba japonica 'Picturata', *Berberis thunbergii* 'Aurea', *Choisya ternata* 'Sundance', *Euonymus japonicus* 'Aureus', *Philadelphus coronarius* 'Aureus', *Spiraea japonica* 'Goldflame'

Trees
Acer palmatum 'Lutescens', *Chrysalidocarpus lutescens*, *Elaeagnus* x *ebbingei* 'Limelight', *Fagus sylvatica* 'Aurea Pendula', *Gleditsia triacanthos* 'Sunburst', *Robinia pseudoacacia* 'Limelight', *Sambucus nigra* 'Aurea'

Above, from top to bottom: *Carex elata* 'Aurea', *Lysimachia nummularia*, *Spiraea japonica* 'Goldflame' and *Ulmus glabra* 'Lutescens'.

Did you know? When tomatoes first arrived in Europe, their fruits were gold.

Opposite: This gorgeous hot border is filled with textural and foliage contrast as well as flowers. The strap leaves of New Zealand flax contrast beautifully with some of the flowering shrubs, such as the black-leafed dahlias, geraniums and canna lilies.

Clockwise from above: Some stunning hot-coloured bulbs include crocosmia, red hot pokers and vallotas.

If you don't live in the tropics, but want some of that sensuality in your garden, it's hard to go past the canna lilies with their striped leaves and speckled flowers in blazing shades of tangerine, carmine, blood and gold. Also useful are red hot pokers or torch lilies (*Kniphofia* sp.), daylilies and Peruvian lilies (*Alstroemeria* sp.) for gardeners wanting to dabble with exotic dancers in a milder climate.

Landscaping materials

The earthy and hot tones of the colour wheel naturally lend themselves to a wide range of materials — from rammed earth to bagged walls with red clay and terracotta. These are all great utilitarian surfaces for both floors and walls.

More refined products, such as terrazzo and polished granite slabs, are perfect for

Potting up some hot colour and flavour

The chilli is one of the most ornamental of edibles. These dwarf-growing types work really well in funky orange plastic pots and will add some spice to a tabletop, sunny windowsill or conservatory. Use them for flavouring a multitude of dishes.

1 Buy chillies ready grown as potted colour (or raise your own from their seeds), then gently tease out their roots.

2 Firm down gently and top with decorative gravel in a complementary colour.

3 Chillies like to grow in a hot spot, but will last well for weeks on a sunny windowsill inside.

large-dimension feature pieces, whether they are step treads or outdoor kitchen worktops. Pink granite setts are lovely for detailed inserts, and work particularly well at boundaries or as edging. Cut sandstone with red streaks or striations can also be beautiful for paving in a hot garden, while stacked stone works well in walls.

For more detailed work, try glass mosaic tiles for water features and red ceramic tiles for garden friezes. Mesh-backed pink travertine (the synthetic mesh on the back of the tiles helps to hold them in place) is also perfect for details or trim.

Mulches like tan bark, crushed stone and scoria will also add tones of red and burnt orange, while glass beads, sand and ceramic inlays are all good for small details.

Rusted iron panels, reinforced iron screens and painted iron effects are part of the metallic selection available, and if you have the budget, you could try gold and gilding on statuary to great effect. If not, rust paint is a cheaper yet still effective alternative. (See page 209 for iron paint effects.)

Stained timber and simple oiled hardwoods also have burnt umber tones that will add a beautiful warmth to the built landscape.

Top: Also known as treasure flowers, gazanias tolerate heat, sun, sand and salt.

Above: In ideal conditions — in moist soil, or even bog gardens and semishade — astilbe can be a sensational plant. 'Fanal' has stunning bronze leaves matched by the garnet-coloured blooms.

Mood board for a hot garden

Sculpted palette

Intense. Advised, intentional, purposeful.
A deliberate dominion over the landscape.
Balance versus form. Exactness and integrity.
Distilled essences. Timeless.

Opposite: This severe clipped beech hedge at Levens Hall in
Cumbria, England, was designed by Guillaume Beaumont, who
trained under André le Nôtre (see page 17).

Above: Carved and sculpted doesn't necessarily mean 'square'. In their own way, sculpted gardens all demonstrate an emphasis on geometry and form. Sven-Ingvar Andersson's garden in Sweden is a fine example of an organic garden.

Right: The topiary garden in yew and box at Levens Hall, an Elizabethan garden laid out between 1689 and 1712.

Right centre: This woven hazelwood screen has the most wonderful texture and sinuous line.

Far right: Another view of the Andersson garden, where climbers cover dead tree trunks to create marvellous living sculptures.

Sculpted design elements

The premise of the sculpted garden is the desire to manipulate spaces and completely alter them from their natural state. Out goes the haphazard, and in comes a carefully orchestrated garden with geometrical considerations — balance, form and a heavily designed outline, all carved into the landscape.

This style is all about controlling your environment. Like no other design style, it takes the house into the garden, fusing the two spaces. In other genres, the practice is to decorate the house, or soften it by planting a garden. In this genre, on the other hand, there are a lot of built elements, such as anterooms and even separate structures. In its modern interpretation, this may be in the form of pathways seeming to float across the water, rooms jutting into the outdoors, or even galleries of garden inserted into the built landscape.

Gardens such as these often relegate plants to the backdrop, utilizing the built landscape to express a theme, so plants may be used as features in pots or, if they have a naturally outrageous form, architectural elements in their own right (see pages 387, 402 and 414). Alternatively, severe shapes or rigid, structured silhouettes may be clipped out of hedging plants. In short, plants are used if they can conform to the design, but omitted if by their very nature they will outgrow their spot and look untamed.

This built landscape can still be very interesting, however. The sculpted garden doesn't have to be boring; it just needs to be executed with precision. After all, if a sculpted design doesn't quite work, it will be hard to disguise this with planting. It has to be strong enough to stand alone. The sculpted garden tends to be a year-round garden, and it has more consistency than other styles.

Control, formal designs, geometry and year-round good 'bones' — whether it's hedging, paving, low walls or water rills — are the trademarks of this disciplined style, as are sculptures themselves. Formal designs can be great as they 'fit' into the boxes that we carve into the landscape.

Pitfalls
Eliminating the non-essentials and emphasizing form and balance mean you also run the risk of eliminating the unexpected delights — the sounds, smells and other elements that surprise. Also, some sculpted design styles rely not just on balance but also on symmetry, so not all spaces are suitable.

Classical gardens

A classical garden implies formality, symmetry and balance, with one side mirroring the other. From the time of its conception in the days of ancient Rome, the classical garden has featured the ordered, restrained look of formally laid out gardens with strong lines and vistas.

Typically, a classical Roman garden was rectangular or square, and based on a geometric design. Enclosed with a wall or hedge, the internal spaces were subdivided with pools and paths or colonnades. In medieval times, this system of division remained the rule in cloister gardens.

This central axis was repeated again later in gardens of the Italian Renaissance, where it remained the most important feature. Slopes were carved into a series of terraces, each linked with steps or ramps. Restraint and simplicity were the key factors governing the design. The range of plants used was small, with box, oleander, rosemary and bay popular choices because they were easily trimmed into solid shapes.

The hydraulic engineering used in the watering systems and fountains of these elaborate gardens was extremely advanced, allowing ornamental fountains, communal and private baths, drinking fonts and the like to be featured, hundreds of years before pumps were invented.

These classical gardens also manipulated the bright sun of the region to perfection. Long tunnels were like cocoons of dark green, created by colonnades and pillars or arched plantings of sombre laurel. They took the intensity out of the sun and directed shafts of soft light to the ground below, before opening out into sun-bathed courts, where focal points of white marble statues

Below: Details such as this urn add references to ancient Rome.

Opposite: This elegantly proportioned and symmetrical garden room at Biddulph Grange, England, comprises refined geometric shapes, typical of the classical style.

Above: The immense and wonderful ground patterning of the Versailles garden in France and its *gazon coupé* or turf and gravel shapes.

and urns or sparkling water features shone like jewels, providing drama and excitement.

Formal gardens no doubt peaked with the landscape surrounding the Palace of Versailles, where the central axis went on and on into the distance as far as one could see, clearing villages in its path (see pages 17–18). So vast is this garden that the River Seine was redirected to power the hundreds of water features.

Today, you can recreate this elegance and order on a small domestic scale in your own garden. Planting tall hedging so that it 'frames' views and reveals a feature, such as an urn on a pedestal, and surrounding paving with low hedges to clearly outline its edges,

both add impact to a formal scheme. Define your corners or main axis with topiary or feature trees to emphasize the geometry of the space. Keeping colours to a minimum — for example, just green leaves and the occasional white bloom — will also focus attention on your design.

Texture in a classical garden is limited to smooth surfaces such as polished marble and pressure-cut stone. Even the foliage suitable for this type of garden tends to be fine textured, such as box and juniper, or glossy, like acanthus and grape. This adds to the feeling of elegance, with contrast limited to detail such as the carving on columns, urns and water features.

Pattern, on the other hand, is very important. Inlays on tiles, architectural motifs, the complexity of a parterre or light shining through lattice all add to the complexity of the classical garden, which may look simple from the outside.

Did you know? The Palladian style of architecture from sixteenth century Italian gardens is named after Andrea Palladio, who also designed many of the best gardens of the era.

A clipped hedge defining a birdbath (below left) or herbaceous planting, such as these irises (below right), is a simple way to use a traditional parterre in today's gardens.

Shopping list

- iron finials or fountainheads
- lattice for screens
- marble for a tabletop or tezzoras
- sawn sandstone
- hedging plants
- edging plants and ground covers
- topiary or standards
- string line and pegs

Places suitable for a classical garden

Classical gardens emphasize symmetry and the main axis so strongly that they are best suited to regular-shaped spaces, where areas can be easily divided into halves and quarters. This design genre lends itself to both inward- and outward-looking spaces, where either a distant vista or a purpose-built focal point can provide an anchor for the whole space.

The geometrical underpinning of such a garden also makes it very suitable for a small space, where patterns and line need to be strong in order to hold the eye. They are useful too for commercial landscapes, such as rooftop terraces, where the design is viewed from above, perhaps from a neighbouring taller building, in much the same way as the Renaissance garden was viewed from the palace above.

Materials for a classical garden

Classical gardens tend to be built with only a few materials from a very restricted colour palette. Cream, white, black and green are always reliable, with touches of red for highlights. Simple, elegant materials with some historical point of interest are best for this garden style.

Marble, long associated with classical art and architecture, is the perfect material for many surfaces, including tabletops. The subtle range of available colours — from leafy greens to inky blacks, warm reds and pure whites — makes marble very versatile. For outdoor flooring, cut stone (especially high-pressure water-sawn slabs that have a

Mood board for a classical garden

Planting a hedge

Planting a hedge correctly is the starting point for a successful classical garden. After all, hedges form the walls of your garden rooms, and they should be as straight as timber fences. And just as a wall should have good foundations, so should a hedge. Give your plants a good start in life by thoroughly preparing the soil with enough nutrients to sustain them. Encourage healthy roots by cultivating the soil so that young plants can quickly establish themselves.

1 Use a string line to mark out the line your hedge will follow.

2 Measure the overall distance of the hedge and work out how far apart each plant will be. Mark their positions, then dig the first hole. Set aside the soil. Remove the first plant from its container, teasing out the roots if necessary. Position it in the hole, making sure that the soil level is the same in the ground as it was in the pot. Backfill with the soil you set aside earlier.

3 Firm down gently around the roots.

4 Mulch with well rotted leaf mould, bark chips or similar material to keep the roots cool and the weeds at bay. Repeat the process for each plant.

Did you know? Flowers were almost entirely absent from the formal English gardens of the seventeenth century. Chiswick House, built in 1726, had an imitation Roman garden.

smooth, clean surface) work beautifully underfoot, although reconstituted compounds such as ground stone and cement, or marble dust and white cement, work if they are well made. Often used for statuary, these materials are also a cheaper option.

Metal, in particular cast iron (which has also been used for centuries), looks great teamed with stone, brickwork and plants. It can be shaped into finials, statuary, table bases, fencing and urns, and adds a sense of stability and tradition.

Enclosing your garden room

After you have finished the hard landscaping, such as building the walls and paving the floors, the next step is to start planting your living walls. Plants in a classical garden are pieces of living architecture. They will obviously take some time to establish, so make planting your first priority.

To choose a hedge that suits your needs, consider how urgently you need a screen, how high you want it to be, whether you require a deciduous or evergreen screen, and the amount of maintenance it will require. The less trimming your hedge needs, the more leisure time you'll have.

Small hedges are great for defining an area or for bordering pathways. Evergreens such as common box (*Buxus* sp.) and *Euonymus fortunei* dwarf cultivars are perfect for this. Larger hedges, which might form a backdrop to other plantings but still be suitable for internal divisions, include orange jessamine (*Murraya paniculata*), sweet olive (*Osmanthus* sp.), bay (*Laurus nobilis*), laurustinus (*Viburnum tinus*) and box honeysuckle (*Lonicera nitida*). Tall hedges of yew (*Taxus* sp.), holly oak (*Quercus ilex*), Leyland cypress (x *Cupressocyparis leylandii*) and the deciduous hornbeams (*Carpinus* sp.) or beech

Above: A simple 'wheel' with 'spokes' of box is a good way of dividing up beds of flowering annuals or vegetables in a classical garden.

Below, from left to right: Taller hedging plants to choose from include *Viburnum tinus*, *Murraya paniculata* and *Osmanthus heterophyllus* 'Variegatus'.

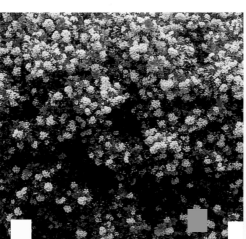

project

Marking out a knot garden

First of all, work out a design on paper and decide what plants you want to grow (see the list of suggested plants on page 352). The design used here is a simple one combining squares and arcs to form a flower motif. A simple combination of silver cotton lavender (represented by the white paint), golden box honeysuckle (the yellow paint) and dwarf English box (the orange paint) would be elegant.

Next, clear and level the site. Although we have painted onto the grass so that the pattern shows up better for photography, make sure that you thoroughly weed and dig over the site with manure before you begin.

1 Transfer the outer perimeter onto the ground using pegs and a string line. Once you're satisfied that it is square, mark out the lines with yellow marking paint.

2 For this design, a second square is to be planted internally, at a 45-degree angle to the first, like a diamond. Measure the mid-point on each of the four sides of the external boundary. Mark each mid-point with a peg, then connect all four pegs with a string line. Again, spray along the lines with orange marking paint, and leave the pegs in for the next step.

3 To create the flower motif, first find the centre of the outer square. Run a diagonal string line from one corner to the other. Repeat for the other pair of corners. Using white marking paint, scribe an arc from the centre of the first square to one of the corners. This line forms one side of the first flower petal. Scribe another arc in the same way to form a whole petal. Repeat this process for each of the remaining three corners of the first square. You now have a flower, diamond and square marked out.

Plant along the marking lines for each motif, using the appropriate plant, and leaving out a plant on any layer that is to appear 'below'. Most plants will need to be placed at 25 cm (10 in) centres, or closer — say, 15 cm (6 in) if you want a faster effect. Remove the lines and stakes, and plant as per usual. Mulch with the decorative surface of your choice, and water thoroughly.

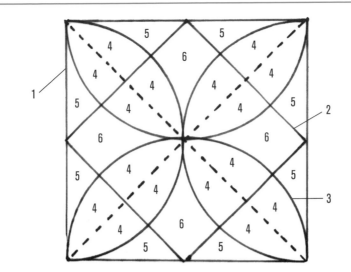

Key to knot garden

1   Outer square

2   Inner square

3   Flower motif

4   Silver cotton lavender

5   Golden box honeysuckle

6   Dwarf English box

Tips

• Plant between autumn and spring as these are the best times for shrubs to establish their roots and for weeding to be kept under control.

• Use different plants or variegated forms of the same plant for each motif to strengthen both the pattern and the 'over and under' effect.

• Keep your design trimmed at least once a year so that it stays bushy, healthy and clearly defined.

Above: One of the criticisms of parterres could be that they are usually flat, with no vertical interest. The addition of upright components, such as tripods and topiary, helps overcome this problem. This herb parterre at Ballymaloe Cookery School in Cork, Ireland, is famous for its home-grown produce.

Right: A simple parterre of box and white gravel is punctuated by spheres and pyramids. The focus is the topiary peacock.

(*Fagus sylvatica*) are all appropriate trees in a wide range of climate zones.

Parterres and topiary

After you have attended to the walls and floors, it is time to consider some of the more elaborate components, such as parterres and topiary, which you'll use to decorate your garden rooms. These will be the focal points of your garden. As topiary is a vertical element, it's great for flanking entranceways, directing traffic and leading you further into the garden. Parterres and knot gardens, on the other hand, are very flat and highly patterned, making them perfect for creating interest on the ground plane and keeping your eye from wandering beyond the bounds of that garden room.

The parterre and the knot

The highly contrived spaces in traditional parterres and knot gardens were planted in patterns and shapes like a decorative motif, rather than a 'garden', and the plants themselves were clipped into shapes. A range of flowering plants was not generally used. These elaborate gardens, which needed a lot of maintenance, were ideal for the period as cheap labour was readily available. (For more detail, see pages 17–18.) Such gardens also provided an excellent visual link between highly ornate buildings and the surrounding landscape.

Parterres and knots are the gardening equivalent of drawings on the ground, designed to be admired from above rather than experienced at ground level. Popular in the sixteenth century, knot gardens contained intricate, geometric designs within a square or rectangle and were often edged with low-growing hedges of lavender or box that showed off the subtle characteristics of the plants. The various species were planted in

Cutting a pyramid topiary

Clipping geometric shapes is best done with some sort of template, as the sharper your lines are, the more effective the look. For a classic pyramid shape, use cane stakes and a length of garden hose as guides.

1 Make a tripod by tying together three bamboo canes at the top. This will serve as a template or frame for trimming.

2 Make a circle out of hose to fit the widest part of your pyramid, and use this as a guide for the diameter of the cone as you work your way up the plant.

3 Starting from the base, trim off any excess growth. Draw the hose tighter as you go upwards to develop a point.

Tip

• Like all hedge and topiary pruning, the more frequently you tip prune, the denser the foliage will be.

Mazes and labyrinths

Above: This turf maze is not only an exciting adventure but also a visual treat of shadow, tone, pattern and line.

An interesting twist on clipping plants into hedges and using them for making patterns is the maze or labyrinth. Both date back thousands of years, and are evident in many Gothic church floors and ancient Greek mosaics, but their use in the landscape is harder to trace accurately. Turf mazes – such as the 1000-year-old miz maze at Breamore House in Hampshire in the United Kingdom, comprising scattered stones laid out in labyrinthine patterns, and also the surviving hedge maze at Hampton Court, near London – show that the concept predated the Victorian era.

Mazes today can be any shape – curvilinear or angular, symmetrical or asymmetrical. They can be crafted out of materials like wood and iron mesh, cut into turf, grown over latticework, laid with stones or clipped from plants. The result can be sheer fun for some but positive torture and tedium for others!

Did you know? Mazes were once known as miz mazes, and these contained pathways so complicated you could easily become lost. Consequently, the term 'mizeree' means a place of unhappiness and discomfort, misfortune and bad luck.

Opposite: The garden at Hatfield House was laid out in the seventeenth century by Tradescant the Elder. It includes many rare plants as well as water parterres, terraces, herb gardens, orchards and a foot maze.

such a way that they appeared to cross over and under one another, like threads in a tapestry. The spaces between the hedging plants were usually left bare, but sometimes they were filled with other plants or with decorative gravels.

The ideal knot garden consisted of four elements, each of a different pattern, which often told a story or incorporated the owner's initials or emblem.

For example, one such pattern at Villandry in France is a combination called *Jardins d'Amour*, Gardens of Love, in box borders, in fancy shapes, accentuated by yew trees (*Taxus* sp.), the 'infill' planted with flowers. There is *L'Amour Tragique*, Tragic Love, with box planted as blades, swords and daggers, and red flowers representing the blood spilt. *L'Amour Adultère*, Adulterous Love, is represented by horns and fans, with yellow flowers, the colour of betrayed love. In *L'Amour Tendre*, Tender Love, hearts are separated by orange flames and masks. And finally, in *L'Amour Passionné*, Passionate Love, the hearts are shattered by passion.

Today the parterre is still a useful tool for creating interest in a small space that may be viewed from above — perhaps a rooftop garden in a cityscape, or on a simpler scale, the front garden of a terrace overlooked by only a few levels.

Plants for parterres and knot gardens

Plants used in parterres should be able to tolerate trimming. Almost anything with short internodes — that is, not much stem length between branches and new leaves — is worth a try.

The second consideration is how often you'll need to trim. Choosing plants that have a similar growth rate to each other will mean easier maintenance, as the whole pattern can be trimmed at the same time. For this reason,

different cultivars of the same plant — such as green, purple or gold forms of box honeysuckle (*Lonicera nitida*), many forms of box (*Buxus* sp.) and dwarf *Euonymus fortunei* with its various leaf variegations — can work well together. A bonus is that they often have similar growth rates.

Finally, consider the longevity of each plant. Some herbs — germander (*Teucrium* sp.), hyssop (*Hyssopus officinalis*), lavender (*Lavandula* sp.), rosemary (*Rosmarinus officinalis*), rue (*Ruta* sp.), thyme (*Thymus* sp.) and winter savory (*Satureja montana*) — will grow quickly but need replacement every decade to look their best, while others, like the slow-growing box, will last for centuries.

Above: Lavender benefits enormously from regular hard pruning, and that is why it responds so well to being grown for hedging.

Right: Some herbs, such as thyme, were also used in the original parterres and knot gardens. Shown here is the pretty variegated form, *Thymus vulgaris* 'Silver Posy'.

Topiary

Topiary, the art of clipping plants into shapes, is often used in formal or classical gardens. A plant can be cut into many different forms — a simple cone, a standard ball on a stem or something more elaborate, such as animals in a clipped green zoo. Topiary works well not only in the formal, structured garden, where it is often used to accentuate paths, intersections and focal points, but also in less structured spaces. Cottage gardens, vegetable gardens and more free-flowing garden styles can often benefit from the addition of a clipped plant, which then forms a contrast with the 'frothy mass' surrounding it. Perfect plants for topiary include bay (*Laurus nobilis*), yew, cypresses, junipers (*Juniperus* sp.),

myrtle (*Myrtus* sp.), lilly pilly (*Syzygium* sp.), box and box honeysuckle.

Plants for a classical garden

To work well in the classical garden, plants need to be able to conform. Screening plants have to be hedged, climbers mustn't grow in a rampant way and ground covers should be almost like a green carpet. Of course, flowers should be discreet, with subdued colours such as cream and white, although perfume is a plus.

Typical plants for taller hedges include cypress (*Cypressus* sp.), Portugal laurel (*Prunus lusitanica*), *Viburnum* sp., *Murraya* sp., yew (*Taxus* sp.), *Thuja* sp. and *Photinia* sp., while medium-sized versions can be

Centre: This yellow flower border is given definition and structure by the golden clipped conifers, which rocket skywards.

Below: Urns and other pieces of statuary are useful for marking the end of a vista.

Above: This stunning Corinthian-style capital — that is, the upper part of a column — is adorned with acanthus leaves.

Above right: The port wine magnolia (*Michelia figo*), makes a stunning medium-sized evergreen hedge with deliciously fragrant flowers that smell of port wine.

achieved with *Choisya* sp., port wine magnolia (*Michelia figo*), gardenia and box hedges. For dwarf plants that are suitable for small borders, see 'Plants for parterres and knot gardens' (page 350).

Train climbers into structure-like features. For a great effect on a boundary wall, train ivy (*Hedera* sp.) up the wall on tall slender stems, then trim it into a neat block at the top. To achieve this look, simply remove the side shoots and leaves from the bottom third of each stem as it grows. Once it has reached the desired height, trim back the central leader and allow it to spread along the top. Star jasmine (*Trachelospermum jasminoides*)

looks terrific when trained onto wires in a diamond pattern, but it must be clipped into shape regularly.

Ground covers can make superb green carpets in the garden. Periwinkle (*Vinca minor*) forms a dense evergreen mat, which weeds find impossible to penetrate. Other choices include the prostrate form of star jasmine (*Trachelospermum asiaticum*) and *Pachysandra* sp., which you can keep in trim by mowing on the highest setting once a year. Dwarf grasses, such as mondo (*Ophiopogon japonicus* 'Nana') and *Dianella caerulea* 'Little Jess', can also be used to edge pathways or delineate pavers.

Maintenance

The classical garden must be consistently and precisely maintained. The stray leaf and wayward branch will look immediately out of place in such a garden. This means that a

Did you know? During Henry VIII's rule in the sixteenth century, the topiary at Hampton Court, near London, was done by a 'topiarus', a gardener who was particularly skilled in shaping plants.

Did you know? The ancient Greeks decorated their columns and plinths with an acanthus leaf motif.

methodical approach is required. Clip hedges with a string line, straight after a flush of foliage for evergreens or immediately after flowering for blooming hedges like camellias. Don't worry too much about cutting off blooms by pruning at the wrong time of the year: after all, the well designed classical garden should still look great without the benefit of flowers. Also, it's easy to locate weeds in such a defined garden, unlike a wild or cottage garden where you may pull out flowers by mistake.

Raking gravel, spot weeding and sweeping paved areas are likely to be the biggest consumers of your time.

Top left: Wearing a garland of leaves, this cherub is a reproduction in the classical style.

Top right: A living carpet of *Vinca minor* edged by a small box hedge.

Above: The ivy on the wall has been trained to grow as a living frieze or motif that functions as much like a painting as a plant.

The potager

Although the French word *potager* literally means a 'soup or kitchen garden' — conjuring visions of a simple collection of carrots, some parsley, a bit of celery and perhaps a few herbs — it can be an elaborate work of art, where vegetables, herbs, flowers and fruit form an exquisite tapestry of colour and texture.

Below: This stunning blue cabbage is one of the most decorative vegetables in the potager, especially over winter.

Opposite: Summer ensures a greater range of produce, including artichokes and mignonette lettuces. The standard roses, which traditionally symbolized monks tending their crops, also add colour and height.

The potager originated in the monastic gardens of the Dark Ages and reached extravagant heights in the sixteenth century gardens of France, where edible plants were used to create enormous decorative patterns, in much the same way as annuals might be grouped in the French *mosaiculture* or in English carpet bedding (see page 62).

The patterns vary, of course, from garden to garden, but a potager may contain grids of planting beds criss-crossed with paths, and there may be two central axes marking out a crucifix, harking back to its origins in the medieval monastery. Within these beds, vegetables and herbs are planted in a rainbow of colours and varieties to add texture and create a tapestry-like effect.

The potager was traditionally regarded as one component of a bigger landscape, just one ingredient of a grand garden, if you like, performing the functions of both a produce and a pleasure garden. The greatest example today is at Villandry in France, where a recreation garden was created from sixteenth century plans at the beginning of the twentieth century. The result is stunningly beautiful and a popular tourist destination.

Today, formal potagers remain the preserve of larger gardens, although in a small space colourful vegetables and herbs can be combined with flower beds and borders, or blended with the cottage garden in an informal manner.

Shopping list

- seeds, seedlings and seed tapes
- peat pots for seed raising
- manure
- lucerne hay or pea straw
- seed markers
- woven willow for edges
- tiles, bricks and paving bricks for edges and pathways
- stakes and canes for taller plants
- some permanent plants such as fruit trees

Places suitable for a potager

In order to thrive, vegetables require full sun and rich earth as well as a fair amount of hard work. Although potagers are typically found in grand gardens with sufficient staff to maintain them, or in country gardens where the owners are dedicated to the craft of growing their own fruit and vegetables, they could also be fantastic in the city. Imagine a twenty-first century update of the allotment garden — rooftops planted with gardens of vegetables, clothing terraces like a beautiful edible carpet.

Materials for a potager

Natural earthy materials work beautifully in this type of garden. Bricks for paths or low walls, hand-made terracotta edging tiles for borders and woven willow or hazel for screens — all have a rustic quality that goes hand in hand with growing your own produce. Detail in the form of seed markers, stakes and wigwams will lend individuality and style to your design.

Top: A fountain is the central point of this potager, which has been divided into wedge-shaped sections by four paths.

Above: Woven willow fencing has a charm of its own.

Mood board for a potager

Above: Espaliered fruit trees provide a productive screen.

Right: Raised beds not only make access easier, they also improve the drainage of a potager.

There are many other practical matters to consider. Mulches should be fertile for soil enrichment, so use high-nitrogen ones such as lucerne and pea straw. Cross-hatched or rough bricks are perfect for pedestrian paths as they provide a better grip. Because a potager is a working garden, and accidents and breakages are inevitable, try to use easily replaced items.

Defining your potager

Due to the ephemeral nature of vegetables, it is important to have a firm structure surrounding your beds in order to give the garden some permanence between the seasons. Raised beds are ideal, as they not only define the shape of your potager but also have a couple of practical advantages: it is much easier to work in a raised bed, as you don't have to bend down as far, and the soil will drain well, one of the prerequisites for growing vegetables.

Installing toothed brick edging

Here's a way to recycle secondhand bricks — make a border for the vegetable garden with bricks laid at 60 degrees. Clean the bricks of any old mortar first.

1 Work out the height of the brick edging and where you want it to go, then lay a string line at the finished height.

2 Dig a trench to a depth that allows for two-thirds of each brick being below soil level, plus 5 cm (2 in) for the bed of concrete. Then make a stiff cement or mortar mix (6:1 cement to water) and push the bricks into it at an angle of 60 degrees. Butt each brick tightly against the previous one, if necessary tapping it into place with a club hammer.

3 After laying a couple of metres (yards) of edging, hold it firm by adding a line of concrete on the garden bed side. Backfill with soil to cover the concrete.

Opposite: This simple path ending in a cul-de-sac allows easy access for maintenance tasks such as weeding.

Above: An organic vegetable patch, making the most of a suburban backyard.

If you don't like this idea, at least incorporate some fixed edging, which will help keep out weeds. This can be decorative — for example, iron edging, bricks on an angle or edging tiles — or utilitarian and disguised by edging plants, such as chives or clipped herbs like rosemary.

The shape of your potager is a matter of personal taste. The traditional grid pattern with criss-crossed paths might work for you, or even a variation of this — a St Andrew's Cross perhaps. Alternatively, a circular shape divided like a wagon wheel might suit your space better.

The organic movement

For some years, concern about the use of pesticides has been mounting. Pesticides have a negative impact on both the environment and our health, and it is no surprise that in recent times there has been a strong swing towards self-sufficiency and growing food organically. This has manifested in many positive ways, from simply growing a few leafy greens in a pot on a windowsill through to the whole permaculture movement.

Devised by naturalist Bill Mollison, permaculture relies on the sustainable growth of food; the idea is that any household, even one with only pots on a balcony, can produce food. It is more a philosophy than a gardening style. Food is regarded as one element in a connective environment, where fruits and vegetables as well as animals, soils, water and microclimate are all considered part of a whole. Plants are grown in 'layers',

Did you know? The 'Dig for Victory' campaign in World War II enabled an estimated two million UK families to be self-sufficient by the end of 1942. In the United States there were 17.5 million victory gardens by 1944. Nitrogen, an essential ingredient in the manufacture of explosives, was in short supply, so a low-nitrogen fertilizer called 'Victory Fertilizer' was used instead. Australia also had 'Victory Gardens', instigated by Prime Minister John Curtin as part of his 'Dig for Victory' campaign. These were mainly tended by women.

reminiscent of the layers of a rainforest, so that different tiers produce. For example, trees produce fruit or nuts at one level, while in their partial shade another crop such as silverbeet may flourish and at the ground level yet another, such as asparagus or wild strawberries, will thrive.

Combining flowers with food

If you are sceptical about vegetables being beautiful in their own right, or doubt that you could eat a whole gardenful, then consider combining flowers with food in your edible garden. This is the way a traditional cottage garden grew, with flowers

Below: Sunflowers come in all shapes and sizes, from 30 cm (1 ft) to 3 m (9 ft). These striking fast-growing annuals are produced commercially for seed and oil, but you can grow them in your garden simply for attracting birds and looking sensational.

Centre: Poppies are among the flowers grown here.

Integrated **pest management**

Nematode-repelling marigolds (above left) can be grown next to insect-attracting fennel (above right) in an IPM-based vegetable garden.

There are many strategies for keeping pests at bay. Companion planting, where plants that complement each other are planted alongside each other, is one method. Typically, this involves planting either insect-repelling plants alongside insect-prone ones, such as basil with tomatoes, or by planting species that attract beneficial insects, which prey on pests. Queen Anne's lace (*Anthriscus sylvestris*), parsley and fennel are commonly used for this purpose. Spraying with non-chemical alternatives such as chilli spray or soap spray, which you can make yourself, is another safe option.

However, these days integrated pest management, or IPM, is becoming more and more popular. IPM takes into account a wide range of options for treating pests. The key factor is to identify the most appropriate methods and the best times for instigating treatment. For example, in one case a single dose of a chemical solution timed perfectly may be appropriate, in another using a predator insect to attack your pest may be the better option.

The trick is to educate yourself about the problem rather than immediately reach for the pesticide without understanding what it is you're dealing with. Some non-chemical solutions are very easy – for example, wrapping hessian around the trunk of a tree and collecting the bugs at nightfall (known as bagging) can catch many nomadic pests that travel in groups. Trapping is another method: pheromones are used to attract the male insects so that you can read exactly when to spray for fruit fly. If lots of males appear, then it's time to spray. In much the same way, sticky yellow paper is used as an indicator for white fly. Planting French marigolds (*Tagetes* sp.), which excrete into the soil an enzyme or hormone that deters nematodes from infesting the roots of tomatoes, is another companion method, so it's worth researching a particular problem first.

Above: Here, flowering roses stand guard while violets and pansies, both edible flowers, busy themselves in the garden.

and vegetables blended together: parsley or chives might form the border, and lettuces were surrounded by pansies (*Viola* sp.). In a larger, more structured garden, the 'kitchen' garden and the 'cutting' garden were often combined into the one space.

Flowers that work particularly well with vegetables include some of the semi-edible ones such as sunflowers (*Helianthus* sp.), love-lies-bleeding (*Amaranthus caudatus*), dahlias, Jerusalem artichoke (*Helianthus tuberosus*) and nasturtiums (*Tropaeolum* sp.), but try some that are strictly for the vase — for example, asters, cosmos, zinnias and carnations (*Dianthus* sp.). Of course, it would

be unwise to blend poisonous plants into an edible scheme, in case an unthinkable accident should befall your dinner guests, so do some research before you start planting!

How to seed your potager

Whether you sow direct into the soil or in seed-raising mix largely depends on your climate and the seeds you are planting. In cool temperate areas, seeds are normally grown in punnets or pots first, so that they can be germinated in a protected environment and grown on until planted out when all chance of frosts have gone. This can be useful in a frost-free area too if you want

Making a cloche

Protecting your vegetables with a cloche tunnel has a few benefits. First of all, a cloche enables you to grow plants in cool temperate areas, as it can keep out the coldest chills and advance seedlings by up to a month compared to their uncovered neighbours. This is vital for frost-prone plants or for growing early season fruit. The other benefit is pest protection. Some insects, but also birds and mammals, love fruit, and you can keep them at bay by using either horticultural fleece or netting over the wire hoops. Finally, in hot climates, a covering of opaque polythene will offer some sun protection for plants that are prone to sun scorch.

Did you know?

Love-lies-bleeding (*Amaranthus caudatus*) was a principal grain grown by the Incas. The seeds, which hang down in long ornamental chains, are sometimes sold as quinoa.

1 Position the metal hoops over the sections of plants to be protected.

2 Place sheets of clear plastic, horticultural fleece or bird netting over the metal wire tunnels as a cover.

3 Anchor the cover at the sides with lengths of 19 x 40 mm (¾ x 1½ in) batten drilled with holes at 30 cm (12 in) intervals. Push 15 cm (6 in) nails or plastic pins through the holes into the soil below. Stretch the cover taut and repeat the procedure for the other side. Cut off any excess.

Above: Raising seedlings yourself is an economical way of planting out vegetables.

Seasonal planting guide to vegetables

For the most beautiful edible garden, combine a mix of beneficial flowering plants, such as Queen Anne's lace, with heirloom and colourful varieties of vegetables. Here's a list of suggested plants, grouped according to whether they grow in the warm or cool months.

Warm season
Amaranthus caudatus
Artichoke
Beans
Beetroot
Capsicum
Choko
Cucumber
Eggplant
Fennel
Helianthus sp.
Lettuce
Leek
Nicotiana sp.
Okra
Parsley
Pumpkin
Silverbeet
Spinach
Squash
Sweet corn
Sweet potato
Tomato
Zucchini

Cool season
Anthriscus sylvestris
Artichokes (Jerusalem and globe)
Asparagus
Broad beans
Broccoli
Brussels sprouts
Cabbage
Calendula
Carrots
Cauliflower
Celery
Chinese cabbage
Kale
Kohlrabi
Leek
Lettuce
Parsley
Parsnip
Pea
Potato
Radish
Shallot
Silverbeet
Spinach
Swede
Turnip
Witlof, including red radicchio and endive

to extend the season of a plant outside its normal time frame — for example, to grow tomatoes over winter.

For some seeds, however, it is advantageous to sow directly into the soil, as transplanting can be stressful for young seedlings and result in losses. Many root vegetables — such as carrots, radishes and parsnips — work better if sown directly then thinned out later on.

Designing with vegetables

When designing with edibles it is important to choose plants according to height, form, colour and season. One of the downsides of the potager could be its flatness. To combat this, incorporate vertical elements, such as tripods for beans and peas, espaliered fruit and cradles for currant bushes. Or you could

Did you know? Crop rotation has been around since biblical times. In fact, the practice of letting the land lie fallow one year in every seven is an extension of this.

include standard roses, traditionally included in potagers to symbolize monks tending their crops. Tall plants such as sunflowers, corn, knotweed (*Persicaria* sp.) and love-lies-bleeding (*Amaranthus caudatus*) also have the same effect.

Most vegetables are annuals and have a specific season or time in which they should be sown, grown and harvested. These plants are broadly grouped into cool (winter/spring) and warm (summer/autumn) season crops. See the lists opposite.

For a vegetable with stunning architectural form, you can't go past the artichoke. Its

Below: This potager is protected by tall clipped hedges and edged with little topiarized walls of box.

Above: A selection of oak leaf and red regency lettuces planted out in formal rows.

Above right: To store apples over winter, wrap them in newspaper and store them in a cool place.

striking grey leaves form a large rosette with notched margins, which are beautiful when not in flower, but superb when crowned with their purple, thistle-like blooms. Rhubarb, swiss chard and ruby chard are similarly outstanding, and the small rosettes of lettuce, kale and cabbages are also great for breaking up the monotony of fine-textured leaves of vegetables like carrots, or rows of strap leaves like onions and leeks. Some tropical herbs are also beautiful and worth adding if you live in a warm enough climate: with their glossy, fragrant leaves, rows of cardamom (*Elettaria cardamomum*) make a great border plant, while clumps of lemongrass (*Cymbopogon citratus*) sway in the gentlest of breezes, making a graceful rustling sound.

Far left: Ruby chard is the red-veined version of green silverbeet.

Left: Tender young shoots of lemongrass are delicious and fragrant.

Making a potato 'pie'

A clamp or 'pie' is a traditional way of storing root vegetables in a cool climate. This looks rather like an African hut, surrounded by a ditch. The clamp is insulated with straw, then covered with soil for extra protection.

1 Choose an area of free-draining soil, then clear and level it. Spread a layer of dry straw to a depth of about 20 cm (8 in). Build a mound of potatoes (if storing carrots, don't stack them higher than 75 cm/2½ ft). Cover the mound with 15 cm (6 in) of straw.

2 Cover the mound with a layer of soil about 10 cm (4 in) deep by digging a trench around the mound and throwing the soil on top of it.

3 Pat down the soil with the back of the spade.

4 Leave a small amount of straw exposed at the top to act as a ventilator and to let warm air escape.

how to...
Pick raspberries

Gently grip a ripe raspberry between your thumb and fingers and pull it away from its core.

Maintenance

A vegetable garden requires consistent and routine work. There are crops to plant in succession, annual vegetables to be replaced by season and harvesting to be done. Add to this a need to vary your vegetables from year to year (called crop rotation or succession planting) so that they don't succumb to disease and you have a fairly high maintenance garden. But the rewards of all this work are enormous if you manage to supply your household with fresh food and superior flavour.

Pests and diseases also love vegetables. Many are easy picking for chewing insects, and may need to be sprayed. Remember to observe withholding periods, or time lags, between spraying and harvest. Even organic sprays and home-made remedies should have a 24-hour withholding period. Thoroughly wash the vegetables before cooking and eating them.

Soils need to be fed, tilled and limed. You should conduct pH tests on your soil before accommodating a variety of vegetables.

Crop **rotation**

Plants are classified into broader groups or families. Each family member not only has similar flower parts, but often also similar cultural requirements, using up similar elements in the soil and suffering from the same pests and diseases. To minimize these effects, farmers have practised crop rotation for centuries. This simply means alternating crops so that members of the same family are not grown in the same spot season after season. For example, don't plant potatoes or tomatoes where you grew eggplant the previous season, as all three vegetables are members of the nightshade family, Solanaceae.

Right: The potager, showing the birdhouse in the background. In medieval potagers, peacocks and other birds were kept as another source of food.

Organic gardens

Not everybody wants a garden that can be mapped on a grid, or indeed the antithesis — a garden that is more like a tamed wilderness. It is possible to interpret the indulgence of nature in a modern garden context, and the organic garden does just that.

Below: Horizontal concentric rings form a turf maze.

Opposite: The circles here are placed on the vertical and repeated one after another to form a fabulous pathway. The focal point is a sculpture facing another part of the garden, designed by Andy Sturgeon for the 2001 Chelsea Flower Show.

Although the Gardenesque period of the late nineteenth century (typified by plantings of palms and brightly coloured perennials and stroll paths) was also closely allied to this meandering sort of garden style, it really evolved into a genre of its own in the early 1900s. The move from regular, geometric shapes to organic, free forms was sparked by the likes of Antonio Gaudi, who designed many great buildings in the early twentieth century but also the spectacular Parc Guell, in Barcelona.

Gaudi left straight lines and rigidity behind, preferring to use bold curves instead. A terrace with mosaic serpentine curves snakes its way through the park's centre, supported by Doric columns with Gothic gargoyles and other features. Palm avenues and woods of pine add to the exotic tropical feel of the Parc.

Throughout the twentieth century, other designers followed Gaudi's inspiration, transforming landscapes with evocative sweeps of colour and extravagance in their plantings. In the 1930s, in his South African sugar cane plantation, Douglas Saunders built a garden that incorporated curves of exotic foliage with cascades and ponds like swirling masses in this same idiosyncratic way. This exuberant, outlandish and flamboyant style of garden design and plant use can also be seen in the fabulous Lotusland, designed by Ganna Walska in Santa Barbara in the United States during the mid-1940s. This garden,

Roberto Burle Marx loved using flora native to Brazil, including bromeliads (right) and orchids (far right). *Epiphyllum* 'Aurora' is shown here.

Above: This wonderful water garden is typical of the lotus garden style used by Ganna Walska in Lotusland, in the United States.

still open today, features an outdoor theatre with stone grotesques and collections of cacti, bromeliads and cycads. There is even a floral clock flanked by topiary animals.

Roberto Burle Marx, the Brazilian architect who designed over 1500 public and private gardens, often collaborating with the likes of Le Corbusier and Niemeyer, is sometimes touted as 'the inventor of the modern garden'. He tended towards biomorphic, organic shapes and borders in his work, but Marx was famous for including bright Brazilian flora in his designs. His use of gargantuan leaves and dramatic flowers coupled with mosaic decoration (as in Gaudi's designs) and moving water have been replicated in gardens throughout the world.

Another designer, the Florida-based Raymond Jungles, has become renowned for this style.

However, an organic garden design doesn't have to be overly bright or brazen. The work of Thomas Church became influential in the United States after he designed a free-form pool in San Francisco in the 1950s. The essence of organic simplicity and restraint, the pool was a simple cell shape, echoing the curve of the landscape in the distance. It contained a white modernist sculpture and was flanked by a lawn terrace and holly oaks (*Quercus ilex*). This pool later became an icon of twentieth century landscape design and the model for pools all over the world. For the next 30 years or so, if someone installed a pool, it was likely to be kidney shaped or something similarly organic.

Mounds have of course been used in the garden for decades. Designer Martha Schwartz used mounds in a minimalist landscape banded by stone paving in a design for a public plaza in Minneapolis, Minnesota. Here, tear drop-shaped grassy hillocks, some planted with trees and bulbs like mini-meadows or woodlands, rise up from the urban scene. Similarly, in the 1990s Charles Jencks designed and constructed The Garden of Cosmic Speculation in Scotland (see also pages 67 and 292). This is the ultimate organic landscape of grand dimensions, where huge earth-moving machines carved up the countryside into spectacular conical mounds and curves like a millennium version of the pyramids.

However, extraordinary feats of construction like this are not necessary in

Left: The wavy edges of these philodendrons, contrasted with the spiky outlines of *Dracaena marginata* 'Colourama' and red cordylines, suit the organic garden.

Above: Although there is no symmetry in this garden (an exhibition piece at the 2001 Chelsea Flower Show), the repeated circular motif provides balance.

Far left: Clipped into tight balls, these box plants at Madoo Conservancy in the United States make fabulous focal points.

Left: The zany foliage of coleus can bring colour to borders and a zing to shady corners.

Did you know? Organic construction in concrete hit its peak during the 1950s with the design (and then creation) of two of the world's greatest buildings, Joern Utzon's Sydney Opera House, a sculpture of sails and seashells, and Frank Lloyd Wright's Guggenheim Museum, in New York, with its curved organic exterior and famous internal spiral walkway. The post-war era was famous for its expressive use of concrete in bold forms. This style was dubbed Brutalism.

order to achieve a garden of sinuous lines. Some landscape designers experiment with brushing swirling patterns onto dewy turf, while others are delving into new materials with exciting possibilities, such as rumbled glass shards, a recycled material that has only been available since the mid-1990s. It comes in a myriad of colours, sparkles with the light and can be walked on barefoot, yet it still acts as a mulch and thereby reduces evaporation and suppresses weed growth.

Flowing curves add a sense of spaciousness, and if they are done well, weighing up areas of mass and void, the space will seem balanced and comfortable without the formality of symmetry.

To make sure your organic garden retains this balance, imagine that the space above each area is actually a volume, and try to weigh it in your mind's eye to create harmony and equilibrium. In structural terms, curved or serpentine walls are more stable than straight ones; this makes them useful for retaining walls.

Places suitable for an organic garden

The relaxed nature of curved garden beds works particularly well when 'making over' or remodelling an existing garden. They make it easier to work established plants into your organic design, in contrast to the difficulty of working with a symmetrical layout where plants have to fit into a mirrored image in order to work well, or one has to be positioned in exactly the right spot as a focal point at the end of a vista.

The organic garden style also works well with level changes and difficult terrain because it follows the topography of the land. This avoids major construction work on features such as terraces and ramps, and this of course helps to keep the hard landscaping costs down.

Opposite: This fabulous garden design by Andy Sturgeon for the 2001 Chelsea Flower Show reveals how sexy curves can be, even in the garden. Another view of this garden is shown on page 374.

Right: Sinuous, shiny and reflective. Stainless steel not only copes with the elements outside (and water as shown), it also looks great.

Far right: Going with the flow, this rusted iron wall doesn't try and stop corrosion, it makes it a feature in itself.

Materials for an organic garden

To capture the mood of discovery, freshness and free-flowing ideas that embody this garden style, you should explore some of the exciting materials available these days. For example, rumbled glass shards and beads made from recycled glass can be turned into interesting landscaping features.

In much the same way as mosaic has been used for hundreds of years, glass beads could be featured on walls or as garden mobiles that sparkle in the light, or even embedded in stepping stones. Mirrors can work in this way

too. Glass shards that are so smooth you can walk on them barefoot make lovely mulches for water features, or even as a growing medium for spirals of lucky bamboo (*Dracaena sanderiana*).

Reinterpreting traditional materials in a modern way also works well for this style. Concrete is the perfect medium for this fluid design, as it can be poured and set into a myriad of shapes. Also, new developments, such as oxides for concrete and quartz additives for render make it a colourful option to explore. Curved metal walls that create fascinating abstract reflections are another option, while small units, such as bricks, or pliable materials, such as plastics and thin timber are all ideal; even poured edging such as concrete curbing may be suitable for making garden edges.

Soft, organic shapes that can be used in the garden include 'lucky stones', those

Shopping list

- glass shards and beads
- pottery balls and woven spheres
- pebbles and 'lucky stones'
- sculpture
- mosaic tiles
- coloured sand
- wild paint colours, such as hot pink
- flexible or modular garden edging
- exotic plants such as euphorbias and echiums, heliconias and banana

Mood board for an organic garden

over-sized pebbles that can be purchased from garden centres and used as natural sculpture if placed artistically. Even ceramic balls or woven wire spheres are perfect for this style. Plywood furniture with sinuous lines or metal mesh chairs with fluid indentations sum up the look. The ultimate decoration would be a sculpture in the style of the British artist Henry Moore, all curved forms and sensuality.

Perfect curves for the garden

There are many ways of introducing free-flowing forms into the garden. It may be in the way you lay out your beds or a section of lawn, or even a naturally shaped rill or water feature, perhaps a simple organic-shaped swimming pool. Mounding the earth on flat sites is another option. Also, island garden beds can be used to great effect in this style of garden, but make sure they are a decent size and that there

is a unifying mass linking the scene together. Grass or gravel is perfect for this. Sweeping driveways and curved paths will also emphasize the continuity of your design.

Of course, there are many examples in nature where organic forms can be reduced to a mathematical formula, following strict rules. Think of the concentric circles of disturbed water or the diminishing spiral on a seashell. Such patterns can work really well as highlights in an organic garden. Lawn spirals (see page 295) or spirals planted using low shrubs such as lavender, spiral topiary (see page 387) and even metal screens with biomorphic-shaped cut-outs would all work in this style.

Remember that curves should be downplayed on plan. From this bird's eye view, using pencil and paper, your imagination can easily get carried away and you might emphasize a curve just a little too

Below: Wild and wonderful. Blue furniture and organic floor patterns add an oceanic feel to this rooftop garden. Designed by Topher Delaney, one of America's most innovative designers, the garden is called Shades of Blue.

Decorating a concrete tile

The wonderful, dynamic mosaics of Gaudi and Marx can be interpreted for a domestic garden in many ways. A mosaic garden bench or wall is one option, but also consider using some of the glass beads available today to create fun and unique detail. A paving stone decorated with glass beads is one way of adding sparkle and pattern to a garden. Make a series of them for a short path, or use some as a feature in a paved area.

1 Using a pencil, trace the design onto a concrete tile. Make any corrections before you proceed with the next stage.

2 Place the beads onto your design, working out how to use each colour.

3 Glue the glass beads onto the tile with a clear silica adhesive.

4 Apply grout between the beads and work it into the gaps.

5 Wipe away excess grout using a damp cloth. Then, once the grout has dried enough to start forming a crust, polish off any powdery residue with a dry rag.

Above: The fluid curves of free-form swimming pools are a legacy of Thomas Church.

Above right: Villa Lante, in Bagnaio, Italy, was designed for Cardinal Gianfrancesco in the 1560s. The swirling patterns of box hedges in this parterre are still effective today.

much. Keep the curves in your organic garden loose and flowing.

For a design that will work well *in situ*, play it safe and go for gentler curves. Also, use a reel of hose (or flexible pipe) to make sure you have created a natural sweep (see page 84). Mark it out with spray paint or powdered lime, then reflect on it for a while before adding any permanent constructions.

Swimming pools

Inground pools are a fabulous addition to the suburban backyard, especially where the climate allows months of enjoyment or where covers and heating extend the swimming season. Pools offer not just a visual treat: they are also a truly interactive part of the garden

that involves the whole family or household in an outdoor lifestyle.

You can manipulate the colour of the water with the surface treatment. Plain concrete will reflect a sky blue, while tiling in various coloured ceramics or mosaics can create brilliant effects. Trowelled-on render finishes complete with quartz aggregates of various sizes and colours, applied to the concrete base coat, can also add sparkle.

Using poured concrete affords you a lot of flexibility with your pool design. Basically, the technique is to spray liquid concrete onto a framework of reinforced steel. This means you can design a shape that fits your block, and also vary the depth from shallow wading areas to sections deep enough for diving.

Spiral shapes

Cutting a conifer into a spiral shape is a quick and easy way to grow a fun topiary, which can be used to flank an entranceway or as a stand-alone feature or folly in your garden. Simply buy a suitable conifer (perhaps a *Cupressus sempervirens* or *Juniperus chinensis*) and run a string line in a spiral from the base to the top. When the string is evenly spaced, use it as a guide as you cut into the foliage, removing a 10 cm (4 in) band of growth all the way around, until you get to the top. It will look great and you can keep it in check with regular trimming.

Above: A spiral is one of the easiest topiary patterns to master.

A pool is obviously an expensive garden accessory, and the costs can become exorbitant if the ground is not level and needs reinforcement, or especially if the ground is solid rock.

On the plus side, a well designed pool can become the focus of outdoor entertaining, but you must be committed to the maintenance involved in keeping a pool clean, which also involves the cost of chemicals, and free of debris.

Another expensive consideration is safe and effective fencing that will exclude young children from the pool area. Check with your local regulatory body on the required heights of fences, and make sure the gates are kept shut and well maintained.

Plants for an organic garden

Gardening in this style is almost like painting with numbers. Large blocks of the same plants work well, with leaf and flower colour being chosen for maximum contrast. These are then punctuated with wild sculptural plants as focal points. Huge leaves are useful as foils for heavily coloured mosaics and the like.

These architectural plants are the eye-catching features of your garden, the prima donnas of garden design, if you like. And, as with all stage productions, you need a chorus as well as the stars of the show, so be careful not to have too many examples within the one space or you won't know where to look.

For gargantuan leaves, consider the banana family. It includes some of the most

exotic-looking plants. There is a range of varieties, including the *Musa basjoo*, which has smooth blue–green fronds that arch majestically. Then there is the live fast, die young Abyssinian banana (*Ensete ventricosum*). With its blood red central vein, it adds drama wherever it grows, although it needs shelter so its leaves don't become tattered. For stunning flowers, don't overlook the pink velvet banana (*Musa velutina*), which has a vertical fan of leaves and makes a great accent plant. Of course, bananas won't tolerate severe cold, so protect them by wrapping their leaves and covering the ground or by bringing them indoors for winter. They grow so fast that you can almost enjoy them like an annual.

Members of the brilliant cycad family of ancient, fern-like plants make other great stand-alone plants. They are very slow growing, so they suit only the patient or wealthy gardener, but they are adaptable to a wide range of climates, which probably accounts for why they have lasted 250 million years. The best known of all cycads is the Japanese sago palm (*Cycas revoluta*), but for sheer drama, the cardboard palm (*Zamia furfuracea*) is hard to beat. It is native to Mexico, and has chunky leaflets with wide swirling branches and a stout trunk.

Other wild and wondrous additions include exceptional palms, like the windmill palm (*Trachycarpus fortunei*) and the wine palm (*Butia capitata*). Euphorbias, with their magnificent heads of green flowers, and pride of Madeira (*Echium* sp.) also work well here.

For the chorus, use swathes of colour from plants like daylilies, coleus, dahlias

Above left: Swirling circular borders of box, like car tyres, house herbaceous plants such as tulips.

Left: The cardboard palm, a fabulous foliage plant.

project

Creating cloud topiary

Creating an unusual Asian-inspired topiary or *niwaki* is relatively easy, due to the informality of its shape, but the procedure does require some patience. Choose an appropriate plant, such as *Juniperus*, which has tightly bunched leaves, grab a pair of sharp secateurs and let your imagination go wild.

1 Take a good look at your specimen. Size it up and analyze which branches you want to feature before trimming anything. Next, carefully clean off the internal leaves to expose the featured branches, then trim the terminal growth to make a tight ball or cloud at the end of each branch.

2 Wire your cloud topiary to help weigh down or place each branch. Secure each piece with a few turns at the beginning of each branch. Use copper wire (annealed or softened if you can get it) for a traditional look. Use cheaper plastic-coated wire if you have a lot of wiring to do, although it won't last as long as copper wire and you will need to check it regularly for ruptures.

3 Arrange each branch to create a pleasing effect. Here, we modified the rules slightly and organized the 'clouds' in different directions, adding to the zany look of this creation.

begonias and border plant (*Alternanthera* sp.), and plant them in large masses so that they swirl across the garden.

Maintenance

Provided your layout has incorporated smooth curves, maintaining lawns should be a fairly simple process as there'll be few tight corners or sharp angles that will need hand trimming. This means mowing in one easy movement. Also, since the organic garden is a little more relaxed, plants can be left to grow naturally. They certainly won't need pruning with a string line.

how to...
Install flexible edging

Pliable plastic edging works well in this garden style, as it is easy to bend into fluid shapes. Bury it so that it sits just above soil level and, once the grass or gravel is in place, nobody but you will know it's there. Hold it in place with tent pegs until you have finished backfilling.

Above left: Abyssinian bananas are used here as giant bedding plants. Their enormous leaves provide the perfect foil for the century plant (*Agave attenuata*) and border plant (*Alternanthera* sp.).

Above: A male banana flower.

Opposite: Playing with shapes, this award-winning garden uses cones, spheres and crucibles as a countercheck to the planting.

Minimalist gardens

Clean lines, a dramatic use of space, geometry, pared down elements and uncluttered surfaces are all synonymous with minimalism. The 'less is more' edict, declared by German architect Ludwig Mies van der Rohe in 1959, eloquently sums up the concept of minimalism — the distillation of an idea into its purest form, making its impact more effective.

Below: *Restio* reeds are fabulous for bog gardens and water features, but can also be used to great effect in pots without drainage holes (see page 406).

Opposite: Simplicity in planting, emphasis on form and delighting in shadow: this garden, planted with *Kalanchoe* 'Flapjack', reveals how minimalist design can result in maximum impact.

The Modernism movement of the 1930s and '40s is also an enormous influence on this garden style. Modernism was an attempt to use the plethora of new materials and technologies along with old materials that had been given a new expression due to advances in engineering. Concrete, glass and steel allowed the previously impossible to become real, such as the first skyscraper built in the late nineteenth century by William Le Baron Jeney in Chicago. By the 1930s these had developed somewhat in their sophistication. Architect Le Corbusier in particular was famous for his towers that combined often white, magnificent roof terraces with a limited range of plants and walls that framed distant trees.

The minimalist style of the 1950s and '60s onwards also incorporates the lessons of the European Renaissance gardens, with their abstract patterns of parterres, designed to be seen from above (see page 349). However, a more significant influence is the eastern garden, especially the Zen Buddhist gardens of raked gravel and rocks, such as the Ryoanji garden in Kyoto (see page 198).

After World War II, as the world opened up and there was an open exchange of ideas, this straightforwardness was reflected in garden design too. Boundaries were unplanted and uncluttered. There was a realization that plain walls, if built well with

good proportions, were pleasing in their own right. Typically the walls in a minimalist garden are made of superb materials and often reveal views through framed slots or display a pattern of shadow and light.

Places suitable for a minimalist garden

Both the urban environment and the countryside can be suitable for a minimalist landscape. Natural environments especially can be very exciting when juxtaposed with a simple, sleek built landscape, creating an electricity of its own. In fact, one of the most famous examples of such a garden is at Fallingwater, a house designed by Frank Lloyd Wright deep in a forest in Pennsylvania

in the mid-1930s. Here, hovering above a waterfall, is a modern private house that is cantilevered over a stream and waterfall. Water rushes through its 'garden', blurring the distinction between wilderness and yard.

The opposite can also be effective. In a city where action and activity can almost be dizzying, a Zen-like domestic space of order and refinement offers an antidote of peace and calm.

Materials for a minimalist garden

Crisp and clean lines and superior materials, with an emphasis on quality, not variety, is the way to construct this sort of garden. Polished granite and laser-cut granite or sandstone make beautiful flooring for

Below: This modern take on a waterfall reflects the essence of minimalism. Rapids and rocky outcrops from nature are distilled into these sheer drops over vertical concrete and platforms at various levels.

Beyond 2000

Avant-garde designers of today are still combining the Zen-like appeal of early 1960s design with minimalist landscapes. The American designer Ron Herman created a chequerboard-like garden with a twist in a central courtyard of a William Wurster 1961 Modernist house in San Francisco. Here, the squares are staggered like steps and built out of steel; some are filled with baby's tears (*Soleirolia* sp.), others with black pebbles. The ground plane is planted with dwarf mondo grass and the clean trunks of gold bamboo rise up through it, creating vertical interest against a cement-rendered backdrop.

Similar fusions by Czech-born landscape architect Vladimir Sitta are being created in Australia. In one very elegant inner city garden, black bamboo is planted in rows between strips of stone and polished black granite. Water flows over the granite and into a trench below, reflecting back the sky and the fronds of the bamboo, and creating the illusion of light in what is actually a small, shadowy space.

A unique chequerboard pattern of glass shards and baby's tears (above left), and the Vladimir Sitta garden of black bamboo and granite (above right).

Above: A minimalist beach garden
displaying Zen-like austerity.

entertaining areas. These are natural materials that improve with age and are highly desirable in such a garden. Decking floors and pebbles combine beautifully and are a cost-effective alternative to stone.

Streamlined boundaries made with concrete and even false walls are sometimes used as backdrops to create a stage where dramatic contrasts might be highlighted. Glass and steel are often used on the exterior

of the house, inviting the landscape into the home. This is married with styled metalwork for overhead structures and pots as well as with marine cable tensioned from posts — perfect minimalist veranda rails.

Water, especially still water that is reflective or narrow rills bordered with stainless steel, works well as a feature, and floating steps jutting out across expanses of shallow water are popular. Wet-edge swimming pools and drops of sheer water from wall fountains are also suitable.

Colour is kept to a restricted palette of grey, black, charcoal, birch and white. No ornamentation is needed because of the strong geometry, unadorned beautiful materials and a few stunning plants in this

Shopping list

- large-format paving in granite, sandstone or concrete
- stainless steel furniture and pots
- stainless steel cable and turnbuckles
- plants with an architectural form
- decking tiles
- pebbles

*Mood board for
a minimalist garden*

how to...
Tension a turnbuckle

Stainless steel cable is a great alternative to the traditional veranda rail. It looks streamlined, opens up views and, like a timber rail, lets the air flow through. To attach it, simply screw some stainless steel eyestraps into your wall or post, wherever you want to secure the cable. Next, thread the cable through the eyestraps and secure the ends with a looped section of cable held tight by wire rope grips. Repeat this process on either end of the wire, hooking up and extending the turnbuckle as the connector piece. Tighten until the correct tension is reached.

type of garden. Sometimes the juxtaposition between old and new — for example, an ancient pot or a gnarled tree singled out for attention — can provide tension and excitement in a minimalist garden.

Elements of the minimalist garden

The white box may epitomize the minimalist home, but what then is the minimalist garden? Is it a concrete slab with a carefully composed potted plant? We demand more from our outdoor space. It still has to be beautiful, functional and provide an escape from the outside world.

Below: This floating walkway reflects sky, silhouettes and shadow to create drama on the ground.

Making a moss bowl

The Zen-like simplicity of moss and rocks in the garden can easily be re-created on a small scale. Here, a black, slightly porous stone bowl is used to hold some velvety green moss. Less is more.

1 Cut the moss to fit the bowl. We've used some moss we found growing on the side of a concrete tank, so take a look around your garden before you visit the garden centre.

2 Remove the moss, and fill the bowl with sphagnum moss.

3 Place the moss on top of the sphagnum, which will keep it moist.

4 Water well.

Adding a stone facelift

The inspiration of Frank Lloyd Wright and his famous Fallingwater home is easy to see in these stone panels, which can be applied like a veneer to walls. Made of superb quality stone, they have a split face on the exterior side and a smooth, sawn finish on the back. This allows them to be glued onto an existing wall. You can apply these panels to both interior and exterior surfaces, providing you use a suitable adhesive and the substrate is of exterior quality. This further dissolves the boundary between inside and out.

1 Make sure the wall is clean and dry. You'll need a spirit level to check the pieces are horizontal and a tile adhesive suitable for exterior use. Glue the first piece at the top of the wall. Secure the tile with masking tape while the glue cures.

2 Measure down from the top of the wall so you can calculate how many panels are required for each section. If any cutting is required, it's best to cut the bottom piece.

3 Cut the base section, then glue the rest of the panels in the same way as the first.

Park André Citroën, the landscape designed by Alain Provost and Gilles Clement at the old Citroën car works site in Paris, is a perfect large-scale example of how a minimalist garden can be a place of excitement and drama.

Here, rows of ramped lawns are surrounded by a plaza-like expanse of near white, large-dimension paving. The space feels like an amphitheatre surrounded by modern architecture, yet despite the starkness, it invokes a feeling of ease, inviting you to recline on the grass. Groups of Versailles planters (classic square timber boxes), planted with trees, are a contemporary variation on the famous French landscape of the Renaissance, which used symmetry and scale in a traditional sense. Water, in the form of a reflective surface and playful jets, adds the element of movement.

In fact, water is a useful implement in the minimalist gardener's toolbox. It can effectively add intrigue to what could otherwise be a bland space. Both still water, with its moody depths and reflective qualities and calmness, and moving water, which is

Above: Parc André Citroën, Paris, renowned for its minimalist design and modern planting schemes.

Below: The malleability of metal allows reflective forms, such as these fabulous sensual curves.

full of energy, can be used to great effect in such a minimalist landscape.

A really exciting example of a sophisticated water feature can be found at the Garden of Fine Art in Kyoto, Japan, where, lying under a thin film of water is a reproduction of one of Monet's 'Water Lilies' series. This life-size panel is actually a photograph transferred onto ceramic, which can be viewed from a walkway surrounded by large planes of glass. The concrete, steel and glass surrounds add to the modern yet Zen-like space. Similar dramatic effects could be achieved in a domestic landscape using advances in technologies — perhaps a slab of laser-cut black granite or a photo or painting on ceramic.

In a domestic garden space, one of the key features of the minimalist garden is to blur the distinction between one space and another. Large-format paving is often used, with a uniform material between the outside and in, chosen to link one space with the other. The large-dimension pavers also help make an area feel less cluttered and spacious, so this style of paving works particularly well in small areas. Clever tricks, such as

Did you know? 'Less is bore' was architect Robert Venturi's famous rebuttal of Minimalism in the 1960s. His American colleague Philip Johnson was also quoted as saying 'we are getting bored of the box'.

Above: The strengths of modern and oriental design are combined in this relaxation area.

expansion joints running away from your eye, can add to this illusion of space.

Other features — such as a floating walkway, an indoor garden spliced into the interior of the house and a pool that flows from the outside into the house — are all used to further blur the distinction between outside and inside.

Plants for a minimalist garden

Following the 'less is more' philosophy in your planting scheme requires discipline. However, this doesn't mean that plants are not important in the minimalist garden. On the contrary. A minimalist garden can really emphasize the natural beauty or form of a particular plant.

A spectacular tree, or something else with a striking silhouette such as a clump of black-stemmed bamboo or a copse of silver birch or spotted gums, could be used as the one element to highlight such a space. Think of it in terms of displaying a plant as if it were a sculpture in a gallery. Tree ferns (*Cyathea* sp.), grass trees (*Xanthorrhoea australis*), frangipanis (*Plumeria* sp.) and cactus, such as the silver torch cactus (*Cleistocactus strausii*), all have forms so striking that they are worth singling out.

The critical factor is to choose only a few important plants and repeat them. You could create a monochrome pattern by using plants that have no showy flowers and rely on texture for their beauty and interest — a precision row of *Festuca glauca* or a swath of restio perhaps.

Grey foliage (refer to page 276) can work beautifully in a minimalist garden setting. With no bright colours trying to compete for attention, a plant's form and texture coupled with the strength of the design make an impact. Plants that look particularly great include massed sedums, clipped cotton

Above left: A minimalist bed of sedum backed by grasses such as blue–green *Festuca glauca*.

Above: This silver torch cactus is a spectacular, hair-covered column that really makes its presence felt.

lavender balls (*Santolina* sp.) and rows of *Helichrysum petiolare* trimmed into blocks.

Ornamental grasses too have a special place in this style. Rushes and sedges, many of which are native to Australia and New Zealand, have a striking outline. Some, like the stripy club rush (*Schoenoplectus lacustris* subsp. *tabernaemontani* 'Zebrinus'), also called zebra rush, have a horizontal banding that adds to their outstanding appearance.

For tricky spots, you can't go past umbrella sedge (*Cyperus involucratus*), as it grows anywhere, from the damp and shady garden to the neglected corner. Also suitable for both damp areas and hard, commercial landscapes is the swamp foxtail grass (*Pennisetum alopecuroides*). The finer, waving heads of tassel cord rush (*Restio tetraphyllus*), with its fine, gently arching stems, are particularly beautiful, making them popular for floral arrangements.

The largest member of the grass family, bamboo (refer to page 195) has many forms and habits. The black bamboo is often seen in the minimalist landscape; however, this is a running bamboo and needs to be planted

how to...
Polish a metallic surface

To maintain the reflective, polished surface of many metals, such as stainless steel or aluminium, you will need to keep them clean. Simply spray on window cleaner and, using a circular motion, polish with a soft cloth. Never use an abrasive scourer or gritty cleaner as these will scratch the surface. Finish with an application of car wax to help your polish last longer and to repel water. Metal containers can heat up, so planting into plastic first then slipping those into the metal pots will save the roots from overheating.

project

Decorating with air plants

For the ultimate low maintenance plant, it's hard to go past a plant that survives on nothing but thin air. Yet that is true of air plants, or *Tillandsia* as they are more correctly called. Although mostly grey in colour, some air plants have reddish tinges in their centres and they can vary enormously in texture, from the very fine textured, such as the hair-like threads of Spanish moss (*T. usneoides*), also known as old man's beard, to the chunky-leafed types. You can create a sculptural centrepiece by placing bamboo stems in a tall metallic container, then 'decorating' the stems with air plants. You could also do the same thing with a piece of driftwood.

1 To keep the stems apart, put some pebbles in the bottom of the container.

2 Using a hot glue gun, put a dollop of glue on one of the plants.

3 Attach the plant to the bamboo stem. Hold it until the glue sets.

4 Continue attaching the other plants in the same way, varying the height to achieve a pleasing overall effect.

5 Attach some Spanish moss.

6 Adjust the positions of the stems by placing some more pebbles. Mist every few days in summer, less in winter. These plants really do grow on air, but dislike the cold.

how to...
Grow grass in a cube

This stylish cube pot made of concrete has no drainage hole. This would be disastrous for most plants, but this grass (*Restio* sp.) thrives on wet feet and copes with dry periods. It's not only classy but also practical: you only need to water it every few weeks. This must be the ultimate minimalist concept!

either in a container or with a root control barrier (see page 194). Many clumping bamboos are less troublesome and equally as beautiful, such as the stunning soft-leafed blue bamboo, which has a slight grey–blue tinge to the leaves.

Plain ground covers like ivy are terrific for acting like a carpet. Lesser known ones include *Dichondra* 'Silver Falls', which seems to be drought tolerant once established, coping with shade and root competition. Gold and silver plant (*Ajania pacifica*) has a

silver outline to each leaf (like clouds) and a gentle spreading habit. The gold refers to the yellow flower. Some succulents, such as the silvery blue tones of chalksticks (*Senecio serpens*) can also be sensational planted en masse as a living floor.

Maintenance

The problem with clean, uncluttered surfaces is that the overall look can easily be spoilt if you don't keep them that way. Fallen leaves on your paving and fingerprints on your

Right: This refined garden of black bamboo teamed with reflective, shimmering stainless steel is thrown into stark relief by a muted ochre wall.

feature pots can easily detract from the minimalist effect. The answer is elbow grease. Sweeping, cleaning and polishing take over from the traditional gardening tasks such as weeding and raking. The high-pressure water blaster may be as handy a tool as the spade in a more traditional garden. Also, keep corrosive metals off pale-coloured pavers where they may leave permanent stains, and treat any metal surfaces with anti-rust to stop them corroding.

Above: The feathery foliage of tassel cord rush.

Living stones

Living stones (*Lithops* sp.) would have to be the ultimate low maintenance, minimalist plant. They look like rocks, or even the footprints of some ancient quadruped, and need no attention. *Lithops* are a type of very slow-growing succulent, which means they never need repotting, rarely need watering and even cope with air-conditioning, provided they are positioned near some natural light. These unusual plants come in various shades of stone — soft greys, muted green and weathered brown — and look stunning planted simply in a tray among pretty pebbles of similar tones.

Above: Living stones growing en masse in a shallow container.

Bold gardens

Fearless, brave and intrepid landscapes are typical of this style. Colour use is daring, and the look is thought provoking. 'Dare to be different' could be the catchcry of such a garden. Bold in this context means courageous, enterprising, confident, forward, immodest, vigorous, free, well marked, clear and conspicuous.

Modernism, or 'going where no one has gone before', probably sums up this bold approach to design. It is an endless search for possibilities; try to resist any preconceived ideas or notions. Look at it this way: it's a bit like handing over the minimalist white box to a child, who then uses colour and naive self-expression to transform the box into an unrestrained, exuberant and bold one.

This whole era, post-World War II, should be seen in its larger context too. It was much more than just architecture, building and, in a small way, landscape design. This was a new frontier characterized by a drive for world peace and space travel, and there were also communal living, rock music and liberating labour-saving domestic appliances, mass communication and rapid change. The whole atmosphere was one of experimentation and seeking new forms of expression. Cheap housing for the masses and tall buildings that would free up ground space for parks and public areas were all Modernist dreams.

In garden terms, it meant the addition of brightly coloured blade walls to divide a space, or vertical falls of water. A garden like this is often a collaborative effort, with an architect, artist, garden designer and interior designer all working together to link the house and exterior as one integrated space. Its attraction lies in the relationship between the horizontal and vertical planes. Typical of

Below: A pineapple-like sculpture in silvery tones makes an impact.

Opposite: Like meteors from outer space, sculpted boulders transform this spacious lawn in the Jack Larsen Longhouse Gardens in the United States into a bold landscape.

Above: Magondii Gardens in the United States have an ethereal quality about them.

Opposite: Woven wicker balls have a bold effect, but on a small, domestic scale.

Post-Modernism

Post-Modernism of the 1950s and '60s saw a rejection of intrepid design, but only in part. For sentimental and conservative reasons, designers wanted to retain some elements of past design schools, so there was a revival of the Arts and Crafts Movement, including its emphasis on handmade, high quality objects (see page 253). However, many designers still wanted the progressive elements of the new era: open plan living areas, modular building materials and prefabricated buildings had changed the world forever and there was really no going back. The result of this is an ironic mix-and-match approach to construction that combines several traditional and modern styles in one structure.

the bold garden are concrete screen walls painted in different colours.

Influential designers in this genre include the Mexican-born Luis Barragán. Although trained as both an engineer and an architect, Barragán loved landscape design and incorporated the outdoor space into his buildings. Famous for using vivid, bright colours, he frequently combined influences from his Mexican roots with ideas from Le Corbusier and Ferdinand Bac, an artist whose work with colour and Mediterranean-style gardens was also designed to delight and enchant. (See the discussion of colour and modern designers on page 254.)

Places suitable for a bold garden

This style of garden would look completely at odds with a timber cottage, just as a cottage garden would look ridiculous planted around some twenty-first century design with concrete-rendered pillars, a wet-edge swimming pool and frameless windows. Enter the bold garden, where brazen design and the use of colour in both plants and landscape materials continue to challenge the norm and push boundaries, refusing to play it safe with what has worked before. This bright and colourful way of treating space is so captivating that even the dreariest of environments can be enlivened. A borrowed

view can be worked into the space and framed, but it is by no means a necessity in this contemporary style.

Materials for a bold garden

Embracing new materials as the Modernists did back in the 1930s and '40s is also a characteristic trait of post-1970s design. Concrete, steel and glass as well as plastics, new polymers and resins can all be used to create exciting and original effects. Paint too, with its amazing range of colours, can be used to brighten concrete walls.

Typical of this movement is the contrast between an organic form and its non-organic materials. Furniture that can be organic yet ultra-modern is characteristic. Philippe Starck designs furniture in this style.

New developments in technology have also had an impact on outdoor design. Blow-up plastic furniture, outdoor sound systems, movement-sensitive lights and optical fibre lighting are just some of the new developments featuring in the bold landscape. Underfloor, lit perspex panels and the outdoor cinema are just a few of the possibilities unleashed by this technology.

Maintenance

The biggest maintenance job in a bold garden is probably regularly refreshing the paintwork. The intensity of colour is one of the features of this style, and the brighter the colour, the more prone to fading out in the elements it will be.

Also, any garden containing water will need maintenance (see page 246). One of the

Below: Walls of incandescent colour light up this garden.

Mood board for a bold garden

advantages of this style, however, is that the water is usually flowing and recirculating, which means it stays reasonably clean.

The plants themselves are generally undemanding, other than the warm climate plants, which may need protection in the cold, and plants like bromeliads and cannas that will look fresher if divided and replanted every few years.

Plants for a bold garden

The biggest and the best plants of the world can slip into a bold garden and not look out of place. Plants such as the New Zealand flaxes (*Phormium tenax*) and their ever-growing range of coloured leaf types — from almost black through to pinks, greys, orange, red and acid yellows — are well suited to a bold design. They are also perfect for a wide range of climates, tolerating temperatures down to –5°C (23°F).

Also from New Zealand, and tolerant of the occasional frost and salt spray, is the New Zealand cabbage tree (*Cordyline australis*). These too have strap-like foliage and a multibranched habit, growing to about 6 m (18 ft) tall. There are several cultivars, including those from the Purpurea group, such as 'Red Star', 'Red Sensation' and 'Sundance', with leaf markings in various tones of pink, red and cream. Other cordylines from more tropical climates are called 'Ti' plants (*Cordyline fructicosa* and

Above: This tiered display of various plants in galvanized pots makes a fearless picture.

Garden furniture for a brave new world

Philippe Starck, famous for his homewares designs for Alessi, has even created some furniture inspired by the humble garden gnome for Kartell. This iconic garden ornament has been recast, this time out of its concrete constraints and into a plastic version that's bright, funky and versatile, yet still captures the whimsy of this popular ornament.

Other designers dabble with designs for the outside. Tokujin Yoshioka's Tokyo barstool, table and pop chaise are fine examples of a style that is made from modern colourful plastic yet has an organic shape. In collaboration with Piero Lissoni, Kartell have also designed a series of plastic outdoor lounges and sofas, such as the bubble chair.

Adding colour and texture to the garden

Making your perimeters a feature in themselves is part of that bold approach to gardening in the new millennium. Rather than screen all your walls, you can make them a stunning part of your design. But what happens when you already have a garden and want to update its look? Paint is one of the best and cheapest ways of revitalizing a space without making irreversible or costly changes.

This weathered bagged wall has been brightened up and given a whole new image, thanks to a cheap, easy to apply, textured paint-on finish and some plants in complementary colours. The colours in this acrylic-based, textured exterior paint are colourfast and resist fading, which means you can change your mind and repaint if you want to each year, but it should last the distance if you're happy with the result and don't want to change the colour. Being acrylic, it is flexible, resists cracking and peeling, and actually protects the surface beneath from deteriorating.

1 The first step is to thoroughly clean your wall. This paint product can be applied straight onto galvanized iron, brick work and rendered surfaces, wood (if primed) and even steel if it has been treated with a sealant first.

2 Next, apply the paint either with a roller for a more textured finish or with a medium to wide brush for a softer, suede-like finish. The first coat will be quite patchy.

3 The second coat, applied with a brush in a criss-cross pattern, will start to show the end result. Always work in small sections, keeping a wet edge as you go.

4 It will take about 48 hours for the paint to dry properly, and it will gradually improve in patina and stone finish as it cures. Use your bright new wall as a highlight in itself, or plant in front of it something that will really zing. Here, an aqua-coloured wall is highlighted by bright pink tones in *Berberis* 'Rosie Glow' and *Cordyline* 'Baby Ti'.

Propagating bromeliads

After bromeliads flower they may start to produce a 'pup', or sucker. Once this has fully matured, it can be removed from the mother plant and replanted (or potted on) easily. This is known as division.

The other way to propagate bromeliads is the way pineapples are grown. The top of the fruit is simply cut off and replanted and this will continue to grow (see page 419).

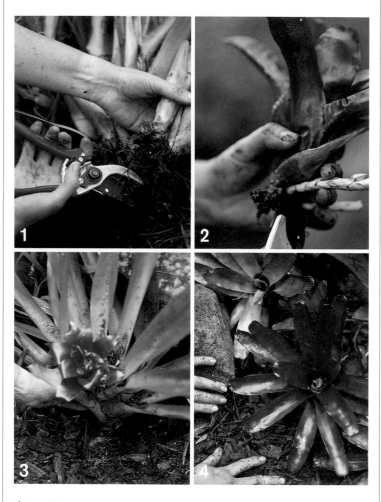

1 Cut off the pup from the mother plant. Once it has started to develop some roots of its own, it will easily grow.

2 Divide the mother plant.

3 Bury the base of each bromeliad section in a very open planting medium, like bark chips, where it can grow without risk of rot.

4 Add some rocks for support. Water in well. It's that easy. A new garden will grow.

cultivars), and include broader-leafed types with lime, pale pink, green, purple and cream markings, even black, such as the 'Caruba' hybrid (see the black and white pot on page 268).

Bromeliads are also popular choices. Many of these have striking leaves as well as bonus bursts of flowers. They grow happily where most plants refuse to cooperate, such as in heavily shaded areas with root competition from trees, and even on rocks, provided their central well is filled with water.

Then there are what could be termed the 'rocket plants', with great spiky foliage reaching skywards. Look for the exotic bird of paradise (*Strelitzia reginae*), and its reed-leafed form called *S. juncea*. For other stunning flowers and leaves, look no further than the gymea lily (*Doryanthes excelsa*). This Australian native has brilliant red blooms that shoot upwards upon 3 m (9 ft) high, asparagus-like spears. A cluster of red flowers opens up like a ruby-encrusted crown, and lasts from spring through to summer. The leaves are a treat too. Their sword-like rosettes are a rich Granny Smith apple green, shiny and handsome additions to any garden.

The *Yucca* genus, many of which feature acid yellow stripes and grey markings that accentuate their bold form, is another rocket plant. The red hot poker (*Kniphofia* sp.) is popular because of its striking torch-like flowers, while many cannas have stunning foliage and flowers that will radiate like fire.

Fabulous dracaenas

The fantastic colour and shape of draceanas are also suitable for a bold garden. The

Opposite: This stunning plant is an Australian native, the gymea lily. The whorls of glossy, apple green, sword-like foliage are sensational too.

Above: With its magnificent bird-like orange flowers, bird of paradise flowers all winter.

Above centre: *Phormium tenax* 'Dancer', with its strong architectural shape, is eye-catching and dramatic.

Above right: Carnivorous plants are always intriguing. This is black-eyed sundew.

dragon tree (*Dracaena draco*) is probably the best known worldwide. With its dramatic whorls of stiff, grey, spiky leaves, it is the perfect architectural plant, but it takes an age to grow, is expensive to buy and prefers arid conditions. A close relative, the Chinese lucky bamboo (*D. sanderiana*), is the opposite. A cheaper plant to buy, it revels in moisture, and is often found growing as a cane in nothing but water throughout Asia, where it is thought to bring good fortune. The stems can easily be trained into spirals, or plaited into bizarre nets or columns.

D. marginata 'Colourama', covered in splashes of carmine, is one of the many hybrids available. Others include the pinkish 'Tricolor', and the plain green-leafed form, or a near-black variety called 'Black Knight'.

Bold bromeliads

There are many different types of bromeliads, some with spectacular flowers, others with striking forms, so they suit various styles of gardens and situations. From the desert to

the tropics, these interesting plants have made a niche for themselves all around the world, but the best known bromeliad is the pineapple.

Bromeliads can occur naturally in trees, on rocks and even hanging from branches like the fine threads of Spanish moss (*Tillandsia usneoides*). Some are known as air plants, as they seem to grow from nothing, but they take their nutrients from mists and fog (see the air plant project on page 404). As these plants are mostly epiphytic — that is, they use plants and rocks as supports, not hosts, for feeding — they can be grown on literally anything. They are easy to propagate, so are useful for thrifty gardeners who want to fill up a spot in the shade or grow some stunning houseplants.

If you're planting bromeliads in containers, make sure you plant them up in a really open mix, like orchid compost, of charcoal, bark chips and decayed leaf mould. Keep the well in the centre of the plant full of water as bromeliads enjoy humidity.

Planting pineapple tops

Pineapples will grow from their tops, so you can recycle them from the fruit bowl into your bold garden, or even use them as potted indoor plants for a while. Their spikey grey rosettes are quite sculptured and make a great feature. Look out for the black variety too.

1 Cut the top off a pineapple.

2 Trim the flesh off so that you are left with the leaves and a short length of core. Let the cores dry out for a few days before planting them.

3 Peel off the lower basal leaves.

4 Plant the prepared tops. Add some gravel to the pot.

Opposite: Even the most staid of plants, like these yews in Levens Hall, Cumbria, can be clipped into outrageous forms.

Left: The bizarre pitcher plant.

how to...
Trim a grass tree

Native to Australia, grass trees are wild plants used to a severe trim by bushfire every few years. When they are grown in cultivation, they may start to yellow off. This is a sure sign that they need reinvigorating, and either a blast with a torch or a haircut back to the base should do the trick.

Carnivorous plants

These wonderful-looking plants scent the air with nectar and keep insects like flies and mosquitoes under control. The most famous carnivorous plant is, of course, the Venus flytrap (*Dionaea muscipula*), which adds to its nutrient supply by snapping shut two spined lobes on live insects and digesting them. The nectar liquefies the insect, except for any hard bits, which eventually blow away the next time the 'trap' is open.

The lesser known, but stunningly beautiful pitcher plants (*Sarracenia* sp.) secrete nectar from glands around their hoods. The nectar lures insects down a slippery slide of death into a fluid that breaks down the insect body. Australia has its own carnivorous plants, known as sundews (*Drosera* sp.). These bind insects with a sticky honey until they dissolve all the nutrients.

Carnivorous plants thrive in humid conditions, so it's essential to keep them moist. Revamp a terrarium or fish bowl, and plant them up in sphagnum moss. Keep the container on a sunny windowsill or outdoors under some cover. Cut back any dead growth at the end of winter.

Did you know? Pineapples were introduced to Europe from the West Indies by Christopher Columbus. They made such a huge impact, in fact, that specially heated pineapple houses were constructed in the seventeenth century just to keep them alive. They also became a popular motif in architecture during this time.

Glossary of terms

Some terms used in this book are known by other names in the US and the UK.

Australia	US	UK
asphalt	asphalt	tarmac
bar and brace	ledge and brace	ledge and brace
beetroot	beet	beetroot
blood and bone	bonemeal	bonemeal
Bobcat	mini mechanical digger	Bobcat/mini mechanical digger
broad bean	fava bean	broad bean
brush cutter	string trimmer	strimmer
budding tape	budding tape	grafting tape
capsicum	bell pepper	pepper
choko	chayote	choko
club hammer	dead blow hammer	club hammer
Condy's crystals	potassium permanganate	Condy's crystals
dibber	dibble	dibber
eggplant	eggplant	aubergine
eyestrap	eyestrap	lacing eyes
fishmonger	fish seller	fishmonger
geotextile material/membrane	landscape/garden fabric	geotextile material/membrane
glasshouse	greenhouse	greenhouse/conservatory
ha-ha	sunk fence	ha-ha
hessian	burlap	hessian
horticultural fleece	garden quilt cover	horticultural fleece
iron lacework	ornamental wrought ironwork	iron lacework
kerb	curb	kerb
op shop	thrift store	charity shop
paling fence	picket fence	paling fence
perspex	plexiglass	perspex
potting mix	potting mix	potting compost
railway sleeper	railroad tie	railway sleeper
render	cement plaster	render
rill	runnel	rill
rumbled marble	tumbled marble	tumbled marble
sandpit	sandbox	sandpit
sash window	double-hung window	sash window
scoria	crushed volcanic rock	scoria
scutch chisel	mason's chisel	scutch chisel
secateurs	garden shears	secateurs
silverbeet	chard	swiss chard
skip	dumpster	skip
soldier course	jack-on-jack course	soldier course
spirit level	carpenter's level	spirit level
stretcher bond	running bond	stretcher bond
strimmer	string trimmer	strimmer
string line	mason's line	string line
sump	oil pan	sump
timber	lumber	timber
timber rounds	log rounds	timber rounds
transpiration bed	transpiration bed	reed bed
tube stock	plugs	plugs
tufa	tuff	tufa
wacker packer	wacker packer	wacker plate
weatherboard	clapboard	weatherboard
weed mat	weed mat	weed control fabric
willow wand	willow stalk	willow rod
witlof	chicory	belgian endive
zucchini	zucchini	courgette

Index

232, 242, 264, 267, 276, 330, 400, 401, 407
paving patterns 103
pear trees 103
peat-based soil 34–5
pebbles 295, 300, 314, 384, 396
Pelargonium x *hortorum* cv. 327
Pennisetum alopecuroides 403
pennyroyal (*Mentha pulegium*) 82, 100
Penstemon sp. 263, 278, 314
Penstemon 'Midnight' 305
Penstemon 'Pink Cloud' 278
Penstemon 'Sour Grapes' 305
peonies *see Paeonia* sp.
peony poppies 278
perennial gardens, 'new' 263
perennials 58
    for beds and borders 56, 58, 59
    for colour 260, 262, 263, 271, 276, 310, 312, 316–17, 327
    for cottage gardens 260
    for flower borders 260, 262
    for meadow gardens 130–1
    for rock gardens 155–6
    and spacing 60
    for tricky places 53
    for woodland gardens 142, 144–5
perfume 114, 115, 187, 237, 262, 274
pergolas 67, 92, 95, 97, 105, 113, 117, 119, 237
periwinkle (*Vinca* sp.) 53, 82, 354
permaculture 363–4
Persian gardens 13, 17, 226, 228
Persicaria sp. 263, 369
persimmon 115, 191, 325
Peruvian lilies (*Alstroemeria* sp.) 319, 327, 328
pest management 365
    see also insect pests
pesticides 363
Petasites sp. 106
Petiphyllum sp. 106
Petrea volubilis 'Albiflora' 274
Petrovskia utriplicifolia 281
Petunia sp. 53, 254, 278, 307
Phacelia sp. 130
Phalaris arundinacea var. *picta* 179, 274
Philadelphus sp. 144
Philadelphus coronarius 'Aureus' 327
Philodendron sp. 106, 241, 378
Phlomis sp. 222
Phlox sp. 53
Phlox condensata 155
Phlox divaricata 145
Phlox paniculata 'Nora Leigh' 274
Phoenix canariensis 166
Phoenix dactylifera 237
Phoenix roebelenii 237
Phormium sp. 53, 108
Phormium tenax 168, 171, 179, 182, 241, 326, 414
    'Dancer' 418
    'Purpureum' 310
    'Variegatum' 327
Photinia sp. 79, 353
Photinia glabra 'Reubens' 259

Phyllostachys sp. 106
Phyllostachys aureosulcata 'Aureocaulis' 322
Phyllostachys aureosulcata 'Spectabilis' 322
Phyllostachys nigra 116, 271, 395, 402, 403, 406–7
Physalis sp. 325
Picea sp. 143
Picea glauca 276
Picea glauca var. *albertiana* 'Conica' 156
Picea pungens 'Glauca' 59
pickerel rush (*Pontederia cordata*) 179, 181
picket fences 73, 76, 78, 284
Pieris sp. 144
Pieris japonica 142
pig face (*Mesembryanthemum* sp.) 168, 210
Pimenta dioica 115
pincushion cacti (*Mammillaria* sp.) 202
pincushion flower (*Scabiosa* sp.) 271, 281
pine *see Pinus* sp.
pineapple lily (*Eucomis* hybrid) 268–9
pineapples 419, 421
pink dianthus 157
pink lotus (*Nelumbo* sp.) 12, 179, 181, 238, 244–5
pink mulla mulla (*Ptilotus exaltatus*) 131
pink paper daisy (*Helipterum roseum*) 131
pink velvet banana (*Musa velutina*) 388
pink vygie (*Lampranthus spectabilis*) 168
Pinus sp. 53, 143, 197, 278
Pinus ayacahuite 212
Pinus canariensis 109
Pinus palustris 111
Pinus pinea 196
Pinus strobus 'Nana' 109
Pistacia chinensis 91
pitcher plant (*Sarracenia* sp.) 246, 421
Pittosporum sp. 79, 171
Pittosporum tenuifolium 'Stirling Mist' 264
Pittosporum tobira 108
plane tree (*Platanus* sp.) 91, 103, 110, 146
plant associations 54–5
plant patterns 103
plant quantities 59–60
plant spacing 58–9
Plantago sp. 106
plantain lily *see Hosta* sp.
planting plans 51–2, 64
Platanus sp. 91, 103, 146
Platanus x *hispanica* 110
playroom 100
pleached plants 17, 80, 102
Plectranthus argentatus 276
Plectranthus ciliatus 313
plum pine (*Podocarpus* sp.) 53, 103
Plumbago sp. 20, 304, 403
Plumeria sp. 115, 238, 247, 274, 402
poa 106
poached egg flower (*Limnanthes* sp.) 130, 272
Podocarpus sp. 53, 103
poinciana (*Delonix* sp.) 246, 247, 322, 322–3
poinsettia (*Euphorbia pulcherrima*) 322, 325
Polemonium sp. 304
Polianthes sp. 274
polka-dot plant (*Hypoestes phyllostachya*) 284
pollarding 145, 146

Polygonatum sp. 145, 263, 288
pomegranates 12, 14, 191, 221, 233, 237
Pompeii 13, 21
ponds 14, 66, 117, 174, 178, 202–3, 236, 245, 264–5, 273
Pontederia cordata 179, 181
ponytail palm (*Beaucarnea recurvata*) 212
poppies (*Papaver* sp.) 222, 270, 271, 286, 364–5
Populus alba 59
porches 42, 96
port wine magnolia (*Michelia figo*) 354
Portugal laurel (*Prunus lusitanica*) 353
Post-modernism 410
pot plants 220, 221, 241, 268–9, 329, 414
potagers 16, 356–73
potato 'pie' 371
potato vine (*Solanum jasminoides*) 304
Potentilla sp. 109
Pratia sp. 53, 156
pride of Madeira (*Echium* sp.) 162, 388
primrose 16
Primula sp. 53, 142
Primula veris 144
privet (*Ligustrum ovalifolium*) 79
prostrate grevilleas 82
protective clothing 63
Provost, Alain 400–1
pruning rock gardens 157
Prunus sp. 197, 237
Prunus 'Amanogawa' 59, 108
Prunus cerasifera 'Nigra' 59, 310
Prunus laurocerasus 109
Prunus lusitanica 353
Prunus maackii 111
Prunus serrula 111
Prunus x *blireana* 59
Prunus x *subhirtella* 59
    'Pendula' 59
Pteris sp. 53, 296
Ptilolus exaltatus 131
Pulmonaria sp. 274
purple cabbage 310
purple gardens/plants 59, 112, 113, 302–15
Pyracantha sp. 80, 325
Pyrus sp. 53, 144
Pyrus calleryana 91
    'Chanticleer' 59
Pyrus nivalis 59
Pyrus salicifolia 276
    'Pendula' 59, 109

quaking grass (*Briza* sp.) 126
Queen Anne's lace (*Anthriscus sylvestris*) 130, 289, 365, 368
queen of the night (*Epiphyllum oxypetalum*) 274
Quercus sp. 22, 103, 144, 222
Quercus ilex 345, 378
Quercus palustris 91
Quercus robur 91
Quercus suber 111
quince *see* flowering quince
rabbit ear iris 40–1
raised garden beds 358
ramps 96, 97

Acknowledgments

My sincere thanks go to Sarah Baker, who has been the most dedicated editor, motivator and friend any writer could wish for. Always efficient, she has been the driving force on this wild ride. Next, to Sue Stubbs, who once again has made me look good. Also, to the designer Alex Frampton who has transformed these pages with her wand. And thanks also to Lynne Spender for her advice.

On the home front, my sister Nicola, a wordsmith in her own right, has helped me enormously. She was never too busy to drop everything and be my thesaurus. Thanks to my uncle, Graeme Kidd, for his help with proofing. Last, my profound thanks must go to my 'support team'. Without Moira Rien, Jada Bennett and Sally Nash this book would simply have not got off the ground. The love and kindness they have shown to my children over the last year will not be forgotten.

The author and publisher would like to thank the following companies for their assistance with this project.
A Turkish Bazaar, (02) 9565 4007, aturkishbazaar@bigpond.com; Architectural Heritage, (02) 9660 0100; Bali Exotic, (02) 0450 0099; Country Floors, (02) 9326 2444, www.countryfloors.com; Eco Concepts, (02) 9698 7355, www.ecoconcepts.com.au; Eden Gardens and Garden Centre, (02) 9491 9900, www.edengardens.com.au; Ken Lamb of Imperial Gardens Landscape, (02) 9450 2455, www.imperialgardens.com.au; Lumeah Limestone, (02) 1300 669 077, www.lumeah.com.au; Porters Original Paints, (02) 9698 5322, www.porterspaints.com; Stile Tiles, (02) 9719 9969; The Art of Tiles, (02) 9565 1066, www.artoftiles.com.au.

Photographic credits

Alan Benson 233, 421 (L).

Joe Filshie 7 (centre), 26, 28, 34–5, 42, 46, 48, 60, 67 (R), 71 (btm L), 81, 85, 90–1 (top), 92 (top L), 95 (R), 97, 99, 100 (L), 105 (R), 107 (R), 109 (middle), 113–15, 119, 122 (btm), 124 (L), 128 (L), 131 (top L), 132 (top), 136–7, 143 (btm), 148–9, 150 (centre), 152, 172 (L), 174 (top), 197 (btm R), 198 (top), 219 (btm R), 210–11 (cacti), 242 (top), 247 (top L), 251 (btm R), 252 (purple, green), 258, 262, 263 (second & third from btm), 264–5, 270 (top L), 273, 278 (L), 281 (top), 291 (top), 292 (centre), 293, 300–1, 302 (L), 304 (L), 305 (top & btm R), 309 (top R, btm L & R), 325 (R), 330 (top), 345 (top), 353 (R), 354 (R), 355 (top L), 356–7, 358 (top), 360 (top), 362, 364–5, 365 (R), 366, 370 (btm R), 372–3.

Marcus Harpur 39, 282 (btm), 339 (btm R), 340, 348 (top), 360 (btm), 369, 406–7 (btm), 412, 414.

Andrea Jones 5, 10, 13, 14–15, 17–25, 70, 92 (btm), 132 (btm), 133, 138 (R), 154 (top), 160–1, 162 (L), 168–9, 183, 186–7, 188–91, 196–7 (top), 200–1, 214–15, 220–1, 221 (btm), 224, 226–30, 232, 234–5, 261, 288–9, 294–5, 332, 334–5 (top), 335 (btm R), 336–7, 338–9 (top), 342–3, 351, 374–5, 376–7 (top), 379 (top & btm L), 380–1, 384, 387 (L), 388 (top), 391, 394–5 (btm), 396, 400–1 (top), 403 (top L), 408–9, 410–11 (top), 420.

Chris L Jones 184, 186 (btm L), 187 (btm R), 214, 216, 218, 219 (top L), 222, 225 (L), 354 (L).

Meredith Kirton 16.

André Martin 4 (L top & centre), 29 (top), 41 (btm R), 47, 118, 119, 123 (btm L), 136–7, 142, 143 (top), 147 (top L), 199 (L), 202–3, 205, 206 (L), 208 (L), 210 (far L), 339 (btm L).

Murdoch Books Picture Library 4 (btm R), 8, 53 (btm R), 65 (btm R), 126 (top L & btm), 147 (top R), 275 (top R), 278–9, 284 (btm), 289 (btm), 291 (btm R), 292 (L & R), 306–7, 310 (top in box), 311 (top R), 316 (L), 320 (top), (middle two pix), 328 (top L), 330 (btm), 345 (btm R), 368, 390 (top R), 418 (L & R).

Robin Powell 182 (top), 370 (btm L).

Howard Rice 68, 71 (top L), 72, 75–8, 94 (btm), 98 (btm), 120, 123 (btm R), 128 (R), 141 (btm R), 153 (L), 164, 194 (top), 195, 196 (btm), 206 (R), 296, 335 (btm L), 358 (btm), 382 (R), 401 (btm).

Lorna Rose 7 (top & btm), 12, 36–7, 40–1, 42–3 (top), 44, 49, 53 (all but btm R), 55–8, 59 (all but middle), 61, 67 (L), 71 (top R & btm R), 73, 79, 82 (btm), 91, 92–3, 94 (top), 96, 98 (top R & L), 103 (top), 104, 105 (L), 106, 106–7, 109 (all but middle), 111 (top & btm — second from R), 112, 116–17, 124–5, 126 (top R), 129 (top), 130, 131 (btm L), 140, 141 (top), 145, 150 (L & R), 155, 156 (R), 157 (L), 166 (top), 169 (btm L, btm R & centre R), 170 (btm), 171, 172–3, 174 (btm), 179, 192, 198 (btm), 199 (R), 208 (R), 212 (top),

220 (L), 237, 238–9, 240–1, 242 (btm), 244 (L), 245 (R), 247 (all but top L), 248, 250, 251 (btm L), 252 (red, blue, yellow, orange), 253 (btm), 255–7, 259, 263 (top three pix & btm), 264 (L), 266, 270 (top R & btm), 272, 274 (top & btm), 275 (top L), 276 (second from top & btm two pix), 280, 281 (btm), 282 (top), 284 (top), 286–7, 290 (R), 302–3, 304–5, 308, 309 (top L), 310 (all but top pic in box), 310–11 (btm), 311 (top L), 312, 314, 316–17, 318–19, 320 (btm), 322–4, 325 (L), 326, 327 (btm), 328 (top R), 345 (btm L and centre), 348 (btm), 350, 352 (top & btm L), 352–3, 355 (top R & btm), 363, 364 (L), 365 (centre), 370 (top L), 374 (L), 376 (btm), 377 (btm), 378, 386, 387 (R), 388 (btm), 390 (top L), 392 (L), 395 (top R), 403 (top R), 407 (top R & btm R), 417, 418 (centre).

Lindsay Ross 100–1.

Sue Stubbs 4 (btm L), 6 (top), 35 (box), 36 (top R), 50 (btm), 52 (btm), 54, 59 (middle), 83, 84, 86–7, 108, 110, 111 (btm — all but second from R), 127, 131 (box), 134–5, 136 (L), 139, 141 (btm L), 146 (btm L & R), 147 (btm), 151, 153 (R), 156 (L), 158–9, 163, 166 (btm), 167, 170 (top R), 175, 177 (R), 182 (btm), 193, 194 (btm), 204, 207, 209, 211 (top R), 212 (btm), 213, 217, 219 (box), 221 (top R), 223, 225 (R), 231, 236, 238 (L), 243, 253 (top), 268–9, 271, 275 (btm), 276 (top & third from top), 277, 283, 285, 286 (L), 290 (L), 291 (btm L), 295 (box), 297–9, 311, 315, 321, 327 (top), 329, 331, 341, 346–7, 359, 379 (btm R), 383, 385, 389, 390 (btm), 392–3, 397, 398 (top), 399, 400 (box), 403 (btm), 404–5, 406 (top L), 411 (btm), 413, 415, 416, 419, 421 (R).

Juliette Wade 6 (btm), 38, 63 (R), 64 (L), 82 (top), 88–9, 90 (box), 102, 103 (btm), 122–3 (top), 129 (btm), 138 (L), 154 (btm), 160 (L), 165, 170 (top L), 176, 177 (L), 178, 180, 181, 197 (btm L), 244–5, 267, 361, 382 (L), 395 (top L), 398 (btm), 402.

Jo Whitworth 31.

Mark Winwood 29 btm, 34 (box), 36 (box), 41 (top R), 63 (L), 64 (R), 65 (top L, centre & R), 66, 95 (L), 101 (R), 144, 146 (top L & R), 157 (box), 162 (R), 246, 344, 349, 367, 370 (top R), 371, 372 (L).

The publisher would like to acknowledge photography in the following gardens: Abbey House Gardens, Wiltshire, United Kingdom; Alhambra, Granada, Spain; Andersson garden, Sweden; Arcadia Lily Ponds, Arcadia NSW, Australia; Arizona Cacti Nursery, Box Hill NSW, Australia; Ashfield, Sandy Bay, Hobart TAS, Australia; Austral Water Gardens, Cowan NSW, Australia; Australian Wildflower Show, Albany WA, Australia; Ballymaloe Cookery School, Cork, Ireland; Bay Street Nursery, Double Bay NSW, Australia; Bebeah, Australia; Biddulph Grange, Staffordshire, United Kingdom; Bonnie Banks Iris Garden, Gravelly Beach TAS, Australia; Briar Rose Cottage, Motueka, New Zealand; Bringalbit, Sidonia VIC, Australia; Burnbank, Ladysmith NSW, Australia; Burrendong Arboretum, Mumbil NSW, Australia; Buskers End, Bowral NSW, Australia; Casa di Pilatos, Seville, Spain; Chanticleer Garden, Philadelphia, United States; Chatsworth, Derbyshire, United Kingdom; Chelsea Flower Show, London, United Kingdom; Cherry Cottage, Mt Wilson NSW, Australia; Cloudehill, Olinda VIC, Australia; Cockington Green, Canberra ACT, Australia; Cowra Japanese Garden, Cowra NSW, Australia; Craigie Lea, Leura NSW, Australia; Cressing Temple, Essex, United Kingdom; Earthwise Permaculture Garden, Subiaco WA, Australia; Fagan Park, Galston NSW, Australia; Flagstaff Cottage, Bowral NSW, Australia; Flecker Botanic Garden, Cairns QLD, Australia; Foxglove Spires, Tilba Tilba NSW, Australia; Fragrant Garden, Erina NSW, Australia; Fuschia Farm & Mt Tambourine Garden Centre, Eagle Heights QLD, Australia; Gardenworld, Keysborough VIC, Australia; Gary Sobey, Skydancers Orchid and Butterfly Conservatorium, Harcourt VIC, Australia; Gemas, Leura NSW, Australia; Gillespies Cottages, Yarrawonga VIC, Australia; Hahndorf Country Garden, Hahndorf SA, Australia; Hampton Court, Herefordshire, United Kingdom; Hatfield House, Hertfordshire, United Kingdom; Heronswood, Dromana VIC, Australia; Het Loo Palace, near Apeldoorn, Netherlands; Hillview, Exeter NSW, Australia; Kennerton Green, Mittagong NSW, Australia; Kevin Kilsby Ceramics, Mt Albert, Auckland, New Zealand; Kewarra Beach Resort, Cairns QLD, Australia; Kuring-gai Wildflower Garden, Kuring-gai NSW, Australia; Lambruk, Fryerstown VIC, Australia; Levens Hall, Cumbria, United Kingdom; Lindfield Park, Mt Irvine NSW, Australia; Linton Historic House; Longhouse Reserve, New York State, United States; Luberon, Provence, France; Madoo Conservancy, New York State, United States; Magondii Gardens, United States; Menzies Nursery, Kenthurst NSW, Australia; Merry Garth, Mt

Wilson NSW, Australia; Michele Shennen Garden Centre, Willoughby NSW, Australia; Miserden Park, Gloucestershire, United Kingdom; Moidart, Bowral NSW, Australia; Mt Tomah Botanic Gardens, Mt Tomah NSW, Australia; Nooroo, Mt Wilson NSW, Australia; Orange Botanic Gardens, Orange NSW, Australia; Park Andre Citroën, Paris, France; Parterre Garden, Mosman NSW, Australia; Pensthorpe Waterfowl Park, Fakenham, Norfolk, United Kingdom; Pinehills, Bathurst NSW, Australia; Plants of Tasmania Nursery, Ridgeway TAS, Australia; Pockets, Billinudgel NSW, Australia; Quatre Saisons Heritage Rose Garden, Glen Forrest WA, Australia; Radisson Royal Palms Resort, Port Douglas QLD, Australia; Red Cow Farm, Sutton Forest NSW, Australia; Renaissance Herbs, Warnervale NSW, Australia; Rose Cottage, Deviot TAS, Australia; Royal Botanic Gardens, Sydney NSW, Australia; Sorenson Garden; Sydney Wildflower Nursery, Marsden Park NSW, Australia; The Flaxman, Croydon VIC, Australia; The Lilian Fraser Garden, Pennant Hills NSW, Australia; The Wildflower Farm, Somersby NSW; Thompson Brookes, US; Titoki Pt, Taihape, New Zealand; Tomar House, Rosevears TAS, Australia; Versailles Palace, near Paris, France; Villa d'Este, Tivoli, Italy; Villa Lante, Bagnaia, Italy; Château Villandry, Villandry, France; Waterfall Cottage, NSW Australia; West Brook, Mt Hunter NSW, Australia; Wildflower World, Auckland, New Zealand; Wollongong Botanic Gardens, Wollongong, NSW, Australia; Woodlyn Nurseries, Five Ways VIC, Australia; Yabba Yabba, Blackheath NSW, Australia; Yengo, Mt Wilson NSW, Australia.

The publisher would like to acknowledge these garden designers not credited on the relevant pages:
Torquil Canning (designer), 42–3 (top); Topher Delaney, 384, 396; Marcia Hosking, 98 (top R); Lee Jackson & Naita Green, Hampton Court Palace Show 2001, The Spacesavers Garden, 412; Andrew O'Sullivan, 49, 240; Ross Garden Design, 145 (top R); Paul Thompson, Chelsea Flower Show 2000, 414; Xa Tollemache with Jon Kellett. A Theatrical Garden. Evening Standard, RHS Chelsea 2001, 339; Scott Williams, 355 (btm).

The publisher would like to thank the following garden owners in Australia and New Zealand for allowing photography in their gardens:
Olwen Abbott, Huonville TAS; Mrs Dell Adam, Cheltenham NSW; Anthea & David Adams, Waiuku, New Zealand; Sally Allison, Lyddington Garden, North Canterbury, New Zealand; S Baker and Spence J, Leichhardt NSW; A G & L A Barrett, Nooroo, Mt Wilson NSW; Virginia Berger, Canberra ACT; Don Burke, Southern Highlands NSW; Lindsay Campbell, 'The Sorn', TAS; Naomi Canning, Hobart TAS; Heather Cant, Burradoo NSW; Amanda Caulfield and Brad Jamieson, Hunters Hill NSW; F Cavenett; Ted Clapson, Camden NSW; Barbara Cotles; K & P Cox, Thirlmere NSW; Dr G Cummins, Pymble NSW; Shelley Cutler, Tascott NSW; G & D Davey, Castlemaine VIC; Janet Dunlop, Orange NSW; Johnnie Felds, Marulan NSW; Frost-Foster, Tascott NSW; K & M Goddard, St Ives NSW; Mr & Mrs Gray, Wahroonga NSW; J Hancock, Erskineville NSW; Margaret Hanks, Forestville NSW; Don & Vicki Harrington, Balmain NSW; T & J Harris, Orange NSW; Diana Hill & David Potter, Ashbury NSW; S Hill, Thornleigh NSW; Kevin Hobbs, Sydney NSW; Graham & Doris King, Mt Hunter NSW; R & M Klaasen, Cairns QLD; Michael & Sharon Kvauka, Nambour QLD; Kirsten Lees and Mark Woodward, Riverview NSW; V Little, Chatswood NSW; Ree & Wilton Love, Tanah Merah QLD; Robert Machin, Putney NSW; S Magoffin, Marrickville NSW; Jane Mander-Jones, Killara NSW; C & R Marquard Pannell, Willoughby NSW; Josie Martin; Phil Mathews, Port Douglas QLD; Beverley McConnell, Ayrlies, Howick, New Zealand; Ros Mitchell, Canberra ACT; Alice Morgan, Pymble NSW; Peggy & Bryce Mortlock, Cammeray NSW; Mr & Mrs K Munro, Strathfield NSW; E Ommaney, St Ives NSW; Ruth Osborne, Beecroft NSW; Mr & Mrs P Park, Canberra ACT; S Parker, Roseville NSW; Paula Pellegrini, Randwick NSW; J & S Porteous, Medlow Bath NSW; Judy Quigley, Stirling SA; I Rabb, Pennant Hills NSW; Sue & Robert Read, Pennant Hills NSW; G & G Rembel, Dural NSW; Linda Ross, Kurrajong NSW; Janet & Lee Rowan, Newcastle NSW; Kay Scarlett, Cobbitty NSW; Diane Smith, Ranelagh TAS; Mrs Smith, Orange NSW; John Stowar, Mt Murray NSW; Cec & Rita Sullivan, Lindfield Park, Mt Wilson NSW; Sue Swain, Bayview NSW; Mrs E Symonds, High Range NSW; Douglas Thompson, Killara NSW; D & B Thomson, Barkers Creek VIC; Pam & Ross Thyer, Sydney NSW; A & R Tonkin, Orange NSW; Merv & Wendy Trimper, Myrtle Beach SA; Jan Waddington, Kergunyah VIC; B & R Wilkinson, Kingston TAS.

Plant silhouettes

Photocopy these silhouettes to the required size, then cut them out and use them to represent different shapes and forms on your planting plan (see pages 51–2).

Plant outlines

You can either use these plant outlines as guides for your own drawings, or photocopy them to the required size, cut them out and use them on your planting plan (see page 52).

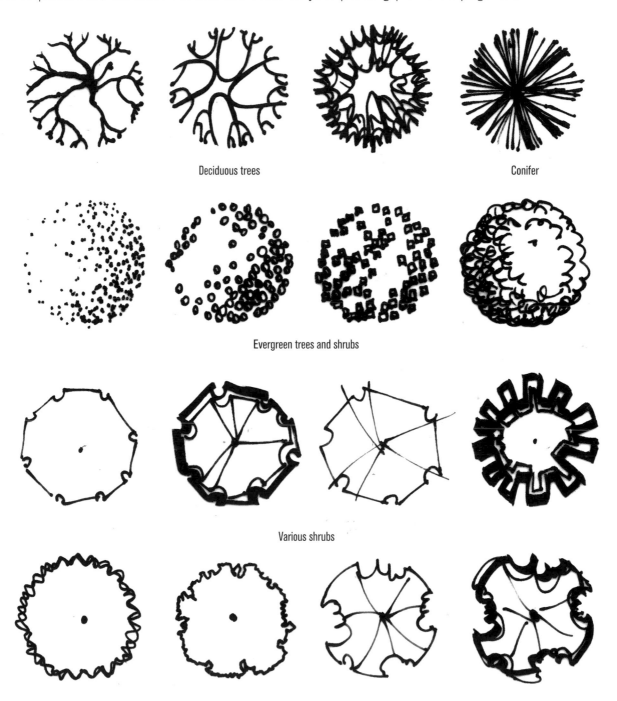

Deciduous trees

Conifer

Evergreen trees and shrubs

Various shrubs

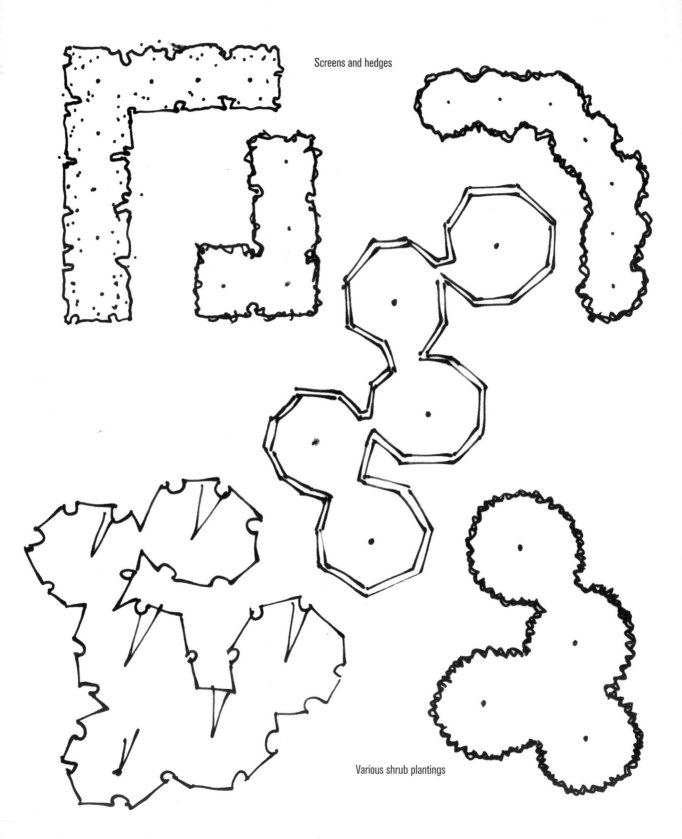

Screens and hedges

Various shrub plantings